A 20ᵀᴴ CENTURY "PORTIA"

THELMA BERNICE KERR-THOMSON

"Here comes PORTIA, with her pitch for mercy!"

~ Mary M. Cushnie-Mansour ~

A 20ᵀᴴ CENTURY

"PORTIA"

BIOGRAPHY
OF
THELMA BERNICE KERR-THOMSON

WRITTEN BY:
MARY M. CUSHNIE-MANSOUR

AS TOLD BY: THELMA BERNICE KERR-THOMSON

Copyright © Thelma Bernice Kerr-Thomson, and Mary M. Cushnie-Mansour, 2011. All rights reserved. No part of this book may be reproduced in any form by any electronic or mechanical means (including photocopying, recording, or information storage and retrieval) without permission, in writing from the author.

Published by
CAVERN OF DREAMS PUBLISHING
Brantford, ON, Canada

First Edition – March 2011

Printed by
BRANT SERVICE PRESS
Brantford, ON, Canada

Library and Archives Canada Cataloguing in Publication

Cushnie-Mansour, Mary M., 1953-
A 20th century "Portia": biography of Thelma Bernice Kerr-Thomson / written by Mary M. Cushnie-Mansour ; as told by Thelma Bernice Kerr-Thomson.

ISBN 978-0-9868169-0-1
1. Kerr-Thomson, Thelma Bernice, 1922-. 2. Lawyers--Ontario--Biography. 3. Judges--Ontario--Biography. 4. Women lawyers--Ontario--Social conditions--20th century. 5. Lindsay (Ont.)--Biography. I. Kerr-Thomson, Thelma Bernice, 1922- II. Title. III. Title: A twentieth century "Portia".

KE416.K47C88 2011   340.092   C2011-900337-6

THE ROAD NOT TAKEN
BY: ROBERT FROST

I shall be telling this with a sigh
Somewhere ages and ages hence
Two roads diverged in a wood
And I took the one less travelled by
And that has made all the difference...

MY STORY IS DEDICATED TO

The two men who believed in me

My Father, Frank Lester Kerr
&
My Husband, David Moffatt Thomson

Madison...
If all men were angels then we wouldn't need "Law"

Robert Frost...
Stopping by a woods on a snowy evening...
Miles to go before I sleep

Ted Kennedy...
"Lust for Life"
Knowledge, joie de vivre and power

Stuart McLean...
Teens skate a thin line between permissible and punishable

Shakespeare's "The Merchant of Venice"...
The quality of mercy is not strain'd
It droppeth as the gentle rain from heaven
Upon the place beneath; it is twice bless'd
It blesseth him that gives and him that takes
'Tis mightiest in the mightiest; it becomes
The throned monarch better than his crown
His septre shows the force of temporal power
The attribute to awe and majesty
Wherein doth sit the dread and fear of kings
But mercy is above this sceptre'd sway
It is enthroned in the heart of kings
It is an attribute to God himself
And earthly power doth then show likest God's
When mercy seasons justice...

~ A Twentieth Century "Portia" – Bio of Thelma Bernice Kerr-Thomson ~

PROLOGUE

There is an old saying that there is strength in numbers, however such was not the case for females who wished to become lawyers in Canada at the turn of the 20th century. The Women's Law Association of Ontario was founded in 1919 by two law school students, Laura Denton and Helen Currie. Originally, it was set up for female law students in the Toronto region, but soon expanded to other areas as increasing numbers of women began practicing law. It became an alternative to the male-dominated professional organizations of the period, which did not allow women the privilege of membership. The Women's Law Association's focal point at that time was on the promotion and support of women's equal involvement in the legal profession.

As time went on the Association began providing networking opportunities for new lawyers, their main concerns still being the welfare of women in the legal profession—lobbying for women's legal and professional rights. Over the years there have been numerous organizations begun across Ontario, but the current challenge for the Women's Law Association in the upcoming century will be to regain focus and solidarity among women lawyers across the province.

On the whole, despite numerous accomplishments, female lawyers still earn significantly less than male lawyers, and the number of women in influential positions is proportionately low. Partners in law firms, senior positions in corporations, and the judiciary and elected benchers of the Law Society are all still male dominated. High numbers of women leave the profession after law school—why? Some of the needs which must to be addressed are related to maternity leave, child care, and gendered perspectives.

(The above is an excerpt from the Archived Newsletter – Fall/Winter 1999 – Message from the President, Barb Hendrickson)

~

Clara Brett Martin (1874–1923) became the first female lawyer in the British Empire. She was called to the Ontario Bar in 1897.

Twenty-two years later a mere eleven women had followed in her footsteps. William Renwick-Riddell (a bencher in 1892) arrived late for the Convocational vote to admit women members of the Bar. The vote was won by one vote—he protested, desiring it be retaken in order to include his opposition. His observation was: "the admission of women is regarded with complete indifference by all but those immediately concerned."

Even the <u>journalistic media of the time described women lawyers with an obsessive scrutiny, bent on examining their manners, style of dress, and discovering a modern "Portia"</u>! To their knowledge, one had not yet arrived. Riddell also failed to note the phenomenon noted by Clara Brett Martin who had retained male lawyers for her clients' litigation, to spare them excessive scrutiny. Nor could Riddell have been aware that a handful of young, would-be women lawyers were about to launch the first Canadian women's legal association, which is still here today.

One might question how the Women's Law Association of Ontario has survived for so long. For one thing, the Association acquired a sense of ownership by its members where the <u>women lawyers found an accepting community even though they found themselves in the "three percent" or less group of those called to the Bar</u>. Their flexibility allowed them to set their own goals and they were small enough to meet individual expectations and large enough to arrange an entire year of programs which took charge of their own interests.

The Association has been a testament to the developing identity of Ontario women lawyers. There was great optimism in the 1920's; the 1930's were lean, but they lead into the vigorous and serious 1940's that promised to shape the next era; which, despite its many challenges, saw a large influx of highly motivated young women in the 1970's and 1980's.

The culture of law practice for women was scarcely defined, but it was changing, as were the rights of women. <u>Women were getting the right to vote, yet a married woman could not retain property rights.</u> Clara Brett Martin successfully challenged the Law Society's opinion that women were not "persons," for the purpose of admission to the Bar, but <u>it took seven years before the Privy Council ruled that women were to be recognized as "persons" in Canadian Constitutional Law.</u> Many of the early members came from families with professional backgrounds, but once called to the Bar it became a question of which social reality women lawyers belonged to. They were confronted with conflicting duties and the question was asked many times—was the world ready for them? Their profession was as segregated as was the society of the time.

In 1919, 22 years after Clara Brett Martin was called to the Bar, five more women stood to be admitted in each of the two following years, and nine in the next. The 1920's became their first era as an identifiable group.

<u>These women were pioneers whom women who embrace the practice of law today should honour and admire. They were subject to scrutiny by press and clients of both genders; they were confronted with choices between their career and family responsibilities.</u> The ones who persevered and returned to law practice after raising their children were eventually tolerated. Their role in society was constantly in the public eye; however, <u>theirs was not a widely followed path and for decades they toiled in highly marginalized numbers,</u> with the anticipated breakthroughs coming much later than expected.

The <u>early members</u> spent the majority of their working careers in sole or small practices. Many of them would be elderly by the time a critical mass of informed women in law would rise. Some of the early members saw little measure of the impact they had on women lawyers, in and on society. Their <u>main task</u> then <u>was to create equality for women lawyers in a man's world.</u> They approached the task with optimism to gain acceptance as fellow lawyers, by proving themselves successful in law.

~

The two co-founders of the Women's Law Association of Ontario, Laura Denton (Duff) and Helen Currie, were the 20th and 32nd women to be called to the Bar in Ontario in 1920 and 1921, respectively. The first meeting was held in the offices of Frank Denton, K.C., Laura's father, with whom she worked. Records are scant of the earliest meetings, but the attendees showed their intention to continue and they planned an annual meeting. In that year every woman ever admitted to membership in the Law Society of Upper Canada, approximately 35 lawyers and law students, were invited to a meeting held at the Inglewood Tea Rooms at the corner of Spadina Avenue and Bloor in Toronto. Clara Brett Martin was the keynote speaker.

The earliest surviving records of the WLAO Constitution dates from 1949. The following is an excerpt from the early constitution...

Article I – Name: The name of the Association shall be "The Women's Law Association of Ontario".

Article II – Object: The object of the Association shall be to encourage interchange of ideas and co-operation among women with legal training.

Article III – Membership: Any woman who has been admitted to practice at the Bar, or who has been admitted and enrolled to practice as a Solicitor in His Majesty's Courts in Ontario shall be eligible for membership in the Association.

Article IV – Associate Membership: 1. Any woman who has been admitted as a Student-at-law and is enrolled as a member of the Law Society of Upper Canada shall be eligible for Associate membership in the Association.

2. Any woman who has been duly admitted to the Bar, or duly admitted and enrolled as a Solicitor to any part of the British Empire other than Ontario, may be elected as an associate member of the Association...

Before the forming of the Constitution, the main activities of the WLAO were: educational seminars, sharing of knowledge, the creation of a welcoming and inclusive community, and celebration of achievements and activities in support of citizenship. From the beginning, membership was open to any woman who had been admitted to practice law in Ontario, and to students-at-law. There were no disqualifying conditions other than disbarment by the Law Society, and no further rights of initiation such as academic standings.

Life-time memberships were available in 1947 to any member willing to pay the hefty amount of $40.00! The first life-time membership was granted to Grace Gordon to honour her efforts as the WLAO representative to the Local Council of Women, where she had served as Convenor of Laws.

Other local branches were encouraged and developed in Hamilton, London and Ottawa. It appears that men were allowed too, and did occasionally attend meetings, particularly as spouses or guest speakers, BUT they could not hold membership rights!

WLAO members enjoyed memberships in many other legal associations as well, but one of their most active liaisons in the early years was with the Local Council of Women; which, at its inception in 1893 had engaged in a letter-writing campaign in support of women's entry to the Bar. This had been at the request of Clara Brett Martin. More than 70 Toronto women's groups belonged to the Local Council between 1919 and 1950. Some of the issues they tackled were: advocacy for Medicare, the abolition of capital punishment, housing for the aged, humane treatment for juvenile offenders, portable pensions, and pensions for women.

<u>Sadly, The Lawyers Club was the lone hold-out when it came to welcoming women as members, or even as a guest, until the early 1970's. It has been noted that on at least two occasions, prior to then, early members were mistakenly invited to attend and then were declined once their gender became known.</u>

~

WLAO activities in the 1920's reflected the optimism of the decade. The records indicate a bold confidence in the community of women lawyers who met through the Association. The first written annual report, 1923-24, reviewed the year's activities, one of which was to establish a scholarship fund. The organizers of the meeting were Helen Currie, Margaret Hyndman, who was a law student at the time, and Irene Maw. Maw, it is said, may have become the first Ontario woman lawyer to practice law out of her home, while acting as a primary caregiver.

In the 1920's educational seminars included such topics as: wills, immigration matters, proposed federal legislation, advice to women lawyers choosing specialized fields of law, practice before juvenile, surrogate, criminal, civil, domestic relations, and bankruptcy courts—just to mention a few. Legal education was always given the utmost priority.

The annual dinner meeting in 1927 toasted the King, the Profession, and three women graduates; and then took an amusing look at the future of women lawyers sixty years from then—*"when only a few stray men would be called to the Bar and when all the judges would be women"*!

~

Clara Brett Martin passed away in 1923 at the age of 49. Thirteen members of the WLAO met and donated $130.00 to start a scholarship in her memory. The prize was to be awarded annually to a final year student with the highest marks in Wills and Trusts.

The historical development of woman lawyers as professionals was important to the early members and this is quite evident in the Association's archives where a set of scrapbooks carefully recorded the biographical information on the first 77 women called to the Ontario Bar by 1933. Whether the subject person was an active member or not was not noted, and the news articles were integrated into the unfolding of a vibrant and living history.

The collection provides a very unique insight into the legal culture *vis a vis* women lawyers, giving a first-hand picture of how early members were perceived by male colleagues and society as a whole. There was a fascination of the media with women lawyers in the early years. Photographs of female graduates of Osgoode Hall were published annually and such descriptive phrases as the "fair but not so stern sex," and "a mere slip of a girl," revealed much about the social milieu of attitude toward these women. The Press was in constant search of an idealized "Portia," without acknowledging that Shakespeare's Portia was most likely in the role of a judge, not a courtroom advocate. Many of the articles appeared on the women's pages, or on the society pages of local newspapers, and there was more attention paid to descriptions of the decorations and the names of the attendees than to the substance of the actual topics discussed.

Ruby Wigle expressed her sentiment to such frivolous reporting in an article in the Canadian Bar Review in 1927:

…In passing, be it known that by women barristers, the expression, "my learned friend" is infinitely more appreciated than "Portia." As women, they may discuss the trend of fashions, or places where cakes may be purchased, just as their brother lawyers ask advice about their spring overcoats, or boast of their gardens; but, in the profession they prefer to be known as the vendor's solicitor, or counsel for the defence, hoping that the practicing lawyer's sex may be of the same importance as their religious persuasion, party allegiance, and financial rating…

The guest list at the annual dance in 1927 indicated just how far women lawyers had come. It boasted, in attendance with their spouses, such dignitaries as: Premier Ferguson, Chief Justice Mulock, Dean Falconbridge of Osgoode Hall, the Attorney-General, and several Justices, including Justice Riddell, whom we noted earlier here was against even admitting women to the Bar.

Unfortunately, that same year a <u>Globe and Mail reporter lamented</u> that of the 53 women then called to the Ontario Bar, "a modern Portia had not yet arrived." The reporter went on to claim that: *"Men in the legal profession … are doubtful if she ever will arise.* <u>*Women, however, are not naturally logical and are too apt to be swayed by their prejudices and emotions. While wishing their fair comrades well and acknowledging their cleverness as solicitors, they are not sanguine regarding their ability as barristers."*</u>

In reply to this—*"But how many men have excelled as court pleaders? … In all the years they have been following the law, not many have become famous. It is true that we may not produce a counsel for many years, but then, we may."*

Gradually, reports became more accepting of women lawyers, even though there still remained a mysterious obsession with finding their Portia—

"Time after time, in the last few years, women lawyers have carried off honours in Toronto courts and left their male opponents wondering if a little genius isn't mixed in with Portia's blonde hair."

By 1925, comments were being made on a trend for married women to cease practice. <u>In 1927</u>, at the retirement luncheon given by the WLAO in honour of <u>Dr. N. W. Hoyles</u>, principal of Osgoode Hall Law School since 1894, Hoyles <u>was noted as saying: "…unfailing kindness to students of the fair sex, pioneers in the invasion of a realm almost monopolized by men … many of his feminine pupils had married and wasted so much study and so much knowledge…"</u> To which the then President, <u>Elizabeth Newton, penned a humorous reply: "Matrimony seems everywhere to be a problem."</u> In the same year, Ruby Wigle wrote: *"Approximately half the number who are qualified give up the active practice for matrimony—a regrettable fact as far as this article is concerned, but too complicated to discuss here."* Many women found that Dr. Hoyle's comments were a challenge to improve the laws relating to women and children.

In the spring of 1933, the WLAO recorded the professional status of all members—practicing or not. In August of the same year, the Globe and Mail reported, by name, the status of the 13 individuals who were called to the Ontario Bar between 1920 and 1924. Four were found to still be practicing law and the others were described as having either "dropped out" or "gave up." The writer gave no further explanation. It was noted in later entries in the WLAO Archives that many of the named women did indeed practice law for a considerable number of years.

The members themselves did not make the topic of conflicting roles between parental duties and *lawyering* a topic at their seminars. That sort of talk was regarded as personal and even though they may have shared information and support in an informal manner, these topics were not actually addressed in seminars until 1989. It is made clear, though, that many of the non-practicing members continued to make contributions to the legal community, as well as to the community at large.

~

By the end of the 1920's, 68 women had been called to the Bar in Ontario. A new problem arose late in 1933, one which the WLAO threw themselves into head-on. The first women who had been employed as lawyers in the provincial government, all members of the WLAO, were singled out by gender, and all received notices of dismissal. One woman was beyond child-bearing years; two were sole supporter for an aged parent. With the support of the Local and National Councils of Women, and other groups, these women were successfully reinstated. In 1934, an articulate Law student observed that there were more things available to men through informal working relationships and *connections* when seeking employment after graduation.

Well into the 1930's, WLOA committees on Law Reform sprung up. The first formal committee work may have been a research project done in co-operation with the "Local of Women." It assessed the employment conditions of women factory workers in Toronto and strove to improve the labour standards legislation. There was an increase in educational seminar topics reflecting a wide range of subject matters of most interest to women, including: patent and comparative corporation laws, criminal and parliamentary procedures, and women's property rights—just to name a few.

Despite all the ground they were gaining, this decade only produced 37 more women lawyers. Some of this may be related to the Great Depression. However, Ontario remained the leader in calling women to the Bar. <u>In the 1941 census there were 8,621 male lawyers listed in Canada; women numbered 129, and 112 of them were from Ontario.</u>

~

Moving into the 1940's, doors began to open for women. Part of this was due to the fact that many of the male lawyers had been called upon to serve in World War II and the Law Society asked women lawyers to take over their offices. <u>By the end of the war, nearly every large firm had one woman on staff.</u> The WLAO also increased their vigour. Early in 1942, there were formal committees on public welfare, and labour and civil liberties. In 1943, in the midst of the Great War, came a long awaited cause for celebration. Helen Kinnear, from Cayuga, Ontario, was appointed to the Bench—the first county court woman judge in the British Commonwealth!

Of course many women were concerned about the impact that men returning from war would have on them—the world had changed. Together with the Local Council of Women, the WLAO began to address such topics as: justice, women and investments, labour legislation, divorce, wills and succession duties, jury duty for women, insurance security, humane justice, home and the homeless, real estate, and "So This is Marriage." The most ambitious project of the time was undertaken by Lily Sherizen and the WLAO Public Welfare Committee—Juvenile Prison Reform. The report was lauded widely in the press and was credited with mobilizing a progressive initiative in the creation of a humane juvenile criminal justice system.

~

The next half of the century brought unique and unpredicted changes and challenges. Women lawyers engaged in activities in step with post-war society—a re-emphasis on the family and expanded opportunities in the bustling economy. Even though additional avenues were opening up for women lawyers, more than one decade would pass before issues of interest would rise and refocus in light of complex changes in law and society—when concepts of equity and diversity would press transformational expectations upon the profession—when larger numbers of informed women in law would ask themselves what it meant to be a woman lawyer. There was a new generation of women on the horizon and together with their predecessors they would give new meaning to old purposes.

The above information was gleaned from The Women's Law Association of Ontario, 2000—History—the early years—Abby Bushby—for its 80th Anniversary Celebration on January 14, 2000.

BELOW THE BORDER THINGS WERE NO DIFFERENT!

A news article in *The New York Times* on February 19th 1950, entitled "On Women Lawyers" discussed some of the issues faced by our American sisters in the early years of law, showing that women below the border were subject to the same prejudices as those in Canada.

Excerpts from: <u>Case (By One of Them) For Women Lawyers</u>
By: Dorothy Kenyon

(Dorothy Kenyon began practicing law over thirty years ago. She has since served as a Municipal Court Judge and a U.S. delegate to the League of Nations and U.N. Commission on the Status of Women.)

"In 1878 it was said that male and female minds were not alike and should not be treated the same educationally." For this reason, Charles W. Eliot shrank from taking the responsibility of introducing the education of women in Harvard College.

... as Eliot so brilliantly foresaw, his beloved Harvard, citadel of Law ... the most conservative, the most powerful of the professions, and the last refuge of the male, will be open to women students next fall ... how has this come about ...

By census count <u>in 1940 there were 4,187 women lawyers in the United States</u>, probably a not appreciably larger number by now. Is not this total proof of failure rather than of success?

Eliot, considerably later in his life, (at my graduation from Smith College to be precise), was gracious enough to observe that, contrary to his expectations, <u>the experiment of higher education for women had not proved an utter failure and that women were demonstrating that they could make excellent "assistants" to men.</u> Having a family consisting entirely of brothers, none of whom I had the faintest intention of ever assisting in any shape or manner, this speech made a profound impression upon my youthful mind, and possibly was responsible for my unorthodox behaviour ...

... <u>certain scientific tests concluded that of the five essential traits of a good lawyer, women may possibly excel in all five.</u>

The first woman lawyer appeared on the scene in 1869. She was triumphantly admitted to practice in the state of Iowa under a statute conveniently interpreted to include her under the description of "white male person." By 1870 there were five women practitioners in a number of states and the movement was definitely under way. But things were not easy. Myra Bradwell, for instance, who was refused admittance to the Bar in Illinois, solely on the grounds of her sex, carried her fight to the Supreme Court of the United States in 1872; but, her application was denied on the ground that it was wholly a state matter ... the fight went on all over the country until, in 1920, the battle of women for the right to practice law was finally won in all states.

Meanwhile, people were beginning to go to law school instead of learning law by reading about it in law offices. And women wanted to go too. The pioneer, in the East, in this field was New York University (where I graduated, and my aunt before me)! In 1892, New York University Law School opened its doors to women ... out of its 800 or so women graduates at least seven of them have served as judges, one of them in the highest judicial position occupied by any woman in the United States (Judge Florence Allen of the United States Court of Appeals, Sixth Circuit).

Next was Cornell, at the conclusion of World War I; Yale gracefully succumbed, and then in the late twenties Columbia made a graceful capitulation and admitted women to all its regular Law courses.

Bar associations were important to the practising lawyer because of their frequently admirable law libraries, as well as their opportunities for contacts with fellow-craftsmen. Occasionally, they fancied themselves as private clubs and the prospect of women members was, in many cases, anything but agreeable. Perhaps the greatest battle took place in New York City's Bar Association ... The clubhouse, practically closed to women, had a <u>law library</u>, one of the best, <u>which was open to women for only one day of the year ... It could hardly be because the velocity of thought of the female was supposed to be three hundred and sixty-five times that of the male.</u>

The opponents of change were gradually forced to their last stand ... Nothing short of Elizabeth Arden or Helena Rubenstein powder-rooms were worthy of ladies of such note ... <u>women</u> entered whatever law school they could get into, graduating and trying to get jobs in law offices. Many <u>found themselves</u> somewhat less than welcome. But they accustomed themselves to <u>having to work twice as hard as their male colleagues in order to get half as much recognition.</u> Many got discouraged and dropped out of the ranks. But the hardcore stuck it out and made good, whether in government or private practice, as associates in large firms, or in their own offices—brilliantly good in many instances ... Rather than fitting themselves into a narrow groove, as some of our Harvard young gentlemen would have us think, these women are spreading their work, just as men do ...

The real bottleneck nowadays remains the law office. It is to the lawyer what an internship is to the doctor ... for the development of skill ... Many a promising young legal mind is stopped in her tracks by the reception she receives in the average hardboiled law office.

"What use can we possibly make of you? You'd make a fool of yourself and us in court. We can't work you late at night as we do the boys. What would the clients say? <u>You may be a disturbing element, falling in love</u> with people, and vice versa. <u>We'll have to stick you in a law library out of sight.</u> In the contingency that you turn out to be good, <u>you'll probably marry as soon as we've finished training you</u> and we'll have had all our trouble for nothing. Thank you, no, we'll play safe and take a boy."

It's a lucky and nervy girl who can break through these barbed-wire entanglements and serve her law apprenticeship in an even reasonably good law office. It is still the rare exception to crash the gates of the gilded firms, the law factories that possess a monopoly of the big-business clients.

Occasionally, the fears of the traditionalists are realized ... girl law clerks have been known to fall in love ... A friend of mine started her clerkship in the firm of two highly eligible bachelors. In no time both proposed to her ... she was forced to choose. And, having chosen, it seemed the part of wisdom to resign her clerkship. Thus her career ended rather abruptly; however, not permanently. After a brief maternity leave, she came back to practice law with her husband. This is a common procedure. There are many husband-and-wife law teams and they work extremely well.

Fears as to women making fools of themselves in court have proved groundless ... <u>There are plenty of fools in our courts, but they are not all women.</u> In fact, women seem to have a "flair"—a sixth sense—possibly our old friend "intuition," and that can make the difference between persuasion and the reverse, between success and failure.

Gone are the days when a woman lawyer shocked the court by appearing in close fitting trousers; gone even is the shock of the plea; which, as solemnly announced by the United States Court of Appeals for the Second Circuit, was probably being made for the first time in history—a plea for adjournment on the grounds of pregnancy. All these *things have passed into history. The woman lawyer who is: neat, adroit and eloquent is not exactly a common figure in our courtrooms, but she is at least an occasional and a sympathetic figure there!*

Are we really miscast as lawyers? There is a growing school of thought, including such <u>an eminent authority</u> as <u>Judge Jerome Frank</u> that <u>regards the entire field of law as feminine rather than masculine.</u> If the subject matter of law is human relations, the rules of conduct of human beings in society, can it be that law is peculiarly a woman's field—after all, women are supposed to be experts in human relations ...

~ Mary M. Cushnie-Mansour ~

THE BEGINNINGS

In this, the final epilogue of my life, I think I am finally finding emotional balance through my love of music, which recalls so many wonderful memories for me. I especially love opera. I believe opera should not only be a release for the elderly, but a safety valve for those with raging hormones in this age of repressed fruition. I have never inflicted upon others great bursts of emotional episodes, but that does not imply I am a cold and unfeeling person. I feel deeply. I was trained from an early age to keep my emotions under control; it would be inconsiderate of me to expect people, other than those nearest and dearest to me, to be exposed to such a thing. I learned to give vent to my emotions through: painting, dance, and music. Even though this suppression has been difficult for me, it was something I had to learn to do when I was representing clients. When I got too emotionally involved, I was less effective.

I have had a purposeful life. I was constantly setting goals and I was good at postponing expectations and gratification. I did my best to honour my father and live out his goals and dreams for me. The only time my dedication to Father's dreams for me was threatened was when I met the fascinating Scot—I shall relate that part of my story to you later.

Now I am in my golden years and I realize the emotional toll that those "Roads Not Taken" may have had on my life. The giving up of my first love and having to suppress feelings for him has been painful. But of course, having said that, the mate with whom I shared my life was a wonderful man. We had the same passion for law, both using it as an instrument for peace.

Here is my story ...

~

My name is Thelma Bernice Kerr-Thomson. My mother claimed to have named me after someone from a 1920's novel. I had many nicknames while growing up—*Skeezix*, from my father; *Ducky*, from my maternal grandfather; *Pitou*, from my Quebec family; and *Butchie* from my husband—prior to the current connotation. I am the only child of Frank Lester Kerr and Madeleine Violet Courtney. I was born in Toronto's Grace Hospital on Wellesley Street. My birth was recorded as September 28, 1922, but my mother swore I was born on September 27. In those days the hospital resembled a cottage and our family doctor lived just down the street. I am one of the "female pioneers" who studied law in Ontario, having passed the Bar exam in 1949. As mentioned in the prologue, there were only 129 women lawyers in Canada at the time of the 1941 census, 112 of those women were from Ontario. That was in comparison to 8,621 males. I still feel the privilege of having been counted as a trailblazer for my sisters who have followed.

But the best place to begin my story is where all stories should begin—at the roots...

GRANDPARENTS

MY FATHER'S FAMILY

Front Row: Ralph, Margaret (Grandmother), Hugh
Back Row: Hugh (Grandfather), Ethel, Eleanor, Frank (Father)

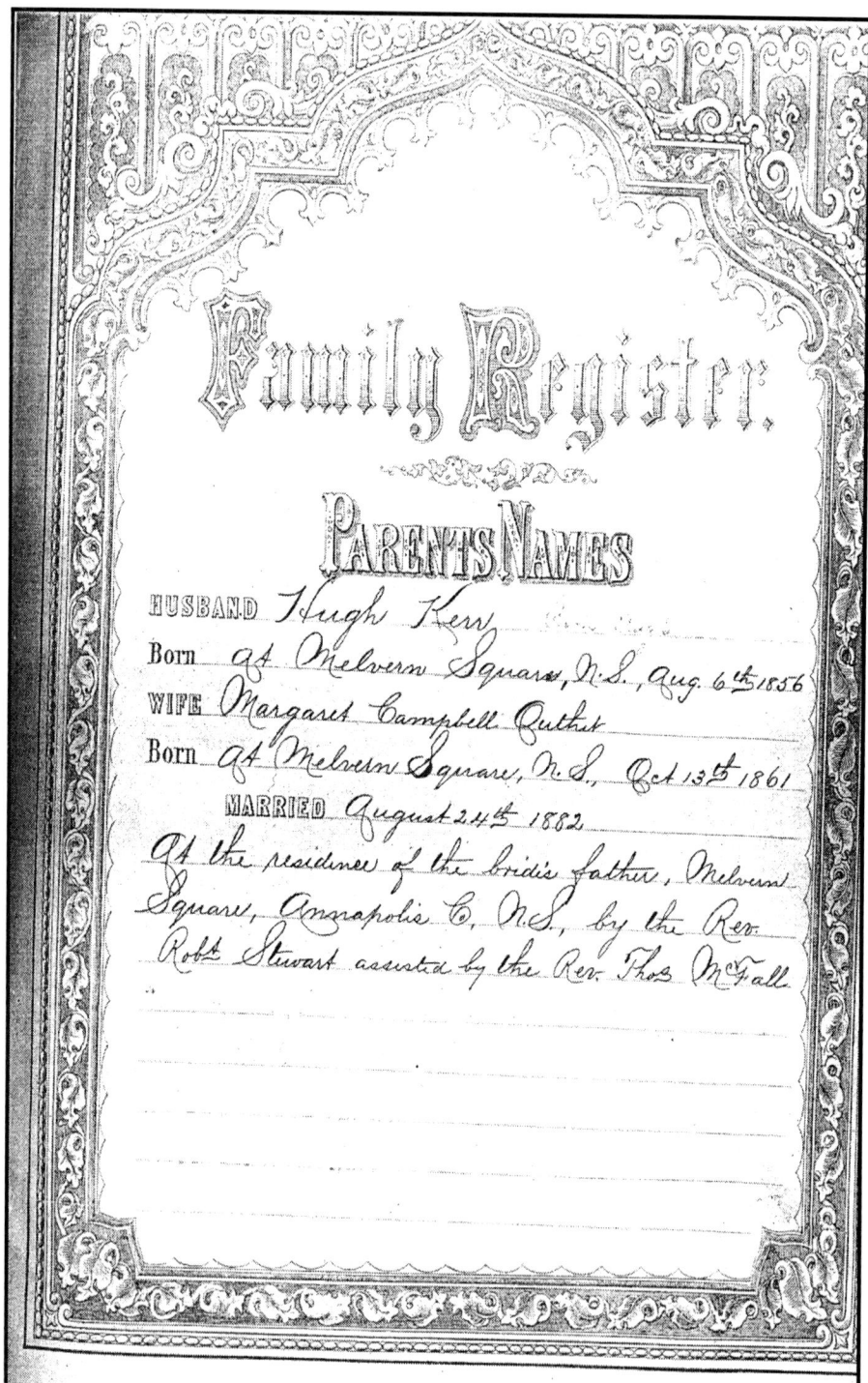

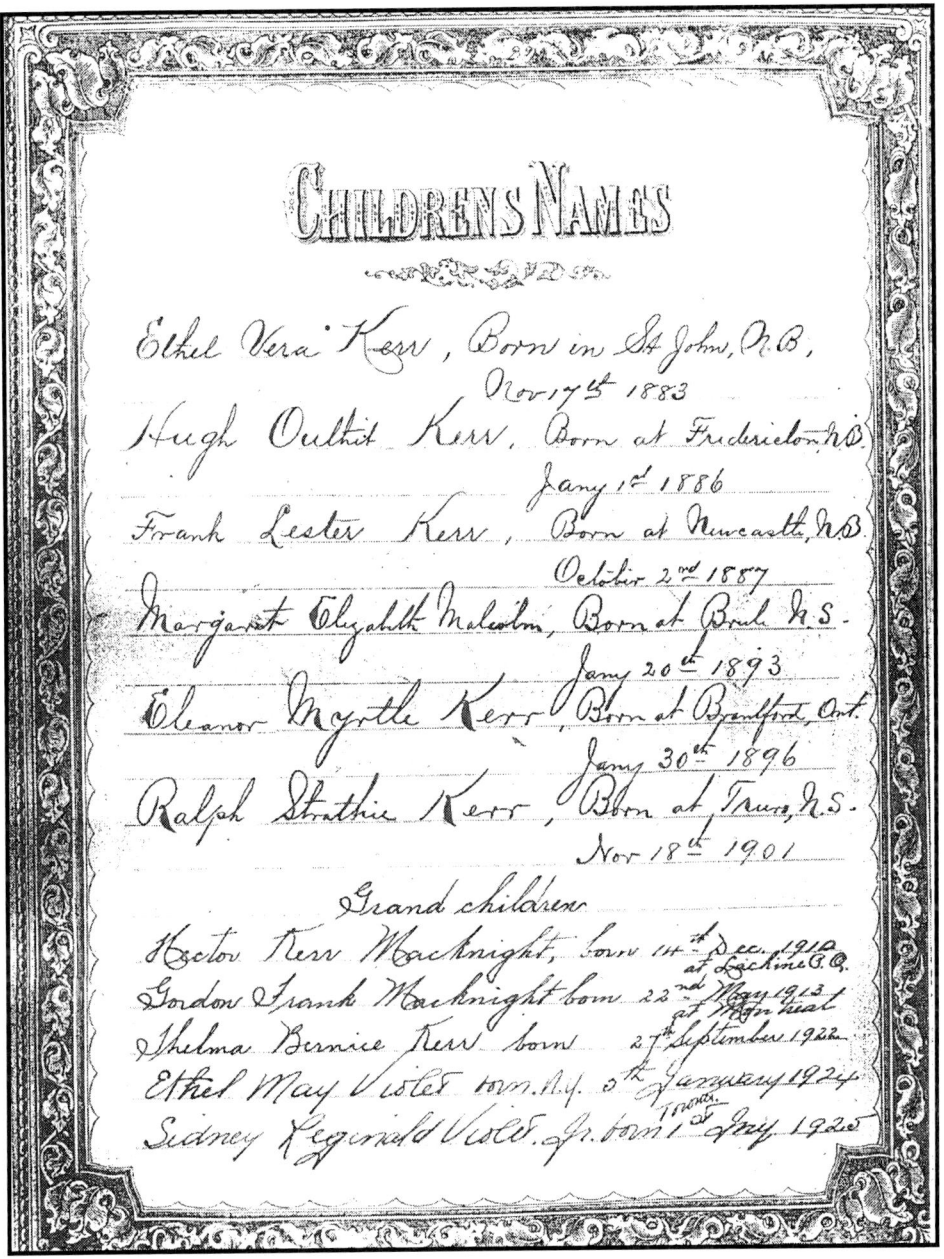

CHILDREN'S NAMES

Ethel Vera Kerr, Born in St. John, N.B. Nov 17th 1883

Hugh Outhit Kerr, Born at Fredericton, N.B. Jany 1st 1886

Frank Lester Kerr, Born at Newcastle, N.B. October 2nd 1887

Margaret Elizabeth Malcolm, Born at Bul, N.S. Jany 20th 1893

Eleanor Myrtle Kerr, Born at Brantford, Ont. Jany 30th 1896

Ralph Strathie Kerr, Born at Truro, N.S. Nov 18th 1901

Grand children

Hector Kerr Macknight, born 14th Dec. 1910 at Lachine P.Q.

Gordon Frank Macknight born 22nd May 1913 at Montreal

Thelma Bernice Kerr born 27th September 1922

Ethel May Violet born N.Y. 5th January 1924

Sidney Reginald Violet Jr. born 1st July 1925

The Kerr family hailed from Scottish roots, even though the family immigrated to Nova Scotia from Ireland. Grandfather Kerr moved his family to Montreal, from Nova Scotia. He speculated in the stock market and apparently the family went from feast to famine overnight, when he lost everything. Because of the family's financial downfall, my father was forced to leave school. He worked as a bookkeeper, in order to help support the family.

Before the family demise, Grandfather Kerr had been quite well off in Montreal, having a fine home with beautiful furnishings and travel souvenirs that Grandmother Kerr had gathered during her trips to Europe. My father had attended McGill University where he studied economics under Stephen Leacock.

J. Frank Outhit, QC, Passes In 90th Year

J. FRANK OUTHIT, QC

KENTVILLE—J. Frank Outhit, QC, a member of the Nova Scotia Bar for 62 years and a practising barrister in Halifax, and later Kentville, for 54 years until his retirement in 1949, died in his 90th year Friday following an illness extending over the last eight months.

Mr. Outhit's long career included school teaching, editor of a weekly newspaper, clerk of the Nova Scotia Legislative Council, 1907-26, solicitor for the Municipality of Kings for 35 years, presidency of the Kings County Bar Association, and Registrar of Probate for Kings County from 1945 to 1952, and in many elections campaign manager for the Liberal Party in his constituency.

Born at Melvern Square, Annapolis County, son of Thomas and Ellen (Morrison) Outhit, he received his early education in the local school and then went to Pictou Academy, and following graduation entered Dalhousie Law School, graduating in 1895.

He was admitted to the Bar at the same year, and in 1916 was made a King's Counsel.

Mr. Outhit, before taking his law course, taught school in Parrsboro. Later he served as editor of The Parrsboro Record. He first practised law in Halifax, where he was associated with the late Fred T. Congdon, KC. He came to Kentville in 1911 and was associated with the late W. P. Shaffner in the firm of Shaffner and Outhit. Later, the present Chief Justice of Nova Scotia, Rt. Hon. J. L. Ilsley, became a junior member of the firm, and it became known as Shaffner, Outhit and Ilsley. Following Mr. Shaffner's death and Mr. Ilsley's removal from Kentville to become Minister of National Revenue at Ottawa, the late Harry Dennison, KC, entered the firm with Mr. Outhit.

Following the former's death, he continued to practise on his own until retirement.

Mr. Outhit was a member of the Masonic Lodge and the Kentville United Church and an honorary life member of the Kings County Bar Association.

His wife was the former Jennie Lambert of Springhill. She passed away in 1936.

Surviving are one son, William D. Outhit, QC, chairman, Nova Scotia Board of Public Utilities, Halifax; one daughter, Margaret, wife of Lt. Col. Kenneth A. Harrison, Kentville; and six grandchildren.

Surviving also are one brother, Daniel M. Outhit, 94, of Melvern Square, who retired last year as treasurer for the Municipality of Annapolis County, and one sister, Margaret (Mrs. Hugh Kerr), 95, Vancouver.

The body, now resting at the W. C. Hiltz and Son Funeral Home here, will be taken to the United Church of St. Paul and St. Stephen for funeral services at 2 o'clock Monday afternoon. The Rev. Kenneth G. Sullivan will officiate. Burial in Oak Grove Cemetery.

Leacock's economic view of history dominated my father's thinking for the rest of his life. Father loved history, as well, and was able to relate past events to current economic circumstances. He used to draw up charts illustrating his theories, and then point out that a great many of the wars had been started in order to protect trade routes. Father often quoted Leacock.

My father had an uncle, Frank Outhit, (my grandmother's brother) whom he deeply admired, and in fact, was named after. This uncle was not only a lawyer, but also a Member of Parliament during the Ilsley wartime coalition government. (see Outhit's Obituary)

MY MOTHER'S FAMILY

Mother's family was "very Irish" and as long as I ever knew them, they were quite well off. Grandfather Courtney was an import merchant dealing in Irish luxury goods such as: linen, lace, china and crystal. I have the fondest memories of him; he was a jolly man, even though he was ill for the majority of the time I knew him. He had been crippled with a stroke while in midlife. I remember my mother was quite devoted to her father. She would always take him for a walk in his wooden wheelchair. She would place me on his knee and he would tickle me and tell me stories. Grandmother Courtney, on the other hand, was a hard taskmaster. One of her goals in life was to make sure her four daughters married well.

Mother's eldest sister was Kathleen. She was the most highly educated of the family, although all the girls had obtained their Grade 13. That was quite unusual for girls during those times. Aunt Kathleen was very gifted in the arts. She painted on china cups, some of which I still have; and she translated a French book into English. She married Harold, a pompous British engineer, who found it difficult to hold a job. They moved to the West Coast and had one son, Harry, the only boy cousin on my mother's side of the family. He, too, was artistically gifted and after his discharge from the Air Force he pursued a career as a graphic artist.

Aunt Florence had a statuesque beauty with a great presence that would have served her well on the Opera stage. She preferred singing over playing the piano—I guess you could say that she was a wannabe opera singer. She had a beautiful voice and had been designated as one of the contralto soloists at Toronto's Anglican *Grace Church on the Hill*. My mother would accompany her sister on the piano, when she practiced her vocals at our house. I could hear her singing when I was studying, painting, or sketching. Grandfather Courtney was upset when Aunt Florence took a job at a bank—he thought it was beneath her, and a poor reflection on his ability to support his family. I believe she worked there in order to pay for her vocal lessons. I also learned, not long after my marriage, of my aunt's involvement in The National Council of Women—she held the very prestigious role of president in 1949.

Aunt Lillian was next in age to my mother. She was a dear, loving person. She used to babysit me whenever my mother needed to run errands. I have the fondest memories of her. Aunt Lillian loved children. Unfortunately she only had one child—a lovely baby boy who died about a week after his birth. I was around eight at the time, and I can remember seeing this beautiful baby in a tiny coffin. I believe the cause of his death was the "RH Factor," a condition caused when the genes of the two parents are in conflict with each other. However, that fact was not absolutely diagnosed at the time.

Mother was the youngest daughter. She was an amazing pianist. She had a younger brother; but, unfortunately, he passed away from carcinoma of the throat (throat cancer) when he was 13. Through titbits she imparted to me, I think she had some resentment toward her sisters; it appeared that she did many of the household jobs that they were not willing to do. One of the things she mentioned was that she had to help entertain her sisters' boyfriends, which apparently flocked to their home. All the Courtney girls had beautiful porcelain skin and jet black hair, and from grandmother's photos they were certainly a very attractive group—true Irish *Colleens*!

Mother's family had a cottage at Long Branch, which they commuted to by train. Mother had preferred to remain in town and keep house for her father who would stay back in order to manage his business. She cited that the cottage was the scene of so much entertainment for her sisters and their boyfriends. When I perused through old picture albums I would see snapshots of big tables sitting under the trees, laden with great quantities of savoury looking home cooking.

When the time came, even though the family had a maid to help maintain the home up to Grandmother Courtney's high standards, my mother was the one who did a lot of the bedside nursing for her father and brother. During the Spanish Flu epidemic of 1918, Mother said that people were dying at such a rate in Toronto that her father decided she had better take the train and join the family at the Long Branch cottage. She said when she went to the station to catch the train it was filled with the caskets of people who had died. It must have been a most horrid experience for her!

I, who was the only granddaughter on my mother's side of the family, felt I must have been quite a disappointment to my grandmother for I took no great interest in the setting of tables and the serving of tea, as a proper young lady should. Around the age of nine, I discovered fishing with my father, and that was that! During my first year in Law School, Grandmother Courtney passed away. She had been upset that I had gone to university to study Law, thinking it disgraceful for me to be attending classes with all of those boys. As a result of her feelings on the subject, she cut me out of her will!

PARENTS

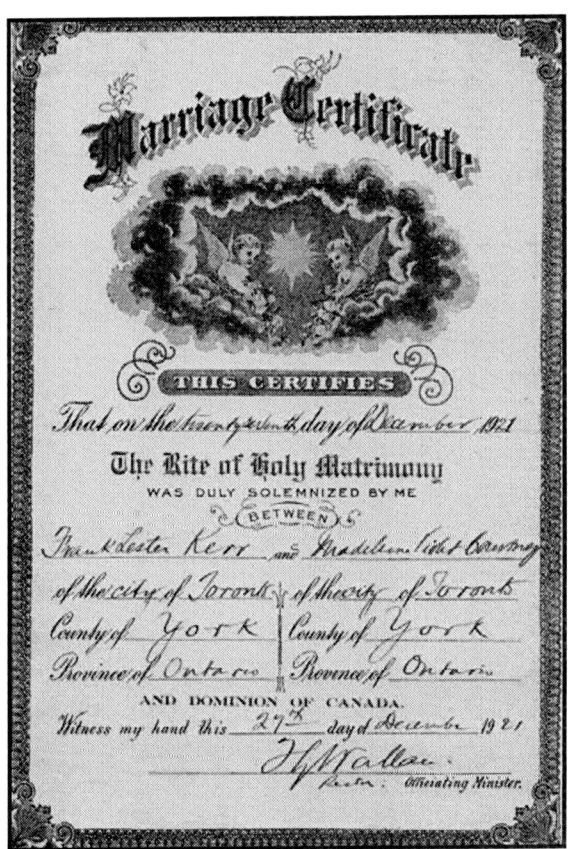

My father, Frank Lester Kerr, was born in Newcastle, New Brunswick, Canada, on October 2, 1888. His sister Eleanor was born in Brantford, Ontario, in 1896. She was the same age as my mother. When the cornerstone of the Victoria school was unearthed, there was an Ethel Kerr listed as a kindergarten student there.

Father was a remarkable man! He was quite brilliant at what he did, even though he was a very unassuming man, with a shy reserve. He obtained his Canadian CA (chartered accountant) degree while working for Clarkson, Gordon and Dillworth on Temperance Street in Toronto. When I was a toddler we moved to Chicago so he could attain his American Public Accountant accreditation. I always felt that because he had had to drop out of university to help support the family, that it had impacted his outlook on life. He was continuously taking night courses at the University of Toronto to improve himself.

My father's quiet personality made him rather diffident about getting out there to acquire new clients, which was an expectation for partners of the firm he worked with, Thorne Mulholland. This firm eventually became an international firm known as "The Thorne Group." The partners, Howston and McPherson, were constantly urging Father to join social clubs. He finally broke down and joined the "Caledon Fishing Club" in order to satisfy his partners. However that did not serve the

purpose it was meant to, because father would just go off and fish by himself!

~

On the other hand, my mother, Madeleine Violet Courtney, was quite the social butterfly. She was born in Toronto, Ontario, on September 18, 1896. Mother was an "expert homemaker." She knew how to work a dining room better than anyone I ever knew, obviously something she had learned from Grandmother Courtney. In fact, Mother was so interested in culinary arts that she studied Dietetics for two years at the Margaret Eaton School. I found it quite amusing when she told me that Grandma Kerr would frequently come over to tell her what to cook for Dad's supper! Mother was a wonderful hostess and a great asset to my shy father, when it came to assisting him with business connections.

Mother's upbringing had considered that "ignorance was innocence." I assumed, from things my mother would occasionally mention, that her wedding night was a terrible surprise to her, and that my birth just nine months less a day afterward was another shock! She spent the first week of her honeymoon in New York City, where she and my father attended the Metropolitan opera every night. I think I was conceived after my father's favourite opera, "Tales of Hoffman!" My ever-thrifty father had an audit to do the first week of the honeymoon, so the client paid part of his expenses. From New York, they took a boat to Bermuda. Mother was seasick all the way!

Mother found it difficult to speak to me about *growing up*, as was the case with most women of that era. When it was time to enlighten me about sex, she placed a booklet on top of a *Kotex* box, along with twenty-five cents—the twenty-five cents was for samples—the booklet was to inform me of what would soon happen to me as a young, blossoming girl.

As I mentioned earlier, my mother was very musically gifted and I think that is what brought my parents together—their mutual love for music. Mother's original ambitions had been to be a concert pianist. She especially loved the Russian romantics, Rachmaninoff and Tchaikovsky, and she played them with such flair that it would make my father's eyes sparkle. As a child I remember the d'Oilly Carte Opera Company that presented a season of opera at the great Massey Hall Theatre in Toronto. We always attended the opera to celebrate Mother's birthdays.

> **SALMAGUNDI GROUP HOLD FIRST MEETING**
>
> Believing that Canadians should have a greater knowledge of their government's structure and the duties of each division, a group of women has formed the Salmagundi club which will meet regularly at members' homes to hear an authority on the subject, followed by discussion.
>
> First meeting of the group, which is non-political, takes place this evening at the home of Mrs. Frank Kerr, 17 Elderwood Drive, Forest Hill Village, the speaker to be Prof. B. Laskin of the University of Toronto law school. He will speak on the House of Commons. Functions of the cabinet and the Senate will be outlined in detail, in subsequent monthly meetings.
>
> The few women who got together to form the group went to Webster's dictionary for a name, choosing "Salmagundi," meaning "a mixture." It also was the name of a periodical devoted chiefly to political matters, published in 1807 by Washington Irving and James K. Paulding. The organization aims to be a cross section of women of varied interests, religions and political leanings. Many of the members are active in other organizations. Membership at present is 40, and it is keen to add more. It hopes to interest new Canadians so that they, too, may learn more of Canada's government set-up.
>
> *October 1945 – Daily Star*

Mother told me about going to a dance with a fellow whom she was not particularly keen on and that is where she had met my father. Father was a wonderful dancer. His sister, Eleanor, had studied ballet and art in Paris, France. When she returned to Toronto, she had set up a ballet school in the front room of the Wellesley Street house where Grandma Kerr lived. This was next door to the house Father bought for his bride; Grandma Kerr was a formidable neighbour! I assumed that because Aunt Eleanor ran a dance school that my father and his brother Ralph had been pressed into partnering the young ladies who were taking lessons from their sister––the obvious explanation for Father's expertise in dance.

My mother was a political "mover and shaker"—as was Aunt Florence.

MY EARLY YEARS

This baby had a life!

Father travelled extensively with his job, so for the first few years of my life I barely saw him. When we lived in Chicago he worked for the big accounting firm Erikson-Lee, and then Price-Waterhouse. He also took evening courses at Northwest University, where he earned his U.S. Public Accountants certification. He would leave for work before I got up in the mornings, and not return until after I was in bed. We lived in an apartment and I slept on a "Murphy Bed" that was pulled out of the closet at night. Mother used to take me for a walk every morning; I remember occasional, cold walks along the beach on windy Lake Michigan. Sometimes we would take the elevated railway into downtown Chicago, where Mother would shop at Marshall Fields department store. We would have lunch in the mezzanine area—Mother enjoyed watching the people from there.

I remember one little friend from Chicago. He would knock on the door in the mornings and yell out, "Thelma Bernice! Thelma Bernice's mother, can Thelma Bernice come out to play?" We would play in the apartment building courtyard—always under the watchful eyes of my mother.

During the Chicago years I was not privy to public education; however, Father, when he was able, taught me basic arithmetic, and Mother taught me to read. I believe my parents feared to send me to the local schools because of the atmosphere in Chicago in the 1920's. The city was full of gangs and bootleggers. Al Capone's gang fought for regional control. There were constant shoot-outs in the downtown and many innocent bystanders were shot.

One of the parlour jokes my parents and their friends enjoyed telling was when I was asked what I wanted to be when I grew up. I would put on a pair of my father's boots and say that I was going to be a bootlegger—they seemed be running the city and had all the money! Of course everyone laughed that such a statement would come out of the mouth of a small child!

We returned to Toronto in 1929, when I was seven. While in Chicago, I had learned to speak *Chicago-ese*, as I called it. Uncle Earl teased my *offensive* accent out of me!

I feel in many ways that I had a privileged upbringing. Being an only child, though, I also felt that my parents might have over-sheltered and pampered me a bit, too. I was fortunate to have ballet lessons from an early age, beginning these while in Chicago. I loved dancing. I remember my first ballet recital. The MC was Ben Bernie.

He used to open the program with the statement: "Youser, youser, ladies and gentlemen…" My ballet career was cut short at the age of 14; the ballet mistress advised my parents that I did not have a suitable body for ballet. Dad decided to buy me a black cocker spaniel, much to Mother's horror—it would dirty her perfect home! Mother's only experience with animals had been with her brother's pet rabbit. In the end, she became quite fond of Shadow. Shadow helped me to feel not quite as lonely in my life as an only child.

Of course there was no way to escape having to play the piano, it being ingrained into my mother's family history. I never really knew why, but my mother did not teach me. I went through a succession of piano teachers. I was easily bored with scales and finger exercises—I just wanted to play like my mother did, and the music the piano teachers had me play had no melody whatsoever that would inspire me to practise! Other instruments I played in the Forest Hill school band were the: ukulele, banjo, and the marimba (similar to a xylophone). I also loved to sing, so I joined any choir I could.

Upon our return to Toronto, we stayed with Aunt Lillian and Uncle Earl, in the second story flat in Uncle Earl's old family home on Spadina Road, just south of Dupont. My mother enrolled me in a school close to my Aunt's home, St. Mildred's College, a High Anglican school. Mother had attended there as a young girl. I was a bit of a misfit because I was relatively advanced for my age, having had a good grounding in mathematics from my father and an advanced level of reading due to my mother's teachings. But the nuns were kind and patient and I believe they helped to prepare me for a regular school system.

Eventually, we moved to an apartment in a duplex on Avenue Road. Father and Mother then went house hunting. My father wanted to live near the northern boundary of Toronto because of the open space there; he loved the solitude of the outdoors.

While living there, I attended my second school, Allenby Road Elementary. I think I made quite an impression on my first day. Mother had me decked out in my white bunny coat and bonnet, and when I first appeared on the schoolyard a most cheeky boy came up to me and said, "Who do you think you are? Lady Allenby?" A teacher had to intervene when I had the boy down on the ground, kneeling on him and punching him out! I showed him that I was no lady!

That was a splendid school, and in spite of my shaky start, they must have been kind to me because the only bad memory from there that I have was their method of teaching swimming. The school had a beautiful swimming pool and we were given swimming lessons during our gym periods. This was my first introduction to a swimming pool. I recall we had to stand on the edge of the pool and then a teacher would come along and whip our legs out from under us by hitting our ankles with some kind of a stick—that is how I took my first plunge into a pool!

~

My immediate family did not suffer too greatly during the years of the Great Depression. I would not say we were lucky, but then again, maybe we were. My father was working. My parents were very thrifty people, as well, their motto being—"re-use, save, make do, and take care of what you had." My father even helped support some of his family who were having a difficult time making ends meet. I was somewhat sheltered from the actual suffering of The Depression that many people faced, but I would sometimes hear my parents discussing the hard times. One memory that has stuck with me was seeing well-dressed men lined up at the soup kitchen at the Scott Mission, just west of the University. As young as I was, it struck me as a terrible social injustice. I considered myself quite fortunate to have the home I had.

FOREST HILL ELEMENTARY SCHOOL

Once we were established in our own home at 17 Elderwood Drive, I attended Forest Hill Elementary School. At the time (early 1930's) this was a "demonstration school" for Ontario, where new ideas in education were being implemented. At Forest Hill, in my time, there was a beautiful green area that I played in after school. I was to come home for supper when the street lights came on. In the summer my parents joined one of the community badminton groups. In the winter a large area was flooded and everybody in the neighbourhood gathered there to skate.

Pupils who did well in their core subjects were offered "opportunity classes," many of these consisted of art and music. I was drawn toward music, joining the choral society and the school band, which is where I learned to play the marimba. I also took a typing class and the elocution class taught by Dora Mavor Moore, who said it was essential to learn how to descend a flight of stairs, how to walk with proper posture, and how to sit like a lady! This class helped me a great deal throughout my life, especially when appearing in the court rooms. Dora was a well-known actress who became memorialized in the city. She also taught me how to properly enunciate my words. In fact, I believe even deaf people can *hear* me well, even when they cannot hear others!

One amazing event, which came out of these opportunity classes, was getting chosen to attend art classes at The Art Gallery of Ontario. A limo would pick me and one other classmate up on Saturday mornings, for a special art class at the AGO, which was taught by Arthur Lismer from the "Group of Seven," and his wife. I felt quite special when I was chosen for this.

When I was in grade ten, my final year at Forest Hill, I have no idea what prompted me to run for President of the Student Council—no girl had ever been president before. Maybe it was my overdeveloped sense of justice that I wanted to run against a boy who was the school bully. I had noticed him bullying all the boys into voting for him.

My pal, Jackie, (Jacqueline Kay) organized a committee of girls to run my election campaign. They put up wonderful banners in the school corridors, to promote me for president. My father helped me with my campaign speech. I think at one time my father must have attended political meetings organized by his uncle, Frank Outhit. Father certainly demonstrated the know-how of how to promote a political candidate—he even taught me how to pound the podium when I made a point during my speech. Here is my campaign speech as I presented it on that day…

Girl Wins High School Office for First Time

Thelma B. Kerr, daughter of Mr. and Mrs. Frank L. Kerr, Elderwood Drive, was elected president of the Students' Council at the Dunloe Road School this week.

The president-elect, who is in the second form of the Senior School, won in a contest with three girls and four boys and is the first girl to be so honored.

Mr. Chairman, Headmaster, Teachers and Fellow Students…

The issue in this election is not to make a "Big Shot" out of some fellow pupil by making him President, but to make sense of an organization that will work together in the best interests of all of us. You all know that there are a number of things that an active, clearheaded council could improve. We have been particularly weak in forming

> **Over School Books**
> By Students of The Class in Journalism,
> Village of Forest Hill School.
>
> **THELMA KERR WINS SCHOOL PRESIDENCY**
>
> Amid the din of campaigning and coloured banners, the students of the Village School nominated and elected as president of the Students' Council, Thelma Kerr, popular second former. Campaign speeches were given in the morning assembly. After nomination papers were received, each candidate advocated his or her platform in two-minute addresses to the senior students.
>
> Voting took place in the group rooms at 1.15 p.m. Ballots were counted and checked, and results were announced by the returning officer at 3.00.
>
> The new president, a la campaign, stiffest competition from Ross ("Slug") Lindsay whom she narrowly defeated. The other candidates were Elizabeth McGibbon, Robert Spratt, Glen Brockett and Frank Birchall respectively.
>
> Much credit is due the poll clerks for the smooth manner in which the election was run. These were: Barbara Tomlinson, Evan Fraser, Len Davis, Kay Wallace, Allan Bathurst, Jacqueline Kay, Madeline Sixt, and Frances Allen.
>
> Miss Kerr, the new president, has the honour of being the first girl elected head of the Students' Council in its historic three years of operation. She defeated Ross Lindsay by the narrow margin of 23 votes, having a total of 121. Those "in the know" were certain that Lindsay would walk away with the election. However, they received a jolt when the girls banded together to elect Thelma.
>
> The new president, ala campaign, promised "bigger, better, and more, social evenings" this year. She is off to a fine start, having already all her committees from the ranks of the defeated candidates.
> —Dick Black (4B)

committees with definite jobs to do. As you all know everybody's business is nobody's business, it never gets done.

I propose to have a committee formed to improve social evenings; we want more and better evenings. There are too many wallflowers at these meetings. Perhaps it would round out a livelier group if we were to extend invitations to our friends and former pupils of the school. We should have a suggestion box at a point of vantage in the school so everybody would help the committee improve the social evenings. And to receive suggestions addressed to other committees.

We want real, constructive, co-operation with our teachers to eliminate the bunching up of homework. If each teacher was given a prearranged night for homework in each subject we could level it off without overdoses. There should be two committees on sports, one for the boys and one for the girls. The problem of getting more time in the gym is a large one and needs the best brains we can muster to deal with it.

The Junior 4 and Senior 4 should be properly represented on these committees so they won't be muscled out of the picture.

Now about movie pictures, we are proud of our equipment but we are not getting the most out of it. There are lots of good pictures and we should have a committee to see that we get them.

This is my platform—I have confidence in your judgment.

My speech won the day, much to the ire of the big bully!

THE HUNT CLUB

There was another great love I had as a girl—a love that has remained with me throughout my entire life—I was wild about horses.

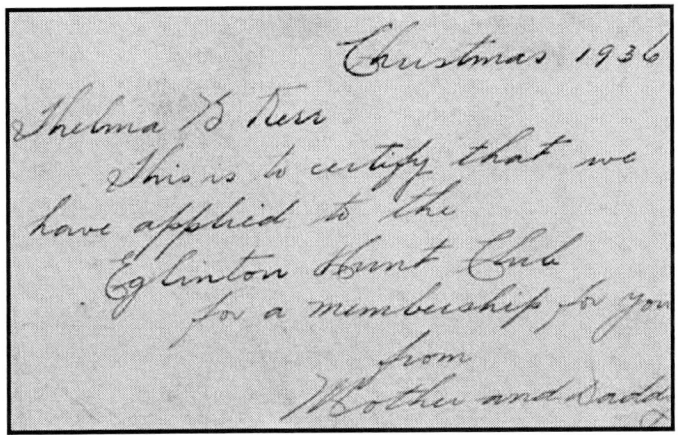

Christmas 1936, my *Mother and Daddy* gave me a junior membership at the prestigious Eglinton Hunt Club. It was another push in the social climbing effort to meet *the right people*. I was *a nobody* to the club members, but I loved the horses. I had been riding since I was very young, at a livery stable, with my dad. He had wanted to join the army with his elder brother, Outhit, but when he was rejected because of his faulty feet, he joined the Cavalry Reserve. I think I inherited my dad's faulty feet.

Even though I did not have a horse of my own, while growing up, I remained a member of the Eglinton Hunt Club on Avenue Road, north of Toronto, for a number of years. They had established the first pony club in Canada (British Institute of the Horse), and they had a wonderful junior program. I felt, though, that there was quite a class distinction between those of us who did not have our own horse and those who did. This was one beef I had with my father. Every time I would beg him for a horse he would retrieve a piece of paper and prove to me that it was less expensive to rent a horse than it was to buy one. Of course that did not mean anything to a horse-crazy girl who wanted her own horse!

The horses the Hunt Club rented out were usually donated by owners who were finished with them and needed a younger horse. My favourite horse was *Old 97*. He was full of energy, whether we were showing, or following the hounds. He had been a Cavalry horse and he was all heart. *Old 97* loved to jump, and when I was not handling the jump approach correctly, he did his best to take me over. Of course I fell off a lot in those early riding classes, but the other kids at the Hunt Club told me that you were not a real rider until you had fallen off at least three dozen times—I sure made it well past that number!

The Hunt Club was struggling to find something that would keep the young people involved, because interest in the hunt was beginning to dwindle. It was starting to be considered as a bit of an anachronism by many of the population in those days. The Hunt was conducted just to the west of Avenue Road, following the hounds into what is now a built up area of Toronto.

Because of the loss of interest in the Hunt, the Pony Club developed a great Saturday youth program. To encourage the junior members to stay more then a few hours, a buffet lunch was provided. Then, in the afternoon, we would practice musical rides, simulating the Royal Canadian Mounted Police performances. This was great training for learning how to control a horse. Every year, at the Royal Winter Fair, our junior team would be called upon to give a demonstration.

We did things like bobbing for apples, where one would gallop their horse from one end of the arena to the other; dismount, bob for an apple in a bucket, and then remount and return to the finish line. We also played musical chairs, riding around a row of chairs until the music stopped, and then dismounting and grabbing a chair. If you were successful in getting a chair, you would mount up again; if you were not, you were excused from the ring. These games were great fun and full of camaraderie amongst fellow riders.

There came a time when I finally became a good enough rider that a member lent me a wonderful polo pony to ride in the final *gymcana*. The groom who had helped me to mount advised me that the owner had paid $3000 for that polo pony; he figured I had one of the best horses in the ring. That was quite a daunting thought! When I informed my parents of this, they secured a box for the family members to sit in, to see my grand entry into the ring. My father even bought me a new, tailor-made riding jacket for the occasion. The band struck up a big drum roll as I entered the ring. The polo pony had never experienced such an entrance—he dashed to the opposite end of the arena, and I fell off—with the family watching!

I spent four years at the Club and acquired some Pony Club certifications, but quit at eighteen when I was no longer a junior, and when the fees went up. I was starting to think about law school and I knew Dad could not afford the time or money to maintain my riding.

BRANKSOME HALL SCHOOL

Forest Hill School only went as far as grade ten, so I had to find another school. I had met some girls from Branksome Hall School at Timothy Eaton Memorial Church. I attended there because they had the best Sunday school picnics, and ferryboat rides to Port Dalhousie. They were some of the nicest girls I had ever met. I guess that between that, and the fact that my mother was partial to private schools, was how I ended up at Branksome Hall Private Girl's School for my high school years—Grades 11, 12 and 13. I had quite a distance to travel from where we lived in Forest Hill, which was in

Rosedale. Mother was instrumental in getting a bus service instituted for the girls from our area, who were attending Branksome Hall. I used to catch the bus in the very early morning.

Father was actually opposed to Branksome Hall. He felt that such a school was not on par with the public school system, and that they were set up in order to promote a young woman to become just like her mother. He also did not like the fact that most of the teachers had no formal teacher's training or certification. Many had been brought in from Nova Scotia because they would work cheaply—most also lived at the school.

There were some aspects of the school that I found to be unduly strict. I remember, in particular, the school secretary. She had a booming voice and a commanding manner that sent shivers up and down my spine. Apparently she sent notes home to the parents of the girls whom she did not think were shaping up to school standards. I don't think my mother ever received one.

Branksome was steeped in Scottish traditions, which did please my father. We girls were divided into different Clans and had to wear kilts. I was part of the *McAlpine* Clan which wore the green hunting plaid. The head girls wore the *Royal Stewart* kilt, which had a red background. Branksome was known more for its sports than for its academic scholarships. I, being quite petite, was too short to make the first team in basketball. I did have a special love for the water, though, and was lucky that Branksome had a pool. There were a few times I almost missed the bus home because I was usually the last one out of the water. There were no actual swim teams at Branksome, but while there I took the St. John's life-saving course.

My keenness for swimming was another influence my father had on me. He had a fancy swimming and diving certificate from the YMCA in Montreal. Father felt that I should learn how to swim by the age of ten; however, I actually had not had much of an opportunity to learn—other than the few gym lessons at the Allenby School. Father enrolled me in the Baracca Club on Spadina Avenue. It was off the circle, around the site of the first Ontario Legislature building. Ernest Vierkotter, who had won the CNE (Canadian National Exhibition) Swim contest for several years running, was the instructor. He gave me a strict regiment to follow. I came out of those swimming lessons a pretty good swimmer. I mostly enjoyed doing lengths of the *Australian Crawl*. Later, when I was in university, I used to go back to the club and swim with Ernest's daughter who was studying medicine at the same time I was studying law. I also swam with some of my fraternity sisters who were in the Physical and Health Education program at the University. We would walk about a mile from our frat house on St. George Street, to the YWCA east of Yonge Street. The pool there was more adequate than the one on campus, under the Margaret Eaton Building. We swam for fun and also trained for competitive synchronized swimming. Unfortunately, this program was cancelled during the polio epidemic.

I remember a few teachers who had an impact on me, while at Branksome. One was a Math teacher. She was brilliant, but there were more times than not that she would get absorbed in what she was doing on the blackboard and forget all about her students!

We had a wonderful French teacher, Mlle. Lenoire, who came from the south of France. When I was studying in Quebec, during the summers, my friends used to tell me my accent sounded just like hers. She was a role model for me, being so chic and smart, making many of the other teachers appear quite dowdy. I tried to imitate everything she did, including mouthing silently all the French vowel sounds and rolling my *r's*. It was because of Mlle. Lenoire that I took such a keen interest in learning French.

Like my father, I was very interested in history, and one of the teachers who taught Modern European History fed my desire to learn more—she also gave me quite good marks. One English teacher commented on my writing style, asking me if I would be interested in a Journalism career. Little did I know then that most of my future writings would consist of writing wills and pleadings! Even now, when I try to write anything, it comes out sounding like a legal document.

I made some very precious friends while at Branksome. By Grade 13 we were divided into two groups—those headed for a furtherance of their education, and those who were headed for a debut into society—kind of like the girls in the movie, *Mona Lisa Smile*. There were several Grade 13 classes; the one designated to lead into university was the one I chose. Of that particular class, though, there were only two that I know of who actually completed a four-year Honour degree at the University of Toronto (U of T).

All of my closest friends were in the academic stream. Many of them enrolled in General Arts at the U of T, with the intention of finishing an Honour degree. With the outbreak of the war there was so much public feeling that university students should not be permitted deferment from conscription. Many citizens felt that students should either join, or become involved in some aspect of war service. Two of my best friends joined.

Mary Ritchie-Kinner joined the Red Cross. She drove for them for years, even after the war; she was an expert driver. Mary was taught how to take care of her truck—she knew how to change spark plugs and tires! Mary finished a three-year General Arts Degree.

Joan Vanstone joined the Navy. The drill-training and route marches ruined her feet. The Navy issue shoes she had to wear were not very supportive! Joan had originally been enrolled in Commerce and Finance at the U of T, but when her fiancé was killed at Dieppe, it took the heart out of her—that is actually when she joined the Navy.

Another best friend of mine, whom I had met while at Forest Hill School, was Jacqueline Kay. She married the boy next door, on his last leave, before he went oversees as an Air Force Pathfinder pilot. He located targets for bombers and paratroopers, and towed in gliders. Jackie managed to complete a three-year Arts degree, even though she immediately became pregnant. The fourth special friend, Elizabeth, whom I called Phoebe, (Tilt was her married name) finished a Fine Arts degree. We still correspond.

Branksome Girls—Class of 1941— (Thelma, front row, left)

Similar to Forest Hill School, Branksome had classes for debutantes. Mother encouraged me to attend these, continuing on with her thoughts of how important it was for me to learn how to be presented to Society, and to learn how to be a good hostess. Of my own accord I took an Art Appreciation course, which I thoroughly enjoyed. Eventually that class dwindled down to one student—me. However, the teacher said she would continue to teach the class as long as I was interested. I guess because of my lust for learning, I got the best of both sides of the school!

I and my regular friends at Branksome were always doing extracurricular activities together. To this day, I am still in touch with two of them. Phyllis Tilt is now in a nursing home; Mary Ritchie is living in Guelph. We try to celebrate the Annual Branksome Spring Luncheon together, in a mutually convenient place, rather than travelling to the school.

I graduated from Branksome in June, 1941.

~

Despite his soft demeanour, my father was a highly principled man who lived by the "Golden Rule"—*do unto others as you would have them do unto you, and its converse, do NOT do unto others what you would NOT have them do unto you*. I found, throughout my life, I was constantly trying to please him. Education was of the utmost importance to my father. It was his influence, more than my mother's, which persuaded me to a higher level of learning. He felt I should attain the education he thought he lacked, and he leaned particularly toward having me study law. Father believed that legal training would sharpen my mind so that I would be able to handle whatever problems life might throw at me. Of course, I am not sure if he was aware of the prejudices that I, as a woman lawyer, would have to face—from both society and my fellow male lawyers.

SUMMERS IN QUEBEC

Top Picture—Rue des Rampart—my view of the dry docks
Bottom Picture—far right, my two-room apartment, 14 St. Famille St.

Lester Bowles Pearson (April 23, 1897 to December 27, 1972) was a professor, historian, statesman, diplomat, and politician. He played an important part in founding the United Nations and N.A.T.O. (North American Treaty Organization), and served them both from 1927 to 1946. Pearson was awarded the Nobel Peace Prize in 1957. I admired his work and decided that when I completed my education I would like to join him in whatever he was doing. When I began to consider studying law, I felt that brushing up on my French would be a good way of preparing me to get into Pearson's Department of External Affairs. I actually had no intention to practice law. To improve my French, I spent my summers in Quebec. Between Grades 12 and 13, I attended the University of Western Ontario's Trois Pistoles School, where I took French summer classes. I also went to the Université Laval, where I studied Spanish.

It was my wonderful French teacher from Branksome, Mlle. Lenoire, who spoke to my parents about advancing my French studies. She had noted my strong interest in French, and that I was doing exceptionally well. She recommended I have the experience of total immersion in the French language when I completed my Grade 12. Mlle. Lenoire, who subsequently became head of the French Department at McGill University, made all the arrangements for me to attend the University of Western Ontario French summer school at Trois Pistoles. Most of the other students were University students who had flunked French—they were trying to make up their credit. I used to get the feeling that they hated me because I was just a high school kid who was so keen about French that I would not even chatter in English to them! My main contact with these students was in the line-up for the *one* bathroom at chez Madam René Rioux.

I hung around mostly with French speaking kids. I had shipped my bicycle to Trois Pistoles, so I was able to ride to the beach on the St. Lawrence River, where I made friends with the sons and daughters of the families who had cottages there. This helped me to be totally immersed in the French language—a lot of the time, though, I had no idea what was going on!

I stayed with a Quebecois family, the Rioux's, who had moved into their father's garage beside the home. They vacated their bedrooms in the summer months, to rent them to students. We were provided with breakfast and supper, most days. René, the mother, was a wonderfully dedicated woman and a devout Roman Catholic. I figured, when I had been out late in the evenings, improving my French with the locals, that I had better get up for early morning Mass so that Madam Rioux would not tell the director of the summer school anything negative about me!

The only thing to do on a date at Trois Pistoles was walk up and down the main street; or, if somebody had a car we could go out of town to a place where there was a jukebox so that we could dance. The Parish priest ran that community like his fiefdom—he thought that boys and girls dancing together was a sin. I loved dancing. When they had a final evening where everybody was supposed to present something, I wore my kilt and performed the sword dance. I noticed who was sitting, front-row-center, scrutinizing my legs while I was dancing—none other than the Parish priest and his cohorts!

I was selected for Valedictorian at Trois Pistoles. They were impressed with my speech about all the terrible blunders I had made in French. I also recited some of my favourite French poetry. As a result, I was presented with a scholarship to study French the following summer at the Université Laval.

In 1945 I was given a fellowship to teach Business English to a class of boys in a Business Administration course; plus, I was permitted to study both French and Spanish. It was a heavy summer. Instead of boarding with a family, I took an apartment across the road from the University, on St. Famille Street. I even tried to learn to prepare my own meals! Once again, I was chosen for Valedictorian, but it was not by popular vote—the Rector of the University decided. I think it was the novelty of my situation that appealed to the staff there—it seemed I stood out because I was studying French for the love of the language, not just for career advancement.

!EBEC, MARDI 29 JUIN 1943

Bourses accordées par l'université à des étudiants

Comme par les années passées, la direction des cours d'été de l'Université Laval a accordé sept bourses et deux demi-bourses à des étudiantes et étudiants d'expression anglaise, soit des Etats-Unis, soit des autres provinces du Canada. Ces bourses sont de cinquante dollars chacune. Voici comment elles furent réparties:

Deux bourses payées par le Comité Permanent de la Survivance française en Amérique: M. l'abbé Wilfrid Papineau, Acadien de l'Ile du Prince-Edouard, et Mlle Géraldine Mouton, de Lafayette, Louisiane. Ces deux étudiants suivent les cours pour la troisième fois et préparent la Maîtrise ès arts en français.

Deux bourses payees par un professeur des cours d'été: Rév. Sister Joseph Mary Cousins, de Seton Hill, Greensburg, Pa., et Miss Thelma Kerr, étudiante en droit à l'Université de Toronto.

Quatre bourses payées par l'Organisation des cours d'été: Miss Vincie Fastiggi, College of New Rochelle, N.-Y., Miss Betty Maria Schweitzer, Webster College, Webster Groves, Mo; Miss Isa Landels, Collegiate, Institute, Lethbridge, Alberta. Deux demi-bourses: Miss Alice Field et Miss Je Fineman, de State Teachers College, Montclair, New-Jersey.

Cent cinquante étudiants d'en hors de la province de Québec s attendus pour la session d'été cours de français et de philosoph qui commencera le 5 juillet.

TO WHOM IT MAY CONCERN

IT IS HEREBY CERTIFIED THAT

THELMA KERR

took during the Summer 19.45.. at Laval University, Quebec, Canada, the following courses and received the approval, credits and rank as listed:

	Courses	Periods	Credits	Rank
	Histoire de France	30	2	100%
	Phonétique avancée	15	1	92%
	Diction	30	1	75%
Espagnol L	Cours pour débutants	60	4	80%

Québec, le 24 septembre 1945

Alph. Marie Parent
Directeur des cours d'été.

A + = 95%. A = 90%. B + = 85%. B = 80%. C + = 75%. C = 70%.
D + = 65%. D = 60%. E = Failed.

TO WHOM IT MAY CONCERN

IT IS HEREBY CERTIFIED THAT

Miss Thelma Bernice Kerr

took during the Summer 19_42_ at Laval University, Quebec Canada, the following courses and received the approval, credits and rank as listed:

Courses	Periods	Credits	Rank
Le XVIIIe siècle	30	2	B+
Évolution du théâtre français	30	2	A
Histoire du Canada français	30	2	A+
Conversation et Diction	60	—	B

Quebec, August 10, 1942.

Alph. Marie Parent
Directeur des cours d'été

A+ = 95%. A = 90%. B+ = 85%. B = 80%. C+ = 75%. C = 70%.
D+ = 65%. D = 60%. E = Failed.

TO WHOM IT MAY CONCERN

IT IS HEREBY CERTIFIED THAT

Miss Thelma B. Kerr

took during the Summer 19.43..at Laval University, Quebec, Canada, the following courses and received the approval, credits and rank as listed:

Courses	Periods	Credits	Rank
Histoire de France	30	2	A+
Histoire du Canada	30	2	A+
Conversation et diction	30	1	B

Quebec, August 30, 1943.

Alphonse-Marie Parent
Directeur des cours d'été.

A+ = 95%. A = 90%. B+ = 85%. B = 80%. C+ = 75%. C = 70%.
D+ = 65%. D = 60%. E = Failed.

MAKING THE DECISION

I started visiting law lectures at the University of Toronto and found them interesting and stimulating. The Dean of the Law School, William Paul McLure Kennedy, was an Irishman who left you spellbound when he spoke. He had numerous academic degrees. I arranged an appointment for my father to meet him, to see if he would fund me through the four-year Honour course in Law.

We had a fascinating interview with Dean Kennedy. My father was just as spellbound as I was. In spite of being told what the cost for the Law School would be, not a quarter of what it is today, my father was all for me getting my Law degree before entering the Bar admission course at Osgoode Hall.

The Law School was in an old house located at 85 St. George Street. The classrooms were quite small. Dean Kennedy designed the program. He had included a broad spectrum of: Western Arts, Philosophy and Psychology, Political Science and Economics. He was also quite a stickler about proper English usage, emphasizing that was one way we could advertise that we were highly educated people.

Law school was a wonderful experience for me—it opened my mind to many things I had never before experienced. I particularly loved Philosophy; I thought maybe I would like to pursue that as a career. However, when I told my father, he pointed out that a Philosophy professor was not in great demand and they did not earn much money—my father, always the practical economist.

~

At one point I had also expressed an interest in studying medicine, which was my father's second choice of study for me. The two vocations, Medicine and Law, were tearing me apart. In order to help me make my decision, I paid $25.00 for an aptitude test at the YWCA. At the end of the test, the instructors felt that I was certainly more oriented toward law.

~ A Twentieth Century "Portia" – Bio of Thelma Bernice Kerr-Thomson ~

UNIVERSITY OF TORONTO LAW SCHOOL YEARS

Thelma (top left corner) and her university friends

I began studying law in 1942, at the University of Toronto Law School, which was only about three years old at the time. The main criteria for entrance to the University were academics. The University set a standard of a 75% average in order to be admitted, and that average was expected to be maintained. That was difficult sometimes because being a law student meant hours of reading decided cases, plus sixty hours of war work for each term!

The public feeling in the 1940's was quite negative toward university students; because, after conscription most people felt we should be in some form of war service. There was also the attitude that women should not be taking up spaces in the Law School that a man, or a returned veteran, had more right to. The campus was dominated by a wartime atmosphere. It was a rare occasion to see a car on campus. When we did, it was usually for someone special, and for a notable occasion.

All able-bodied men had either enlisted or had volunteered for some aspect of war-time service. Most of the boys I had grown up with volunteered to serve in their chosen branch of the Armed Forces, rather than being conscripted into one not of their choice. I have fond memories of playing *corner lot baseball* with many of them. Most wanted to be *fly boys*—some even lied about their ages and joined the RAF (Royal Air Force) so they could be in the *Battle of Britain*. They figured they could skip their Grade 13 exams, polish off Hitler, see Europe on their summer holiday, and be back in time for the fall university classes. However, the general public was not aware of how badly the war was going for Britain by 1942. Communication across the Atlantic Ocean was slow and heavily censored. Most was done via Morse code, using one finger on a single electrical keyboard. Posters advertising "Loose lips, Sink ships" were everywhere. I felt sorry for my friends who were so excited to join the war effort—or maybe I just worried that I would not see them again—in fact, many of them did not return. To this day, I choke up when I think of some of the boys who never came home.

Becoming a part of the Armed Forces never appealed to me. I hate physical violence of any kind—I especially hate war, feeling it to be a terrible capitulation of man's ability to think and reason. In my opinion, then and now, it is unintelligent to resort to physicality in order to resolve differences that could better be acknowledged and discussed. I was a big fan of the predecessor to the United Nations, which Lester B. Pearson had started at the time of the Suez Canal

Crisis. There had been an attempt at world government and understanding between nations even before the U.N., (League of Nations) and that is where my interests lay.

Physically fit young men had deferment from conscription, as long as they maintained the required academic levels. They did not have to serve overseas, but they were still expected to join the Canadian Officers in Training (COTC). The University campus had lots of marching groups and plenty of bands, but there was an actual shortage of young men to date; or, to dance with. The University even cancelled our *frosh hop* during the *polio epidemic* in 1941. However, despite the shortage of males, there were still some dances. Because I loved to dance, I did my best to give the new recruits a good time—a little levity in their lives. War is a terrible thing—despite being busy with my studies, and the extra projects that I took upon myself, it was not the best of times to be at university.

~

I had several interesting classmates from the Caribbean islands. Normally, they would have gone to Britain to take their Bar admission courses; however, because of the war it was arranged that they take their British Bar exams at the U of T Law School. I cannot forget one man from Trinidad, Rham Persnad. He was of the Muslim faith. He stood up in our first lecture and announced that he would not submit to taking lectures in a classroom that had women in it. At the time, there were three women in my class: Mary Eugenia Charles, a black woman from Dominica; Joan Morris, who was a graduate of Ontario Ladies College, and me. Our professor, Bora Laskin, managed to calm Rham down by informing him that this was how it was done here and he had better get used to it.

The Dean came in with his "welcome to the first year" lecture, which included "look at the man to the right of you, and look at the man to the left of you." He told us that the second year classroom was too small for all of us, so they were only going to pass one-third of us. The fact that a lot of the boys actually went into the armed forces eliminated this eventuality for many of those who might not have made it through to second year.

I think our first Criminal Law lecture was designed to discourage the faint of heart. The subject dealt with "unnatural offences"—I had no idea what they were. I went home and asked my mother—her reply was: "I have no idea either; when you find out will you let me know?" I went to the library, because as far as I was concerned, everything you needed to know was at the library. It was there that I discovered that unnatural offences were sexual offences. The law library and the medical library were in the basement of the main library at U of T, so I snuck around the stacks of law books and ventured into the medical library. I had not only wanted to discover what unnatural offences were, I was also interested in finding out about the male anatomy, and natural sex!

During my first year of law school, I envied the sons of lawyers because a big hurdle I had to overcome was the esoteric language of the law. I was continually consulting law dictionaries to find out what these special terms meant. The sons of lawyers had a tremendous advantage—they could go home and ask their fathers! But I was keen and did what I had to do to succeed in their world!

Blackouts were something we also had to contend with. These were imposed during the war because it was thought that Toronto could be a target, due to the abundance of war industry we had there. We had to buy black shades for all of our windows and we were expected to observe strict regulations. If you were caught showing light when the wardens came around, they would knock on your door and tell you to block the light. This made studying in the law library very difficult because there was very little light in there to begin with. I used to rush to get there in good time so that I could get a desk with a little dim light, in order to be able to see what I was reading!

~ A Twentieth Century "Portia" – Bio of Thelma Bernice Kerr-Thomson ~

Thelma, front row, centre

David, middle row, left

INTERNATIONAL STUDENTS' CLUB INVOLVEMENT

I began taking a special interest in the war refugees and the foreign students who were attending our campus. One, in particular, stood out—Mary Eugenia Charles.

Mary was born on May 15, 1919, in Pointe Michel, Dominica. She was the granddaughter of former slaves, and one of the five children of John Baptiste and Josephine Delauney. Her father's master had recognized how intelligent John was and had sent him to school for an education. He eventually became the founder of the Penney Bank and assisted many of the locals with loans to help them get started in life. John also managed plantations for numerous absentee land owners. Mary's brothers became doctors; her sister entered a convent.

Mary went to Catholic schools in Dominica and Grenada before attending the University of Toronto from 1942 to 1946. To reach Toronto she had to catch a sailing taxi from Dominica to Antigua, and then get on a commercial flight to Canada. After receiving her B.A. in Law, Mary continued her law studies at the London School of Economics and Political Science. When she returned home to Dominica in 1949, Mary became the first female lawyer on that Caribbean island.

I corresponded with Mary for many years. When the Dominica finally built a landing field for commercial aircraft, she urged me to come and see her island home before the tourists discovered it. David and I did manage to visit Mary before we had children. We travelled on a *shoestring*. Mary arranged a wonderful tour of the island for us; she also talked about her island's political climate.

Mary got involved in politics and in 1970 she was appointed to the legislature. In 1975 she was appointed to the House of Assembly, where she became the leader of the Opposition Party. Mary was a co-founder of the Dominica Freedom Party, which helped Dominica to gain its independence from Great Britain in 1978.

Mary Eugenia Charles became the Prime Minister of Dominica in 1980. She served three terms and her primary concern was to improve the lives of the citizens of her country. Mary encouraged some tourism, but was determined to preserve the island's ecology and national identity. There were no casinos, night clubs, or duty-free shops then, and Mary wished to keep it that way. Dominica's motto is *Après Bon Dieu, C'est la Ter–After God, the Earth.*

One situation that I remember about Mary, during our university years, was her fear of water. Unfortunately, in order to graduate we had to know how to swim—I am not sure of the reasoning behind this. Mary took swimming lessons all through the four years of university, but she still had not learned to swim. I remember her struggling to accomplish this so that she could get her degree. I felt sorry for her—she had good marks, but could not get her B.A. in Honour Law until she proved she could swim! Obviously, Mary eventually did conquer the waves!

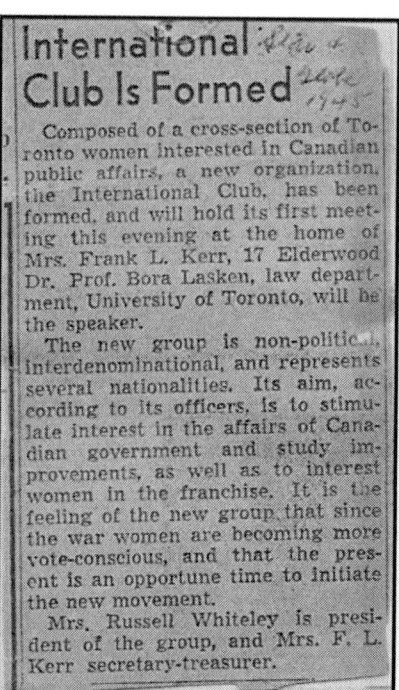

International Club Is Formed

Composed of a cross-section of Toronto women interested in Canadian public affairs, a new organization, the International Club, has been formed, and will hold its first meeting this evening at the home of Mrs. Frank L. Kerr, 17 Elderwood Dr. Prof. Bora Lasken, law department, University of Toronto, will be the speaker.

The new group is non-political, interdenominational, and represents several nationalities. Its aim, according to its officers, is to stimulate interest in the affairs of Canadian government and study improvements, as well as to interest women in the franchise. It is the feeling of the new group that since the war women are becoming more vote-conscious, and that the present is an opportune time to initiate the new movement.

Mrs. Russell Whiteley is president of the group, and Mrs. F. L. Kerr secretary-treasurer.

I felt very sorry for the foreign classmates who had not been accepted in WASP (White Anglo Saxon Protestants) Toronto. Many of them had been in university in Germany and had given up all they had, including their educational opportunities, in order to escape Germany and Hitler's domination. In Toronto, during those times, anybody who was German was thought to be a Nazi and they were treated most unkindly. I guess there was the fear in some people's minds that these young students might be spies.

There were also several students from Communist-dominated countries who had a tough go finding accommodations in Toronto. Many did not have the means to live in the university residences, and they were not socially accepted either. I thought these students should have an opportunity to mingle, in order to promote understanding between them and their Canadian classmates. There were not many Canadian classmates who were interested in my idea, but I decided to push forward and start an International Student's Club.

With the public attitude, I could foresee that many of these students would go through four years of education on the U of T campus without ever being invited into a Canadian home. I felt this was outrageous. I persuaded my mother to put on some Sunday buffet suppers, to which I could invite some of my socially ostracized classmates. I wanted them to see what a Canadian home was like. Our home was not ostentatious, but it was a comfortably, upper-middle class home, and my mother was very gracious. The students were extremely grateful.

One black student from Barbados, Basil Rowe, was a very proper gentleman. He was the son of an Anglican Rector. Basil thought he should invite me for a meal at Hart House—the U of T male bastion. They were allowed to bring a female guest on Sunday nights.

The help had Sundays off, so Sunday meals were packages of cereal. Cereal bowls had been set out so we could help ourselves. Basil took me to a lovely chamber music concert in Hart House, which did not permit women under any circumstances, unless they were escorted by a Hart House man. Apparently, the men swam in the buff at Hart House and they felt that women would cramp their freedom. Of course, I had my eye on their Olympic-size pool because there were not many adequate athletic resources for women in the 1940's.

I also tried to join a camera club at Hart House, which was advertised in the university newspaper, but I was stopped at the door and reminded that women were not permitted in Hart House without a proper escort.

However, back to my committee, I did not have much help in organizing it. People were not consistent about attending the meetings. I did have help from a German woman, whom I sensed was very lonely. We held a Valentine's dance at the Women's Union, in order to raise funds. I also wrote

Student from the British West Indies, Telford Georges (left), is president of the Law Club. He is chatting with Jim Ross of Edmonton.

to the Rockefeller Foundation in the United States, begging for money. Various university campuses in the States already had prominent international student houses (see news article). In my letter, I pointed out the need for the same in Canada. No funds were forthcoming during my time, but my son tells me that an international student house is now on campus, and that it provides housing and social gatherings for foreign students.

There was much to admire about these foreign students—the sacrifices they made for higher learning, and the quality of their minds. They had come from very different cultures. Many of them returned with their new knowledge to their impoverished homelands, wanting to make a difference. Louis Fox, for example, became Chief Justice of Jamaica. I heard that he had an orchard in the country, which was his weekend retreat. When the Chief of Police told him they could not guarantee his security on the island, he returned to Toronto and worked in the Legal Aid office. In later years, my husband and I met him at a Bar convention, and then entertained him and his Quebecois wife, for the weekend at our farm in Lindsay.

Throughout my university years, I continued to take an active part in trying to give some social life to foreign students on the campus. In my final year there was an international gathering of foreign students in France; I thought I should represent U of T, having started this group on our campus. When the time came to announce who would be going, it ended up that a professor's daughter was chosen. Quite frankly, I do not remember ever seeing her at one of our meetings, but she went to the conference I was preparing myself for!

~

In 1942, Britain was on her knees. This was not widely publicized, but there was a sense that the war was going badly for them. Germany had such a head start building up their Air Force and Navy, whereas Britain had been unaware of the need for it and were having difficulty filling that need. Finally, Churchill and Roosevelt swung the Lend/Lease deal that provided us with planes from the United States. A man, Intrepid Stevenson, shuttled back and forth between Britain and the United States. In the Hearst Press—Chicago Tribune, it was reported that many were against the involvement in what they thought to be Britain's war.

U of T Law School was tough during these years with the demand for having to maintain a 75% average, plus the required sixty hours of war work each term. Everyone was buying into Churchill's credo—nothing mattered now but victory. We did what we could and devoted ourselves to every effort possible on the home front, to help toward that victory.

I volunteered as a *ward-aid* at the Toronto Western Hospital. One of my jobs was to assist one RN in a 30-bed female surgical ward. Most of the women were diabetic amputees. My job was "general labour"—holding kidney basins, and cleaning bedpans and linens. After noting the way some doctors treated the nurses and patients, I became cured of ever wanting to pursue a career in medicine. Of course, I did understand that wartime was probably not the best time to assess the medical profession; many doctors and nurses were overseas and the ones who were left at home were run ragged. We were also short on most supplies. So, after my hospital experiences, I decided I had chosen a better path by pursuing law.

During my second year at U of T, I assisted in a wartime daycare centre at St. Stephen's Church. This was the same church that my parents were married in; I was christened there, too. Today, it is behind Kensington Market in Toronto, Ontario, and it has a soup kitchen and gives assistance to the needy.

My training included a series of 12 lectures on early childhood development. I found them very informative, since I had no experience with younger children. Those lectures made an impression on me and are what persuaded me to stay home with my sons for the first few years of their lives. The daycare was open from 7 a.m. to 7 p.m. I was assigned to the three-year-olds and I found them to be quite delightful. When children are past the terrible-twos they start trying to make nice and form friendships. Most of the mothers worked at a shell factory in an Old Massey-Harris plant. The only thing that really bothered me was when the mothers would come to pick up their children—of course they would be tired—some would start cuffing those dear little kids around. That was difficult for me to witness, especially after we had been so careful with the children during the day.

~

I was in my final year of university when the war ended. I had to write my Roman law exam on D-Day, May 8th 1945. My father had the day off. It seemed everybody did! But it was our last exam and the professors decided we should write, despite the festivities that were going on! Lacking a ride downtown, from my father, I took the TTC. The street car was full of people celebrating D-Day!

The returnees from the war did not affect me until I entered Osgoode Hall. They were tough, determined competitors, trying to make up for precious, lost time.

International Student's Club

Women's Fraternity—Tri-Delta's (Thelma, bottom right)

Law School Progress Sets Notable Record

Sixty years ago the Faculty of Law was created at the University of Toronto, with a mere handful of students seeking to take the course. Today the School of Law has more than 300 students from all parts of the Dominion and many from other parts of the Empire, and has achieved one of the most notable records of any law school in the world during its brief history.

Tonight hundreds of students and graduates will gather at the King Edward Hotel to celebrate the diamond jubilee of the faculty. Among them will be many prominent in law, business and politics.

The faculty was created by statute of the Senate in 1847, but prior to that time law was taught and degrees in law were conferred by the university for many years. Only two lecturers were assigned to the faculty in 1847, while at present there are seven full-time lecturers, with two part-time lecturers.

Greatest progress in the school has been achieved under Dean W. P. M. Kennedy, who was appointed head of the faculty a quarter of a century ago. During that time he has modernized the faculty, bringing it up to the standards of the world's leading law universities.

Degrees received from the School of Law have international recognition and are accepted by every university law faculty not merely in Canada and the United States but in the United Kingdom, and before the war in the great university law faculties in Europe. It has the distinction of being the only overseas faculty of law approved by the Council of Legal Education for the English Bar, placing it side by side with certain approved university faculties of law in England.

Graduates of the School of Law are exempt from all examinations for the British Bar except the final professional papers. In several provinces students graduating from the school may practice law after attending law school or being articled for a period of one year, but in Ontario, the graduate must obtain his qualifications at Osgoode Hall.

Many students who came from the West Indies in the war period, are continuing their courses here rather than go to England. When they graduate, they have only one year to complete at a law school in England to practice in their homeland.

Co-operation between the student and the staff is one of the main reasons for the high standard of education achieved at the university. Most of the work is done, according to Dean Kennedy, by individual contact between student and lecturer. Impersonal lectures are avoided.

~ A Twentieth Century "Portia" – Bio of Thelma Bernice Kerr-Thomson ~

~ 67 ~

IAIN

I and my girlfriends decided that with all of the prejudicial attitudes toward students that it was our patriotic duty to entertain new recruits and Air Force volunteers in the Commonwealth air training program. We referred to them as *fly boys*. We wanted to make their enforced stay in our country a pleasant experience. Tea dances for teens were quite popular in the 1940's because a young woman was less likely to get stuck in some dark corner with a *groper*. So it was decided—we issued an open invitation to a Saturday afternoon dance, via the notice board at the Manning Depot at the CNE (Canadian National Exhibition) grounds, where the Air Force recruits were being screened and divided into air or ground crews.

Finally, the day of the dance arrived. We girls were excited to see if our invitation list had been filled. We had been busy making sandwiches, squares, and cookies. It was thought at the time that university girls were not a lot of fun, but we were out to prove the *naysayers* wrong! We lined up, awkwardly, waiting to be approached by the group of LAC'S (Leading Air Craftsmen). I am not sure if we actually looked the part of welcoming hostesses! But the scene was set—a record was put on the Victrola phonograph, and the sound of a waltz filled the room. At first there did not appear to be much response, but then I noticed a handsome six-foot LAC striding across the room. He stopped in front of me and asked ME to dance with him!

So, that is how I met Iain Charles MacAulay! He came to Toronto in 1942, to join the RCAF (Royal Canadian Air Force). Iain had been trained in Scotland as a radio operator for the Royal Navy, but he aspired to be a fly boy. He was assigned to the Merchant Navy, but decided he had had enough convoy duty, especially with all the German submarines picking off boats in the British convoys. Iain jumped ship in New York and then took a train to Toronto.

I picked Iain for a winner immediately, but I had no idea why he had sought me out—maybe it was my plaid skirt, cashmere sweater, and string of pearls that I wore! Iain was a wonderful dancer. He waltzed divinely; I was *blown away*. When a tango was offered, he was accomplished at that too. I could not have been more swept off of my feet! We hit it off wonderfully! Iain said that he had been taught how to dance at his boarding school in Scotland—we danced as though we had taken the same course. The Scot was HOT to foxtrot with! After the dance, he asked me for my phone number.

However, before Iain could actually court me, I had to introduce him to my parents. After the dance I called my mother to ask permission to bring The Scot home to dinner. My mother said yes. On the Bay Street car I learned that Iain had a degree in Natural Sciences from Edinburgh University, also that he was 23 years old.

Of course, my father delved further into Iain's background—he wanted to make sure his little girl was not getting into something over her head, with an older man. He learned that Iain had spent the first eight years of his life in Rangoon, Burma, where his father owned a dry-dock shipyard. At age eight, he had been sent back to Scotland to continue his education at a private boys' school in Dumfries. My father also learned that Iain's father had been taken prisoner by the Japanese when Burma was invaded. He had been last heard from while on a forced march. Iain had no idea if his father had survived—very few had. His mother and sister had escaped to Durban, South Africa.

I was flattered that such a fascinating man found me interesting. I was 20, but Iain was the first man to *make me feel like a woman*, when he looked down at me from his lofty height and told me that I was the first woman he had ever desired! I do not know if I truly believed him, thinking that maybe that was just a clever pick-up line. But I did confide in him that he too had an affect on me, like none other I had ever experienced. I had many platonic male friends; but Iain—well, I was honoured that he was so interested in me.

I began to volunteer at the dances so that I could attend them all. It was great fun, even with all manner of Servicemen, including the prairie boys who could only do a *two-step* and pump handled every dance, no matter what beat was being played.

Iain did his basic training in Toronto and we saw each other on all of his leaves. He was posted at my old Hunt Club for his courses on Theory of Flight and Celestial Navigation. We walked for miles, and while walking we discussed philosophy. He was fascinated with my Humanity courses: Philosophy, Psychology, Greek and Roman History—rare subjects for him, with all the sciences he had taken. I was constantly agreeing with him on issues. One day he said: "Why, you are very intelligent!" I guess I was wise for my years and this surprised him—I believe I can accredit such wisdom to my study of law.

Iain got his *wings* at the Armouries in Brantford, Ontario; I was greatly honoured to attend the ceremony. My father had arranged to do one of his regular audits of Agnew Surpass Shoe Company in Brantford, so my parents accompanied me to the graduation. After the ceremony, Iain and I went outside and sat on a bench that overlooked the Grand River—it was there that he asked me to wait for him. I could not have been happier, but I also had a sense of foreboding that he might not return. I said I would wait and I wrote a few lines to him practically every day that we were apart.

Ours became, for the most part, a long-distance relationship. After Iain earned his *wings* he was sent to Brandon, Manitoba, for night flying and bomber training. When he returned to Toronto I would spend time with him and his crew, mostly Australians, *The Aussies*, as we called them. The Royal York Hotel had a good policy during the war, of letting out rooms according to rank. Iain, being an officer, had a room of his own. Sometimes, he and *The Aussies* rented a suite, and I must admit that they had some great parties there, bringing in racks of beer for their 72 hour leaves! Before going overseas the crews were encouraged to spend time together—bonding!

A proper young woman of my generation and social circle could not openly admit to any sort of sexuality, but when Iain described the physical affect I had on him, as though it were a scientific observation, I haltingly stumbled upon sensations that I had never before experienced. When Iain wrapped his strong arms around me, I felt as though I were entrapped forever. He smelt so clean and fresh, and his pheromone (scent) aroused me for the first time.

It was apparent that Iain had had very little female contact in his life, before meeting me, having gone to private boys' schools and then into the Royal Navy. I set out to show him what the love of a good woman could do for him; and, if I am to be truthful here, I very nearly succumbed to his desire. His intentions toward me were clear. I sometimes wondered if he had been coached by his crew in the methods of seduction because he pulled many ploys out of his hat in order to win me over. He had a different one for every leave.

I remember quite clearly the time when he was staying at my parent's home on his last embarkation leave. He stayed for four days and he asked if he could send his laundry out. I told him I would not mind to wash and mend his clothes. This seemed to surprise him. When he took off his shirt I was almost overcome with an animal desire to rip off mine and then press my pounding heart to his. I was nearly ready to risk my *deflowering,* right there on the kitchen floor! But something deeper inside of me halted that urge; it had been instilled in me NOT to enjoy the privileges of marriage without undertaking its responsibilities.

After that close of a call of letting my guard down, and after the lecture on "unnatural sex offences" at the University, I decided to do some research of my own. I took out some books on sexuality from the university library in order to research "sex" and "the penis." I snuck around with the stack of books, the binding toward me, so no one would be able to see what I was reading. I never thought of the fact that the librarian would be aware of what kinds of books I had taken out, and I was probably also unaware of how many other young women of my age were going through the same emotions. But, those were the times—very different from today. I had experienced the rage of hormones at a moment in my life when my body was ready to experience the next stages in life's cycle. It was difficult because of the turmoil of the war and the constant fear of losing our heroes who were in danger, so far from home and family. There was always the, *what ifs* in our minds. Chaos and uncertainty constantly *dogged* me because the Air Force casualty rate was fifty percent. Every day, at noon, while eating a brownbag lunch at the Frat house, I would listen to Lorne Greene, on the CBC radio, as he called the numbers of those on the casualty list.

Such is the indiscreet admission I have kept in my heart all these years.

~

I continued to see Iain. He even took me one day to Long Branch to visit his aunt and uncle. She had insisted he bring me to her house for tea. I think he was afraid that I might be too much of a snob to accept the humble circumstances under which his aunt lived, since he knew I had been educated at Branksome Hall. I was disappointed that he would think that of me, but what I finally realized was that in Britain there was quite a class distinction for those who graduated from private schools.

This aunt was Iain's mother's sister; she was a delightful Scottish lady. She worked as a bank teller to support herself and her wheelchair-bound husband who was a retired Irish-Cavalry man. He had fought in the Boer War. The uncle shared my love for horses and we exchanged horse stories while Iain's aunt prepared a lamb chop and mushy-peas supper. The couple owned an old car that the uncle could no longer drive. I promised to come and drive them out to visit friends when Iain was away.

The day finally arrived when Iain informed me he would be embarking on his overseas' duty. In the summer of 1944 he left Canada. Iain flew two tours of operations—one piloting a Lancaster bomber with a crew of seven; the second, a Wellington bomber. I wrote a few lines to him every day. I have always wondered if he kept my letters. I hoped they helped get him through his difficult days. They were filled with my dedication to the war effort: giving blood, packing Red Cross P.O.W. boxes, hospital aid, and nursery school work.

Iain wrote to me as frequently as he could, but his letters looked like paper doilies because the censors would take a blade to the names of places he had bombed. Sometimes, there were long gaps between his letters, in 1945. After the 1945 Armistice, one of his letters mentioned that he was thinking of volunteering in the Asian Theatre, since the war was over. I was not surprised with this, given his close connections to Burma.

One day a mechanic from Toronto, who had worked on Iain's aircraft, appeared at my door with an entire bolt of beautiful raspberry-red Harris-tweed material. I was so dumbfounded I did not even ask the young man in. Iain had such a way of making me feel so special.

In the summer of 1945 I received a letter from Iain with his embarkation number, and to let me know that he was going to try to get a ship to Quebec City. I was in Quebec that summer, working hard on a Fellowship. I had been assigned the subject of comparing Britain's romantic poets with the romantic poets of France. I was hoping to return to Quebec the following year to maintain my thesis before a committee of the faculty, but by the end of the summer I realized that with all that was going on in my life I was not going to be able to accomplish that. My French was also not quite good enough to attain a Master's degree level. I had taken an eight week Spanish course with the idea that if I ever had the opportunity to join the Foreign Affairs Department, I would be more prepared if I had a working knowledge of three languages. This was my father's thinking, too. I was also trying to keep myself busy in order to overcome my anxiety of when Iain might be repatriated, and of what we would do when he was!

Iain was discharged from the Air Force in May 1945. He was granted a Medical scholarship at Edinburgh University. He was delighted because studying medicine had been one of his long-range ambitions. In the fall of 1945 Iain sent me 300 pounds and asked me to join him in Scotland. I was very torn, for a number of reasons. My turmoil came from being mixed-up between Iain and another good friend, David, whom I had come to find almost indispensable in my life, while studying law. There was also the fact that I was in my third year at law school and my parents had sacrificed a great deal for my education. I felt obliged to complete the course my father had set for me. My parents had postponed paying off their house mortgage and doing the many needed repairs, until I finished at Osgoode Hall. My father's failing health was becoming a great concern for me, as well, and I was worried about leaving him and my mother.

I contemplated the fact that if Iain helped support his mother and sister, financially, that that might be an impediment to the marriage, he wished we could have. I also wondered if he would return to Rangoon to claim the family home and business. I considered what life for me might be like in post-wartime Scotland, being married to a medical student, and I pondered if such a privileged girl as I was would be able to cope. Iain and I had never discussed the topic of money during our walks—our dates had been cheery and happy—no nitty-gritty things about real life. Many scenarios kept flitting through my mind—would Iain think that I would be equipped to be a solicitor's clerk over there? I felt I would have qualified to be a solicitor, and I began to wonder if Iain was hoping, or expecting me to work to support him. And, would my Scot, who was such a man of the world, and whom I sometimes feared might have itchy feet, be around to help me raise the children I so wanted to give him? My mind was spinning—I needed time to consider which direction I was going to take.

I decided to invest the 300 pounds until I could make this extremely difficult decision. There was a long gap in Iain's communications while I was struggling to make up my mind. Of course, I assumed it was because he was either giving me space, or that he was terribly busy with his studies. With the distress of the decision making, and writing my exams, I came down with streptococcus of the throat. Then came the moment where I was forced to decide. The final crux was my obligation to my father. I felt that if I went to Scotland that might be the end of him.

Iain had loomed large in my life from the moment we had met, until the moment I sat down and wrote that terrible "Dear John" letter to him. I returned his 300 pounds, plus interest. Thinking back now, I realize how terribly inadequate my letter was—I neglected to mention my father's ailing health and the fact that me giving up my study of law would have killed him. In the summer of 1946, I would have loved, more than anything, to use the 300 pounds Iain had sent me, to go to Scotland for a "tumble in the heather," to give life there a trial, as women might do now. But that was the stuff of dreams—not the reality of the times. I am grateful to have known such a wonderful man, but I think my wartime romance was doomed, right from the start, because of: time, work, distance, and somewhat differing life's goals.

I went on to a Fellowship, and then to Osgoode Hall—that was my life—one of long-range goals and postponed gratifications. Over the years, despite the good life I enjoyed, there have been times I wondered where I would have ended had I followed my heart to Edinburgh!

DAVID

David was the fifth child of a Presbyterian minister. He talked often of the good times he'd had as a teenager, when his father ministered in Stroud and Allendale. David had enjoyed boating and water sports on Lake Simcoe, and in Barrie where his father also ministered. But David did not have quite the privileged life growing up, as I did.

I met David, briefly, during my first year at university. He was a year ahead of me. I knew one of the girls in his class; she introduced us. Our initial time together was brief because David volunteered, at first, to bring in the harvest of the bumper crop of grain in Saskatchewan, and then he joined the Armed Services in the middle of his second year. David, like so many other boys, wanted to join the Air Force. He had been in the Officer's Training Course (OTC) at U of T—I believe that all of the able-bodied men at U of T had to be in the OTC. David enjoyed Military History.

When David first joined, they did not have enough planes for all the pilots; so, he was sent to Petawawa as an artillery officer. He was good in math and they had him teaching boys that did not have a grasp of the mathematics needed to aim guns. However, David did not like the cold winter in Petawawa, so he resigned his commission.

He went through another screening and it was discovered he had a higher education. They sent him to "Camp X" (Special Services), for espionage training.

David went through vigorous physical training there. All was going well until they got to the lecture in which they handed out a "garrotte" (a piece of wire with wooden handles on either end). He was taught how to sneak up behind a sentry and take them out by putting this garrotte around their neck, and then pulling on it. David protested, saying that was the wrong place for a preacher's son to be! They sent him to the Gaspé region to visit different units that were stationed around there, and to gather evidence of German submarines that were attacking our convoys as they came out of the St. Lawrence River. It was not generally known that this area was frequented by German submarines, targeting our convoys of merchant ships—supplies carried via the *Lifeline*.

~

When he returned from Service, in the middle of my second year, David was in my class. He was rusty on the first term courses and he needed a refresher course before writing his exams. In that competitive atmosphere no one would lend him their lecture notes, so I lent him mine. David was a kind friend and that is just the thing one did for a friend.

There is one contention I have though—returned Service men were *fast-tracked* through their courses. So there I was, helping David and he got to graduate before me! My one consolation is that I actually had more education than he did, because he missed out on some of the more advanced Comparative Constitutional Law and Ethics courses that were part of our final year's studies.

Because I helped David, he in turn became a very supportive classmate at a time when most people felt that women did not belong in law because they were such *emotional creatures*. Or, maybe it was not actually because I helped him; maybe he had an ulterior motive, known only to him at the time. Whatever the case, David became my most sympathetic confidante. I confided all my worries, including my concerns about Iain who was on his second op in Germany. It was strange, though, that I never told Iain about my friendship with David. Some of my letters that I wrote to David while I was in Quebec show this...

EXCERPTS FROM LETTERS TO DAVID—1945

June

Dear David:

Thank you very much for your nice letters. And congratulations to <u>you</u>-After the way <u>u I scabbed</u>* for the first two months we ended up in the same category. I was especially happy that no one flunked-and chances look pretty good for making it next year too now don't they? ... Life in the Gaspé sounds wonderful. Whenever you get tired of your job I'd be glad to take it over ...

I am leaving for Laval on the 25th and going all the way by boat. I should arrive in Quebec on the 27th ... They are giving me my tuition free this time in return for my teaching English an hour a day. I haven't the vaguest idea about how to go about teaching a roomful of French people English. I guess I'll have to study it up on the way down ... The trouble is when I speak French all the time my English gets rather shaky ... I do hope I can show you la belle Ville de Quebec ... I show it off as tho it was my own special discovery ... It might be fun if you could arrange to come when we go on our excursion to Lac Beauport ... I'll let you know when it is definite ... We usually have a swim, then a dinner and afterwards go out in the canoe singing until dancing starts in the pavilion on the water. Last year I walked around the lake ... It was one of my favourite excursions. I wouldn't miss it for anything and I think you'd enjoy it too. I hope you can make it.

I'm still sort of convalescing (it makes a wonderful excuse for loafing). I've been doing quite a bit of riding lately-and I've also gone all out for domesticity ... brushing up on my cooking--and I've made new curtains for the guest room and my own room. The family are accusing me of having an ulterior motive for getting so domesticated all of a sudden ... If so it looks as though such efforts were spent for naught at this point, as Iain's latest bright idea is to take a job in Burma-involving two years up country in the forests. I like roughing it for awhile-<u>but</u>-that idea has all the earmarks of being too much for me.

I met the "Duke" downtown one day ... He had just flown in from canvassing the province; taking a poll on the forthcoming election ... no doubt he'll regale us with snatches of it between lectures next year ... I went to the races with Karl Morowitz ... afraid I didn't bring him any luck--I just managed to break even myself...

I went to convocation to see my younger fraternity sisters graduate-and I also saw LLB's presented to Ivy Laurence (with honours) and Harold Butterworth. La Brie got his Masters of Law the same day.

That's about all for now. I'll let you know how everything is in the belle Ville when I get there. You can reach me via Université Laval until I find a place to stay.

See you in Quebec-, Sincerely, Thelma

<u>u I scabbed</u>* An expression used when referring to slaves scrubbing the floor—used here to express the way they had to work for the law firms in those days—like slave labour.

July

Dear Dave:

Your nice letter finally reached me this morning-having come through the seminary--goodness knows why-unless the Fathers took it upon themselves to censor it. They are so scrupulous of my well-being it's touching. But I have something on them now. The other day Louise and I were sunning ourselves on the roof of her house when a priest came out on the balcony of the seminary and blew us a kiss!

I don't usually reply so quickly to a letter, but this arises partly from the inspiration to which your letter gave rise-and partly from my uncertainty as to how long I can survive on my own experiments in cooking. There seems to be something incongruous about a career woman batching it in a perfect love-nest--my apartment was just fixed up for a bride and groom ... My little gas range seems to sense the incongruity of the situation ...it plays the weirdest pranks on me whenever I try to bake anything ... However, I can now whip up a really mean scrambled egg so you must come and have breakfast with me when you hit Quebec...

How I envy you swimming in the ocean and lying on the beach! I have that pallid summer school look and it's most uncomfortable for me to be so white in the middle of July, for as you know, I am no hot-house flower.

I've got myself quite a timetable here - 36 lectures a week and my 5 English classes on top of that - all of which require at least 2 hours work every night. So you can imagine how much time I have to get out in the sun ... my main diversion has been French movies ...

I hold my English class in the Law Library ... it makes our 'dungeon' look like a pig sty. You must see it when you come. The class is teaching me a great deal ... we have lots of laughs - most of them on me ... my job is to get them to talk in English and correct any mistakes ... Already I have learned several new words that I didn't even know existed - and they are really putting my spelling to the test. One joke they told, was about a man whose wife presented him with 3 sets of twins. The first set he called Kate and Duplicate, the second set Pete and Repeat, and the third Max and Climax!

My Spanish is coming along now. I hope Kelsick will be back next fall so that I can practice it on him.

I got an invitation to go to a reception to meet "my colleagues" - the other professors at the university - I went fully expecting to feel very much out of place among the learned graduates of the Sorbonne etc ... However two of the profs brought me home - after having imbibed freely in some excellent wine and superb French pastry. I found that they could be quite jolly in spite of their wealth of learning ...

It's hard to believe that my stay here is half over now ... the family keep reminding me that I am expected home the first week of August. This one time I would like to disappoint them, if I could do so and still maintain their financial backing.

It's still a big question when I'll see Iain again. He is considering going to the Pacific ... if he does he should be here in a month or two. If he does not, I think he wants to go back to Glasgow U., but doesn't want to hurt my feelings by telling me that dear old U of T hasn't a patch on his <u>alma mater</u>.

Please give me some notice when you are coming so I can arrange to show you around a bit. Yours, TK

August

Dear Dave:

Thanks ever so much for the etchings. I like them very much...I will hang them in my room... You may even see them in a garret in Glasgow someday-who knows... You must come up for dinner and let me display my newly acquired culinary art.

Please excuse the writing... but my constitution was so weakened by high life in Quebec that I have that throat trouble again. Rolling into bed at 6a.m one week, after farewell parties and getting up at 6a.m the next week to make boat connections was too much for me. As you may have guessed my stay in Quebec was somewhat extended. I stayed 10 days after the course was over, hoping that Iain would land there, until I got a letter informing me that he is <u>not coming back!</u> It seems that the current idea is to study medicine at Glasgow. This was quite a blow to me... nobly I tried to throw myself into my supreme war effort entertaining the navy. There's nothing like drowning your sorrows with the navy... It's a good thing you didn't ask me down to Gaspé- I would have accepted all too eagerly. The trip home was ideal... I stopped over in Montreal and climbed Mount Royal. I took a picture of the cross, just to prove it. I got thoroughly lost on the descent... territory is reminiscent of Muskoka-or the cliffs. I never would have thought that one could be so alone in the middle of the largest city in Canada...

I was crossing Lake Ontario in a glorious storm when the ship's radio picked up the news of the Japanese surrender. Those on board who were not sick proceeded to get drunk. I hasten to assure you Dave, that I was neither sick nor drunk. I sought refuge from that bedlam out on deck enjoying the storm.

... when I got home the baggage checks for my next trip were waiting for me in the mail. I am now trying to get into condition to go up to P.H.E camp next week.

I went to the Prom with Karl Morowitz... he tells me that Mo is deserting us for Dalhousie and Laskin is going to join the staff at Osgoode. Maybe I'll go to Osgoode after all. I also hear that Kelsick is leaving for England next month ... Be good to yourself-and thanx again,   Sincerely yours, Thelma

So it was that, despite my great love for Iain, I had come to depend so much on David for support and encouragement that I was beginning to think I could not imagine life without him. Every time I turned around, he was there, as though he were dogging my tracks. Once I had made my decision in the fall of 1945 not to join Iain in Scotland, I guess David and I officially started dating—going from the pals we had been in law school to something more.

One thing David and I thoroughly enjoyed together was our love for the outdoor life. Most of our dates consisted of hiking and picnicking, and renting canoes to paddle down the Humber River. David and I were also different from many of our classmates who had their eyes set on becoming lawyers for the big law firms on Bay Street—David had talked to me about starting a law firm together in the country somewhere. He had had a happy outdoorsy life during his teen years, when his father had been in charge of a country parish. He wanted the same life for any family he might have in the future.

There was someone else in our lives who had noticed that David and I might make a good couple—Miss McBeth, a librarian in the law library. When I was first taking lecture notes, I would scramble the names of the cases we were supposed to read. A lot of the lectures were about the points of law made in specific cases, which would bear the surnames of litigants involved. Because my lecture notes were a jumbled mess, I would ask Miss McBeth for the so-in-so volume of such-and-such series. She would say: "You're in first year, aren't you?" I would nod, and then she would say: "Well I think this is the book you want." She also helped me unscrambled all my errors.

Whenever David came to Toronto, on his leaves, he would try to come to the law library. I was usually there reading law books for the Company that I worked for, doing *precis* of legal decisions. Miss McBeth would guide him to where I was sitting—so she was definitely a matchmaker early in David's and my association!

In the spring of 1946 David had to make a decision whether to start at Osgoode Hall, or to go to Brazil for the company he was articling for—the legal department of the British American Oil Company. He began to pressure me to totally forget *The Scot* and to marry him. "Look," he said; "I want to know if I can plan to spend the rest of my life with you, because your decision will affect my decision as to what I do with my law. Would you come with me?" he had asked.

I had yet to do my three years of articling, required in order to qualify for the Bar, and not completing that was not an option for me. However, it was also at that point in time that I returned Iain's money to him. In some ways I had procrastinated doing that while I was figuring out which of the two men would win my heart in the end—with whom I could have a life! I told David this. Instead of going to Brazil, he entered Osgoode to finish up his admission to the Bar.

GRADUATION FROM U OF T

Some of the attractive graduates who received degrees at Convocation Hall, University of Toronto, yesterday are pictured above. Left is Helen Halliday, who graduated in physical and health education. Centre are Nancy Fairley and Doris Clark, who received degrees in the same subjects. At right is Ruth Ma, Canadian-born Chinese girl, now a Bachelor of Music.

Graduation ceremonies during wartime were much less elaborate than they had been in pre-war years. I was tired from all of my studying and exam writing; so, to be quite frank, I actually do not remember much about the ceremony when I received my B.A. in Honour Law in 1946. After the ceremony there was a nice, low-key garden party. My parents attended it with me.

There were only five females in my graduation class. I am grateful to the women who had gone before us, paving the way and cheering us on with their kindness. One woman I remember in particular was Margaret Hyndman. She was constantly encouraging us. She wrote a book on Company Law, and she had even started a female fraternity of women lawyers. I was invited to join.

Of course, if I was going to continue on with law, I still had three more years of courses at Osgoode Hall, plus articling for a law firm, before I could actually practice law. To elaborate further, being one of the last veterans, or should I say, *survivors* of the old style of legal education, we were expected to attend lectures at Osgoode Hall Law School and article for a firm at the same time. We would attend lectures taught by professional lawyers, in the mornings. These were meant to prepare us for the nitty-gritty practice of law in the real world! In the afternoons we would work for the law firms where we were articling. During our first year, quite a bit of our service to the firm was the work that couriers do now—delivering papers to other law offices, searching titles, and filing papers at Osgoode Hall.

Admission to Degrees

GRADUATE DEGREES ARTS
COMMERCE MEDICINE
APPLIED SCIENCE MUSIC LAW
PHYSICAL AND HEALTH EDUCATION
SOCIAL WORK PHARMACY
AGRICULTURE

University of Toronto
Friday, November 12th, 1948

BACHELOR OF APPLIED SCIENCE
PRESENTED BY PROFESSOR L. M. PIDGEON

Roy Edward Raphael Abraham
James Albert Agnew
John Edwin Allen
Alfred Robert Askin
William George Beck
Alan Collingwood Bell
Hyman Biller
Richard Joseph Brown
Philip Andrew Eugene Cardinal
William Gould Carter
Herbert Murray Keith Conn
Rex Earl Cousins
David Peter Crichton
John Craig Cringan
Ross Meade Cruikshank
Gerald Edward Blake Daniel
George Donald Day
Alexander Deuchar Duncan
James Arthur Ellwood
William Clark Evans
Jack Albert Farlow
Robert James Fennell
Bertram Douglas Canniff Fleming
William Alden Ebenezer Frost
Raymond Elmer Gainey
Gordon Neil Gillespie
Kenneth Grace
John Alvin Green
William Anthony Grell
James Alexander Grierson
Joyce Margaret Griffiths
Arthur Ernest Guay
Thomas Norton Hayman
Joseph James Heffernan
Leonard John Hudyma
Kenneth Edward Hunter
Howard Joe
Bernard David Kaufman
Donald Graham Kempthorne
Peter Gault Kingsmill
Arthur Adolph Kosnick
William James Charles Lewis
Lawrence Joseph Loebach
William Angus MacDonald
Donald Hobson MacKay
Bruce Alexander MacLeod
Joseph Padraic Bingham McLoughlin
William Denton McMurtry
George Drummond Mahon
John Arnold Maine
Herbert Dingwall Monteith
George Robert Muddiman
Bernard Morton Pullan
Norman Henry Robinson
John William Rutter
Donald John Salt
Michael Kenneth Joseph Schurter
Alan Parkin Sentance
George Robert Smith
Robert Beatty Spence
John MacLaren Spratt
William Burrows Sproule
Albert Charles Suter
Earle Moore Taylor
Ronald Rex Taylor
Robert George Tress
Charles John Urban
Gordon Elliot Wallace
David Edward Alexander Whitfield
James Daniel Wright
Eldon George Henry Yundt
Gordon Allan Zinn

BACHELOR OF MUSIC
PRESENTED BY THE DEAN OF THE FACULTY OF MUSIC

Arthur Bligh Crighton
David James Connelly Hodges

BACHELOR OF LAWS
PRESENTED BY THE DEAN OF THE SCHOOL OF LAW

Walter Ernest Bell
Victor Robertson Butts
Melvin John Cunningham
Michael Earnest Fram

Walter Howard Frere Kennedy
Thelma Bernice Kerr
William Andrew Lencki
James Bryce Lillico
Albert Joseph McComiskey
Harry Ian Manning Mactavish
Joan Weir Morris
Murray Douglas Morton
James Young Ross
Kenneth Gordon McLean Ross
Lewis Samuel Ross
William John Scott
William Lorne Northmore Somerville
David Moffat Thomson
Letitia Sydney Jane Waugh

BACHELOR OF PHYSICAL AND HEALTH EDUCATION
PRESENTED BY THE DIRECTOR OF THE SCHOOL OF PHYSICAL AND HEALTH EDUCATION

Robert Allan Cooper
John Turner Doll

BACHELOR OF SOCIAL WORK
PRESENTED BY THE DIRECTOR OF THE SCHOOL OF SOCIAL WORK

David McColloch Critchley
Gene Margaret Dufty
John Valdo Fornataro
John Elvin Gamble
Cleta Marguerite Herman
Kenneth Barnell Jacobs
Marion Winifred MacKnight
Burton Roper Morgan
Margaret Stewart Morley
Catherine Josephine Mary O'Connor

BACHELOR OF PHARMACY
PRESENTED BY THE DEAN OF THE ONTARIO COLLEGE OF PHARMACY

Jane Mary Adams
Glenna Jean Armstrong
Robert Willson Bevers
Paul Percy Budish
John Francis Cavanagh
John Patrick Carey
Kenneth James Gabson
Malcolm Gerald Day
Walter Arthur Deeley
Harvey Joseph Dembrofsky
Ellwood Murray Derbyshire
Burns Wilfred Foster
John Woodall Gerrie
Bernard Glazier
William Hultay
Gordon Edward Hutchinson
Max Leflowitz
Gordon Victor McKinney
John Vytautas Margis
Harvey Martin Mogk
Patrick Joseph Murphy
Robert Bruce Murray
Seymour Russell Pepper
Jack Frederick Sadler
Rachel Elizabeth Smith
Donald Cameron Thompson
Helen Emily Trevelyan
Ivan Carroll Whiteside
John Frederick Wright

BACHELOR OF SCIENCE IN AGRICULTURE

Robert Harold Strong
William Brock Whale

OSGOODE STUDENTS PASS YULE EXAMS

Christmas examination results for the first-year class at Osgoode Hall law school show that the following have passed:

M. E. Fram, Miss J. W. Morris, W. J. Wheelton, R. E. Barnes, D. A. Berlis, T. S. Farley, R. H. Frith, W. Engoetz, L. C. Winhold, J. G. Fullerton, M. Cadesby, W. D. Goodman, D. R. Steele, E. E. Coutts, A. G. Campbell, J. P. Nelligan, A. B. Rosenberg, Miss S. Dymond, N. J. McLeod, A. A. Russell, W. L. Maddin, D. K. Russell, E. A. DuVernet, F. V. Regan, J. C. Phillips, M. N. Lacourclere, B. W. N. Apple, K. A. Murchison, G. A. Gallagher, Miss T. Kerr, D. A. Smith, G. N. Guyatt, J. H. McConnell, G. J. O'Neill, D. L. Richardson, F. C. Stinson, R. S. Mackay, E. N. Crawford, D. G. Kilgour, N. M. Peters, W. L. N. Somerville, W. M. Carlyle, C. R. Clarke, J. W. F. Goodchild, R. L. Graham, D. Goldberg, D. L. Magee, J. W. deC. O'Grady, L. S. Willoughby, M. L. Magill, B. G. Winters, H. W. Kelly, J. S. Nutt, J. G. Martin, D. J. MacDonald, W. W. Leach, D. L. Shanoff, P. V. Rudden, D. M. Duncan, J. M. Hodgson, R. R. Loffmark, R. C. O'Neal, I. M. Rogers, G. I. Purvis, A. G. Keeley, E. J. Pivnick, F. M. Stark, J. L. Cohen, W. A. Lencki, M. R. Morrow, Earl Brown, M. C. Foster, W. A. Inch, Ian T. MacDonald, D. J. Roche, J. A. Winter, J. B. Aird, T. O. Fraser, L. Maraskas, J. A. McQuarrie, W. R. Buchner, J. Leiff, G. S. MacDonald, R. W. Spratt, G. S. Boychyn, J. W. Brooke, C. H. McGrath, H. F. McKerracher, R. C. White, J. W. Burridge, J. B. Lawson, D. F. Mossop, G. P. Miller, E. J. Myers, A. J. Marck, J. R. Crerar, R. S. Jones, H. A. Black, R. S. Smart, W. R. Poole, H. G. Brewster, J. S. Grant, D. A. Flock, F. R. Lalor, M. N. Mousseau, J. R. Reid, A. J. Bourassa, R. C. Honey, J. G. McNaughton, S. D. Pugsley, J. H. Turnbull, W. R. Waterbury, J. B. Conlin, H. L. O'Donnell, C. E. Clarke, J. R. Kehoe, E. W. Legris, D. J. McNab, G. H. Milsom, E. A. H. Porter, W. J. Robinson, W. T. Wood, K. K. O'Hara, R. S. McCreath, Miss E. Robson, W. A. E. Sheppard, W. J. Whittaker, R. F. Reid, R. Ian Ross, W. R. Allen, D. A. Bales, G. D. Campbell, W. E. G. Young, J. W. Cram, W. A. W. Scott, H. H. Hyndman, P. J. Morris, D. M. McKerroll, E. H. McVitty, R. D. Poupore, N. V. Sawyer, H. C. Arrell, R. H. Honeyford, G. J. Majic, J. B. Trotter, D. A. Elliott, F. J. Chauvin, Paul McNamara, J. A. Pocock, J. L. Roberts, F. Rocchi, J. J. B. Woods, J. L. Agro, C. T. Murphy, D. P. Warren, S. W. Laughlin, A. F. Sheppard, T. H. Murphy, T. E. O'Marra, G. Perley-Robertson, R. J. Colonnier, C. F. Doyle, Miss B. J. Duncan, H. S. O. Morris, G. F. Kinsman, J. M. Greer, M. A. Bitz, G. Carton, W. E. Doxsee, T. C. Byrnes, S. C. French, S. Resnick, H. W. Aitcheson, H. A. V. Dancouse, T. J. Jacob, M. Latendresse, A. J. McComiskey, J. J. Robertson, S. Schwartz, E. J. Newton, J. B. Simpson, C. F. P. Robertson, G. C. Campbell, M. J. Haffey, D. R. Mason, W. H. Reid, L. A. Lillico, W. B. Best, G. R. H. Shaver, H. E. G. Bull.

Tri-Delta's New Year's Dance (Thelma and David on right)

Fraternity Party after graduation (Thelma and David, back row, right)

Thelma with her parents on her graduation day

David on his graduation day

~ A Twentieth Century "Portia" – Bio of Thelma Bernice Kerr-Thomson ~

CALIFORNIA WITH MOM AND DAD—SPRING 1946

In the spring of 1946, my parents took a month-long trip to Europe, to celebrate their 25th wedding anniversary. Later that summer they asked me to join them in California, where my father had been sent on a business trip. I was not having a good summer because I had finally sent Iain that terrible "Dear John" letter, and even though I was now *seeing* David, it had been an agonizing decision for me. It was also during that summer that I had had a terrible strep throat infection, something that was very serious before antibiotics. I believe I might have picked it up from my mother who had returned from Europe with a sore throat.

I had been working at a part-time piecework job, writing *precis* of cases, and had been offered a permanent position. I was thinking that I did not really want to go to Osgoode Hall Law School—I had enjoyed the academic atmosphere at U of T, but Osgoode Hall was regarded as a "trade school for plumbers of the law." The competition and attitude, according to David's reports, were of a cut-throat nature. I began contemplating other opportunities in law—possibly a Court stenographer. They had to have a highly specialized education, and I had heard that the exams were very stiff.

By the end of the summer of 1946, I was still contemplating the decision of whether or not to go to Osgoode Hall. Of course my father was still trying to pressure me into going. I think my mother was worried about the state of my health, though, because I had not fully recovered from my strep throat. As I mentioned, it had been arranged for my father to go to California at the expense of one of his clients, Mr. James Playfair, a wealthy business man who was exploring investments in off-shore oil, which was a relatively new venture in 1946. Mr. Playfair sent my father to check out an *Oil Man* who was negotiating to invest with Mr. Playfair. While my parents were in Laguna Beach, California, they wrote to me that the *Oil Man* had provided them with a beautiful suite at The Pacific Coast Club, and that there was a couch I could use if I wanted to join them. They sent me the money to fly there. They were still celebrating their 25th wedding anniversary—Dad always found a way his talents could be used to subsidize a bit of pleasure, here and there, for himself and Mother.

I decided to fly down and join my parents in Los Angeles. I needed some *R & R* to clear my head while I was contemplating my future. I wrote letters to David, telling him in detail about all of my adventures. In 1946, the flight from Toronto to Los Angeles was quite an adventure! ... *T.C.A uses a very neat Douglas craft, seating 18, but they couldn't carry that many with the full complement of freight* ... I wrote. There was a $100 difference between the airfares for flying at the level of the stratosphere, where you required oxygen, and flying below it; I, of course, took the cheaper flight. On the day of my departure a storm blew in on the East Coast, ... *we were delayed about half an hour until there was enuf ceiling to take off and even then there was talk of our having to turn back...was expecting to have the trip called off at any moment. We went through sloppy sleet and the weather was generally disagreeable* ... Even after arriving in Chicago at O'Hara Airport ... *I haunted the Chicago airport for 8 hours while my connecting plane was grounded in Philadelphia ... the airport gradually filled with people waiting for grounded planes ... Finally my plane came in at 12:30 a.m. and the people waiting cheered it like the pony express* ... It did not help the situation that the airport was under construction; there was a burlap bag over the entrance to the Ladies Room! The airline I was booked with kept giving me meal tickets during my wait—problem was, the only place that provided food was a little kiosk, and they only served hot dogs and donuts.

    From Chicago ... *The T.W.A plane was quite a bit bigger and very powerful. It cruised at 10,000 feet and seemed to get above the weather. It sailed along very smoothly and I managed to get some sleep between the stops at Kansas City, Wichita, Amarillo and Albuquerque* ... Kansas City was the next memorable stop. The accent was so thick I did not know whether I was in Kansas City, Kansas; or, Kansas City, Missouri! The stop there was quite lengthy because the plane was being refuelled and serviced. I wandered the airport, stretching my legs and looking about, even though there was not much to look at. As I meandered around, I kept hearing the PA system calling for someone. Suddenly, I realized it was me; I had not recognized the way they were pronouncing my name! They were holding the plane for me.

    What an adventure the flight from Kansas City to Los Angeles was! I tried to get some sleep. Being a bigger plane then the last one, I was able to stretch across the seats. I woke up to see ... *a sunrise on the desert ... it was desperately hot until I peeled off all the blankets and stuff I had on during the cold night* ... I was sure *glad to be so far above that flat, parched monotonous country. For 8 hrs it sped past at 180 mph—just brown parched grass as far as the eye could see. We went thru a pass in the mountains and that provided some bumps and thrills which at times brought us uncomfortably close to the rugged peaks. We saw the snow-capped San Francisco Mountains. I have never seen anything like it ... I was glad that I was awake and that the plane was late so that it was light enough to see ...*

When we landed in Burbank the balmy temperature of 88 degrees hit me like a ton of bricks. The blue woollen suit I had put on before leaving Toronto did not help! I took a limousine into Los Angeles and was thrilled with the all the sights on the Avenue of Palms, and the California architecture ... *Most of the buildings are one storey high and sprawling all over because of earthquakes. The homes are Spanish-style bungalows ... each on their own level on steps up the sides of mountains ...* The Pacific Coast Club looked very posh as I pulled up to it; I could not believe I was really going to stay there! The *Oil Man* provided us with a nice ocean-view suite, complete with a small sitting room with an in-a-door bed for Mom and Dad, plus a separate room for me.

The first thing I wanted to do was go for a swim, to cool down after my long trip. I had the whole pool to myself. A man approached me and said, "You must be the Canadian girl; no one else swims when it's this cold!" The same man accompanied me on our evenings out. I wrote to David of him ... *My partner reminded me of R. Shepherd, but he could rumba, so I forgave him. He taught me to Samba ...* My, how we were entertained that trip! I could not help but think that, between all the sight-seeing, night-clubbing and parties in our honour, that ... *the main industry here seems to be amusing people, food and DRINK. Bars and cocktail lounges are more numerous than gas stations ...* The *Oil Man* sure knocked himself out showing us a good time ... *we toured the golf clubs and saw some wonderful riding stables with miles of scenic bridle paths especially cultivated ... strange forms of vegetation I have never seen before, plus dates, oranges and grapefruits on trees! ...* We had a special seafood dinner at Sam's, the place for fish ... *tomorrow a luncheon in my honour, a Pan-Hellenic tea ... took a two day trip to Palm Springs ... we certainly saw a great variety of country ... desert, mountain and beaches ...* We went through the date groves ... to the desert, *"lowest of the low down places,"* 20 ft. below sea level ... *a typical frontier town ... We were taken all around Signal Hill where the oil wells are,* (Mr. E. is in the oil business and sold Dad an interest in a little trickle he has up there) ... *went to see Earl Carrol's "The Most Beautiful Girls in the World"* ... my letters to David were just brimming with all the sights, sounds and experiences I was having—somehow I even managed to squeeze in some shopping ... *and procured a pair of shoes with the greatest of ease and a ducky little blue satin bathing suit with a bare spot in the middle! I really have wonderful luck shopping here, everything fits and suits me!*

By far, though, the real "treat of the trip" was when Dad took us down to the Latin Quarter. I wrote ... *to the sound of the Spanish guitars and that velvety tongue we wandered through shop after shop of beautiful handiwork, silver filigree and leatherwork ... They also had the most adorable Mexican dresses ... I'm going to try to duplicate one when I get home. The climax came when we got hungry, and lured by the sound of singing and guitars and the sights of the grate fire, we wandered into what was advertised as the wine cellar of an old Spanish mansion. There we dined and wined and were regaled with Spanish songs and dances on into the night* ... So much for California being a restful trip—the most rest I got was probably either at night, after falling into bed exhausted from being *the belle of the ball*, or in the pool, as I made sure to do lots of swimming ... *I am trying to stay on the beach. The natives consider it cool at 75 degrees and the water cold at 66. I am in seventh heaven living in my bathing suit and toasting the white skin they seen to prize here...*

Eventually, though, it was time to head back to "the real world." Osgoode Hall had already started when I wrote to David of my return home ... *it's sweet of you to want to meet me. I appreciate it very much, mostly because you are the first person I want to see when I get there ... I only hope the T.C.A pilot's don't strike in sympathy with their T.W.A counterparts. A secretary of Dad's clients has reserved space for us on the plane that leaves Chicago on Sunday Nov. 3rd at 5:45 ... I'll be staying at the Palmer House in Chicago* ... I was eager to get home to David; even though the California climate continued to call to me, so much so that I conceded in one of my last letters from Los Angeles ... *Your idea about South America is interesting. If this is at all typical of a tropical climate, I could quite gaily leave Toronto's cold and snow ... I'm afraid that my short course in Spanish wouldn't get me very far, so maybe that's one of the things we'll have to learn together ...*

However, my tropical South American dreams of balmy beaches and David would have to wait, because when I returned from California it was time to gear up to enter the "shark's tank" of Osgoode Hall Law School. My father had finally persuaded me. He impressed on me his desire to make sure that I would be a self-sufficient woman, which included being financially independent. He explained that he did not want to happen to me what had happened to his sisters, Ethel and Eleanor, and to his mother. He had ended up supporting them all, along with his sisters' children. That is why my father had bought two houses on Wellesley Street—one for his bride, one for his mother and sisters. His sister Ethel died of TB—his mother took over the care of her two boys.

~

By the time I returned from Los Angeles, it was past the deadline for starting at Osgoode Hall. I was lucky that I was even accepted, but I think it was because of the fact that I had good marks from the U of T Law School. Admittedly, my fourth year had not been as good as the first three years because of all the *other things* that had been on my mind. Plus, my mother had been very ill with strep throat during the time I was writing my final exams. I had the responsibility of nursing her and making the family meals. I missed a Bankruptcy exam and the professor had me write a supplemental exam.

Some might think that it was a bit harsh that during a time when I was studying so hard that I would also have to look after household duties and a sick mother, but those were the times—I just accepted it. I did write an appeal against my failure of the Bankruptcy exam, stating the circumstances surrounding the period when I should have been studying for it. But if truth be told, I had skipped some of the lectures. In the boom time, after the war, when society was trying to make up for all the goods and services that had been lacking throughout the war you could do no wrong—there was money to be made in any endeavour. I never expected I would ever have to face a bankruptcy on behalf of any client who was willing to work. Basically, I was just not interested—I did not think it was a useful subject for me to have in my bag. Of course, I also realized that I had to pass the course to get admitted to the Bar.

I guess I should have been studying while I was nursing my mother, but David was sick as well. He was not into the bankruptcy stuff either. Economically speaking, it seemed like something way out in *left field*. David was living with his father, in his stepmother's home, and the stepmother loved to travel, so she and his father were away. David was supposed to be looking after his stepmother's father, but he was too sick to even study. I assumed they were not eating properly, so I took some chicken soup and junket for both of them. While David was eating, I read my lecture notes to him. I figured that anything he knew I fed to him, and then he turned around and got a better mark than I did!

So I entered Osgoode Law School late, but was fortunate that I had a very good friend in Sidney Dymond. She had obtained her university degree through matriculation. Back then, you could be admitted to the Bar admission courses on matriculation, which meant that all an individual had to do was meet the academic standard required. I think she actually wanted to pick my brain for the legal terminology that I had studied while at the U of T Law School. Sidney arrived at the Great Hall of Osgoode Hall early enough to get two front-row-center desks for us. Thus, she and I were right underneath the lecturer's nose for the entire year. Something that probably did not endear us to our classmates!

Sidney and I were very serious. Throughout the years, David kept telling me to lighten up, but seriousness was something that my father and mother had ingrained in me. I had grown up as an only child in an adult world. I guess I was just old for my age.

ARTICLING POSITION—FALL 1946

My three years of underpaid service to a lawyer upon whom I depended for the documentation, in order to be called to the Bar, had begun. Of course I could not start at Osgoode until I had somebody to sign a paper saying they would take me on as an articling student. I had tried to obtain a placement without my father's help, but it was difficult because not many firms wanted to hire a female. My father audited the McMillan, Binch Law Firm books, in Toronto. He was highly respected there and had made some good friends amongst the partners. I believe that it was because of my father that they decided to give me the opportunity to article at their firm, even though they thought he was crazy to invest so much time and money into educating a daughter in the field of law. They told him that I would probably eventually quit, get married, and have babies. I began my articling career at $3.50 per week, less than my male counterparts. I had had another firm offer me a position, but it would not have given me the excellent experience, or distinction I would get at McMillan Binch.

    I was lectured quite soundly because of my late start. I sometimes wonder whether that was actually overlooked because of whom my father was. Gordon McMillan, one of the senior partners, informed me that I was the first female that prestigious firm had ever taken on as a student-at-law; and, although they had an office for law students, he wanted me to work in the library so they could *keep an eye on me* and make sure that I was not demoralizing the male students. Such was my initial introduction to the firm!

    I used to wonder about some of those young men. Other than David's friend, Mel Cunningham, who later became our partner, I had no idea what most of the other students were doing. Mel was involved in the firm's real estate department. He became so adept at that part of the practice that they left him to manage it when the British solicitor, who was in charge of the department, went away for his summer holidays. My impression of the other young men was that they were a bunch of *playboys*—sons of wealthy clients, the firm lawyers, or prominent judges. I was absolutely unaware of what kind of work they were doing; however, I was much too busy to find out!

    I remember one student in particular—Jack. His father was an affluent lawyer. Jack liked to live the *playboy* lifestyle. He would stroll into the office about ten o'clock, unshaven. He would say hi to the receptionist, go to the washroom and shave, and then go out for breakfast. After that he would lounge around the male student office. Finally, he got a call from Gordon McMillan!

    "You know, when you're an articled student in this firm, it's not just your country club—you're expected to do some work!" Gordon McMillan informed Jack.

    "Oh?" Jack replied

    McMillan continued on. "You have to come in when the office opens at 9 a.m., and buckle down and do some work, or we can't continue to carry your articles. Now, are you going to start working?"

    Jack's reply—"May I think about it overnight, sir?"

That was the attitude of some of those over-privileged boys!

~

My father had great faith in me, though, and his thinking was way ahead of the times. I came upon a newspaper article in The New York Times, dated February 19, 1950, entitled, <u>Father Was Ahead of His Time</u>. It began with the statement: <u>"Girls", he said, "can be lawyers."</u>

Laboratory of Steven's Institute of Hoboken, N.J., gives surprising confirmation of this theory in a study which it made a few years ago of the primary characteristics common to various professions. In the case of lawyers it found five important characteristics: a subjective personality, capacity for inductive reasoning, an aptitude for accounting, a large English vocabulary, and creative imagination.

"Women," said the report, "were bound to be, on average, more definitely 'subjective' and therefore more the professional type than men, and to rank higher in accounting aptitude. There is some evidence, although it is not conclusive, that women average higher then men in inductive reasoning. Inductive reasoning is defined as the gift 'for sensing relationships, for integrating facts, for generalizing.' Such a gift might be that characteristic of women known as intuition."

The report concludes that "in every aptitude of the lawyer which the laboratory can measure women average higher than men." It winds up by advising more women to consider the Bar as a career and reassuring them as to their capacity for success at it.

<u>*Yes, the small number of women lawyers means nothing except as it dramatizes the fact that the going has been tough and that the struggle for recognition is scarcely over.*</u> *Most of us forget what headway women lawyers, with all their handicaps, have already made…five members of the Federal judiciary, headed by Judge Allen of the United States Court of Appeals; two Federal District Court judges; a Customs and a Tax Court judge; state court judges; mayors of cities; legislators; Federal, state and city commissioners; city solicitors and attorneys—the list is legion—to say nothing of the private practitioners.*

<u>*Years ago my lawyer father said the words*</u> *I should like to hear everybody use today. Holding tight to his hand and skipping to keep up with his long stride,* <u>*the little girl that was me suddenly popped this question*</u> *out of nowhere to him:*

<u>*"Can girls be lawyers, Father?"*</u>
<u>*And he answered, smiling: "Why not, my dear?"*</u>

So like something my father would have said, and so like what he believed, at least fifteen years before that article was written!

~

I do credit the McMillan, Binch Law Firm for the excellent law experience I received while there. However, there was a tradition in those days to test the mettle of the new inductees—that of *hazing*. I was sent out to *arrest* a ship! My job was to pin a warrant to the mast. Back then women were not allowed to wear slacks. I was wearing a herringbone suit—I could only imagine the snickers from the sailors who were peeking up my skirt, as I was trying to nail the warrant to the mast so it that would not blow away. Another time I was sent, on a holiday, to pin to a bank door a "letter of protest," protesting a note that was due that day. Those are just a couple examples of hazing—during my first year at the firm, I got them in spades!

In my second year the Firm started entrusting me with some interesting work. I assisted Larry McCarthy, Counsel for the Federal Government, on one of the few "Conspiracy in Restraint of Trade" cases. I organized the evidence and assisted in the presentation of the case. That was a fascinating experience! There were 17 defendants from different corporations who sold dental equipment to dentists. They were accused of conspiring between themselves to fix the prices. I could have conceived a *Gilbert and Sullivan* operetta out of the performances I witnessed in the court room. We would name an offence they were accused of, and then all 17 Defence Counsels would, in turn, stand up and say, "I object! I object!" As I said—opera material!

One of the jobs expected of articling students, before a trial, was to go out to interview the individuals on the jury selection panel. I was sent to some very seedy sections of the city that I never would ventured into otherwise, to see if these potential jurors had any particular prejudices or fixed opinions that might impinge on their decision on the case they were being considered to decide.

I was also part of the collection team for a law book firm who published annual volumes of important case decisions that had taken place during the previous years. Lawyers had to buy the annual volume in order to keep their sets up to date; we had to pursue the lawyers who had not paid for their books. I attended creditor's meetings where debtors were rearranging their financial commitments.

Another job was to keep the minutes for the Wood Company, which made paper supplies. Their motto was "Sanitation for the Nation." This was a tremendously valuable placement. I developed a good grasp of corporate law, which served me well when I appeared before the panel for my oral questioning upon my admittance to the Bar. When I announced my intentions to pursue a county town practice, the chairman of the panel actually said that it would be a shame to have my knowledge of corporate law wasted on such a venue. Some city lawyers thought county lawyers just *played* at law!

Jack Hammel, an old prospector who had struck it rich, comes to mind as one of the firm's clients who was suing the British American Oil Company for cleaning out some oil tanks just off of his beautiful lakeshore property. One day, when David *called for me* after work, one of the senior partners called me into his office and said: "Isn't that young man that you are seeing after work the law student who works for the British American Oil Company law office?" I responded that he was. That partner proceeded to tell me that during the lawsuit he expected me to discontinue seeing David. I declared to him that David and I were engaged to be married and that we did not discuss cases we were working on—we had other things on our minds when we were together. This was just another example of the poor *attitude* toward a woman trying to be a serious lawyer during those times!

WAITING A YEAR TO BE MARRIED

It was proper, back in the 1940's, for a young man to ask his intended's father for her hand in marriage. David did not even dare to do this until he had his Law Degree in hand. He was admitted to the Bar in 1948 and then he approached my father. Apparently, David had a most stressful interview with my father in our basement workshop. Father raked David over the coals, as to his potential possibilities, and about whether or not he could earn enough money to support a young woman who had grown up with luxury and indulgences. My father's final summation was that David would have one year to prove that he could earn a good living in a county town law practice. Only then would my father bless our union.

David and I researched where we could possibly set up a county law practice. We surveyed several towns where we could enjoy the outdoor life. We consulted with law book salesmen, asking about any possible practices which might be for sale. We checked into towns where there might not be enough lawyers per capita. Lindsay kept showing up on the list. We visited there several times and fell in love with the region, and the beautiful Lake District around it. Lindsay's population in the late 1940's was around 10,000. We learned that one lawyer was leaving private practice because he had been called to the bench. We decided on Lindsay.

So, with my father's words ringing in his ears, David headed up to Lindsay a year ahead of me. We had located an apartment, which had formerly been occupied by a woman with nine children. It was situated over a Chinese laundry and "Lynn's Lunch." This would also become my first matrimonial home. It was in total disarray when David moved in, and I do believe that the disarray did not improve much because he lived there with two other bachelors—need I say more! One of those bachelors was Mel Cunningham, our first partner.

We started our law practice with $3,000. The first $1,000 was my dad's graduation gift to me; the second $1,000 Mel had obtained in a lawsuit settlement for a concussion he had received from an accident. With $2,000 in the account, David and Mel obtained a $1,000 loan from the Bank of Commerce. We bought some second-hand furniture and law books, and the necessary equipment to start our law office.

Our first client was one of Mel's, a divorce. We received a $100 retainer fee to start the action. I can remember sitting down with David and Mel, and dividing it up 40-40-20—the $20 of course was my share because I was still articling at McMillan, Binch. However, I realized later, from my correspondence to David that I was actually doing a lot of work on this divorce—interviewing witnesses, and preparing and filing papers. McMillan, Binch was very indulgent with me, allowing me to work for David's and my firm, while I was on their payroll! I actually did quite a bit of this sort of thing to help David build the practice during that first year.

TRIP WEST WITH MOM AND DAD—AUGUST 1948
(As told through excerpts from my letters to David)

I think my father wanted me to realize that if I married a "poor county lawyer" I would never be able to travel again the way I did with my parents. Almost, as though they wanted to prove this point, my parents took me on a wonderful train trip to the West Coast. I never realized the vast extent of our province until spending an entire day traveling through its northern woods ... *I talked to two women who lived in railway towns; they said they wouldn't live in Toronto for anything. They had spent a short time in Toronto and agreed that they each had had plenty of the big city in two days...*

Our train was three hours late in arriving to Winnipeg, Manitoba. We spent the afternoon in Assiniboine Park and then went back to the C.P.R. Hotel for supper. The park was massive, sprawling over huge tracts of land. Even the buildings were enormous!

We arrived in Edmonton, Alberta, at 6:40 a.m. As soon as we arrived, Dad was paged to the phone. The first thing that Mom and I thought was that the office was calling, but when Dad returned he informed us that a local newspaper had called to see if they might send around a photographer to take our pictures! ... *How desperate they must be for news! A society editor came right over with the photographer—this should give us some free advertising if she prints any of what Dad told her about me. She said that our pictures would be in this afternoon's edition ... I'll send it to you as soon as the papers come out...*

Once we were settled into our rooms, we took a long walk around the town, taking in the Parliament buildings ... *I got a view of the Library—I wish I could have taken some law books for souvenirs, there were so many in the museum and Legislative Chamber...*

In view of the fact that I was a celebrity in town, I thought I better look up my *crazy*, architect frat sister, Mary Imrie. A fond memory I have of Mary is the night we mixed two colours of paint together and then painted the walls of our living room at our frat house. Everyone had been arguing about which colour to use—By the time Mary and I finished, the walls were two shades of pinkish-rose! We ended at her place for cocktails. Later, we joined my parents for dinner at the hotel. They were looking a bit glum, thinking that we would not be making it to Jasper the next day because of some flooding.

The journey to Alberta's Jasper Park Lodge was the most thrilling and scenic of our trip ... *The mountains and the rushing torrents leave me breathless in the sight of their splendour. The havoc wrought by the floods is everywhere apparent. They say that the rain was so heavy that it melted snow that hasn't been melted for years*...

Despite the beauty of the landscape, our first impression of the area was not very good. First of all, we were late arriving, and then it took two hours, during which time we sat in the lobby, before we were shown to our cabins ... *and even then it hadn't been tidied up since the last guests left it. The place is really too crowded for comfort*... Our cabin, which housed about four families, was also quite a distance from the Lodge and the lake—I wondered what price the more exclusive, private cabins on the lakeshore would have cost!

Boy, I must have been a snobby *Victorian prig* the way I criticized the behaviour and dress of the other people at Jasper Park. It was a very expensive resort ... *You would think that people who would pay so much for a vacation would be well-groomed, well-dressed and well-mannered. The fact is that the majority that I have seen sift through the lobby are none of those things. They are frowsy, dissipated and over-indulged, wearing everything from ill-fitting jeans and shorts, to evening and dinner dress. As for their manners, words fail me. They seem to think that an excess of cold hard cash gives them license to ignore the sensibilities of others*...

I wrote to David that evening and told him how much I wished he was with me. I told him that even if we had had to sleep in an *Indian tepee*, it would have been heaven to me just to have him so near. I waited anxiously for a letter from David, hoping to hear news of his first rush of clients. When I did not receive any mail, I felt that it must be because the irresponsible kids who worked at the resort had lost it! Some of the help was terrible—one girl, who was supposed to be serving our breakfast, spent more time talking her girlfriends. Our meal was cold by the time it arrived at our table!

Dad and I went horse-back riding for three hours along the Maligne Canyon. It was a really wonderful way to see the country—I think Dad enjoyed it as much as I did ... *The scenery was breathtaking. We saw several deer and a big black grizzly bear that must have weighed nearly 300 lbs. We also came upon the body of a dead wolf whereupon my horse nearly had a fit and we lost the trail completely. It poured rain and we got drenched, but we were dry by the time we got back to the stable. I think it was the first time that I have ever been glad to see the stable after a ride...*

We met the most interesting lady while at the Lodge—Madame Chevrier, the wife of Canada's Minister of Transport. She was vacationing with her children. She actually remembered having met my mother and me at the Salmagundi Club in Toronto. Her three-year old daughter was the belle of the pool! I enjoyed a couple of swims, but felt that the water was much too warm.

I was pleased to finally receive a letter from David, informing me that he was an uncle to a fine baby boy. I was also thrilled with the news of his opportunity for free advertising at the next Rotary luncheon in Lindsay ... *How I wish I could hear you! Just be your own dear sweet cheerful self and ask lots of advice from the old-timers who would be flattered by your asking... I know you'll wow 'em... You wow me, at anytime...*

It had been a quiet day—for various reasons—one of them being that I was still feeling the affects of various aches and pains from my previous day's riding adventure ... *I spent the morning flicking over the pages of my Contracts notes in an idyllic little summer house on the shore of the lake. I could think of better things to do there, most of them with you...* In the afternoon we took a trip into town and I searched for a birthday present for David. I thought I would get him a cowboy shirt, and maybe a matching one for me. I decided against that when I saw how much they were! Back at the Lodge for the evening meal, I ate quite heartily. When I weighed myself later that night, I discovered I had already gained three pounds on the trip! In the letter I wrote to David I asked him if he thought I should try and cut down to four or five courses per meal, even though we were paying for seven! I also asked David to ... *tell me all about the office, our first sucker and all the doings in our adopted home town...* I asked him to give my best to Mel and the McQuarries.

There was a dance planned for the evening, but I decided not to attend because the Lodge was so jammed with people that there was not even one chair left. I was missing David. I thought to myself that if I had anything to say about it, we would never again be apart for such a long time.

~

I was getting quite antsy at the lack of letters from David, when his letter dated August 12th was shoved under my door. I thought that his choice of a subject to talk about at the Rotary luncheon was excellent ... *You could certainly make it very interesting for anyone who knows nothing about the development of our Legal System, and at the same time impress them with the depth of your knowledge of it* ... I wished I could have been there to support David.

Everyone was raving about a magnificent golf course that was in the area, so my parents and I set out in the morning to investigate. I wrote to David about how ... *each tee gives a different view of the surrounding mountains and they look so different from the different angles --we actually wound up getting lost on the golf course!* We also took pictures of a mama bear and her cub, taking great care not to annoy the mama because she was a very "buxom lass" of around 400 pounds!

In the afternoon we went on a sightseeing bus tour. The bus was driven by Tom Beckell who was in his 4th year of Honour Law at Varsity. He sure swung that bus around the hairpin turns to get us 6,000 feet up Mount Edith Cavell. Even though it was a beautiful hot summer day, it was actually quite cool on the mountain. I walked another 1,000 feet beyond the timber line so that I could take pictures of the glacier.

~

I was delighted to receive another letter from David. In it he had included the *Lindsay Post's* news clipping of the Rotary luncheon at which he had spoken. I was impressed with the publicity David was getting. I set his letter aside and headed out to church ... *the young rector gave a very scholarly and yet highlighted sermon, bringing in the idea of looking up and enjoying the beauty of nature ... also spoke of Karl Marx's theory on the Christian religion —he refuted it very effectively ... I spoke to him after service —he told me that he nearly came to Grace in Toronto—small world. To prove the same point there are 3 other Tri-Dells here now ...*

It was quite ironic that we bumped into my "honorary cousin," Stewart Webb, (Aunt Florence's nephew by marriage) who was working at the Lodge as a gate patrolman. He was also responsible to keep an eye on the young chauffeurs who drove the guests around, making sure that they were not just taking joyrides. Stewart was in his final year at Varsity and very much involved with a young lady. He told me that he really wanted to get married, but that his father was insisting he go to Osgoode. He asked my advice, but I told him that it would be best that he decide based on his own deliberations.

On Sunday afternoon we walked around Lac Beauvert … *the path is all nicely levelled and smoothed, with benches along the way—a perfect lover's lane. It was about 3 miles around, so I had some time to study in the sun when we got back … I am getting a nice tan. Tonight we were to take a twilight tour which is noted for the animals it comes upon, but a storm broke while we were at dinner … it is just teeming rain again. Already this is a record season for rain* … in lieu of the tour, the Lodge showed moving pictures to the flock of storm-bound guests. After the movies I headed back to my room and wrote of my adventures to David, telling him, once again, how much I missed him.

~

We had a pleasant trip to Vancouver Island. We were to stay in the Empress Hotel in Victoria. There was a high wind on the way across the channel, but the water was not rough because the channel was protected by a string of islands, much like the 1,000 Islands near Kingston. The hotel was nice and we enjoyed our stay there.

The first adventure on the Island was a bus tour that included Mrs. Buchard's Gardens, and an old limestone quarry that had been converted into a beauty spot. In the afternoon we walked around the downtown; and, since I had not gotten David a birthday present yet, I thought I might find something suitable. I came across a nice white cable-knit pullover … *but for various reasons I think I had better knit you one myself. I did get you, what I thought was an excellent buy, a maroon sleeveless pullover at David Spencer's. I chose maroon because it will be becoming and won't show the dirt. I hope you'll like it* … I arranged to have the pullover shipped directly to David so that he would be sure to have it in time for his birthday. My mother slipped a matching tie in the box, plus a note wishing him many happy returns of the day.

By the third week of August, I was missing David terribly. I also had not had any letters from him for a few days. Finally another letter arrived. I was so pleased to read his news that I immediately wrote to him of how proud I was of his accomplishments.

As I mentioned earlier, there had been quite a flood before we arrived. The area was having a tough time keeping the railway lines open, so sometimes our schedule was subject to change without notice. We wanted to see some of the northern part of the Island while we were there, so we waited for the ten o'clock train to Nanaimo. From there, we hoped to be able to take a boat back to the mainland. We took a bus to see the Naval Base at Esquimalt, and went on board the ship, *Ontario*. The Master Painter and the cook kidded us about staying at the Empress Hotel—they said the staff there was not nearly as friendly as they were!

~

Finally, it was time to head home. While on the train, I wrote a letter to David … *We have been crawling along the banks of the Fraser River all day, 12 hours behind schedule … there are still traces of the havoc wrought by the mighty river when it was on the rampage. Some sections of the track were washed right out, and the ties flung up on the shore give one an insight into the awful height the river reached.*

The wreck up the line threw a very effective monkey wrench into the operations of several departments at Jasper. It held up traffic from Edmonton where the Lodge gets most of its supplies. It was getting short of food when we left, though some of the boys went with a truck to salvage what they could from the wreck.

The people coming west from Edmonton had to get out and walk around…the train from Vancouver picked them up and then backed up some 50 miles to Jasper. We got it when it got back to Jasper at midnight, having waited since two in the afternoon. The people who were on it have some harrowing tales to tell of their misadventures. A young mother, with 3 children under 5, fainted on the trail between the trains. Another woman had a heart attack … altogether the whole trainload was a sorry sight …

We got a bigger engine at the last station and are making better time now…Take care of yourself, Dearest, because I love you. xoxo—Thelma

FINAL STRETCH OF ARTICLING—PRE-WEDDING

September 1948

Now that I was back from my trip, it was time to crack the books again. This was a tumultuous time for me. I was juggling: studies, articling, assisting David with building our business, and most of all—planning my wedding. We had not set a date yet, due to my father's conditions to David, but I had my heart set on a June wedding. I intended to make that happen! If it meant having to spend extra hours doing legwork in Toronto for David, while he was in Lindsay, then that is what I was prepared to do. Besides, I felt that the busier I was, the faster the time would pass, for I missed David, so. There are even moments now, when I peruse through my letters, that I wonder how I ever managed.

This part of my story is highlighted with segments of my letters to David. The letters have helped me to remember the events of the time. I was of an age where most of my girlfriends were either already married, or were in the planning stages of marriage. Some even had children, or were very pregnant. I felt my clock ticking, plus, I believe I was getting tired of the daily grind of studying. David had been a dear and had loaned me his final year's notes, which eased some of my workload—one advantage of being loved by a man who had taken the same path in life that I was on!

Upon our return from the West, my parents and I drove up to Lindsay to say hello to David and Mel. Of course, Mom and Dad were saying hello—I was dying for a hug from my man! We spent a lovely weekend and then headed home. I could not bear the parting and the only thing I could think of was how long it would be before we saw each other again. Life was moving on—classes—working at the firm—dreaming …

… I went into the office this morning after lectures and all was calm with just a skeleton staff of the usual drones… All were very sympathetic about my cold and I was informed that Mr. Wright got Sandy McGregor to serve that female he wanted to sick me onto. He seems to be getting almost exclusive service from Sandy, (the Combine Commissioner's son), which suits me just fine… Mr. Wright was so demanding and inconsiderate at times that I would not have cared if he got completely browned off with me and did not ask me to do another thing for him ever again! I found

out some good news—we were going to start alternating our Saturday mornings between students. Whenever possible, I took some time to run a few errands for David ... *I ordered you a Seal and some "Will Backs"* (forms used to cover Wills)—*you should receive them this week.*

My mother's birthday was in September; I bought her the most adorable little purse and pair of gloves, to match her flashy Arabian-toed shoes. I wanted to make sure she had a nice present, in case Dad forgot her birthday. As it turned out, he had not forgotten—he had given Mother a nice cheque. She was thrilled to get double-treated, and even more-so that I had actually presented her with a gift that suited her! I was tickled pink.

My friend, Joan Vanstone, was getting married, and our friend Marion gave a luncheon for her at the Granite Club. Her fiancé, Bill, celebrated with a traditional stag party with his friends. I could not believe my eyes when I saw Joan's wedding gifts... *all every bride could wish for in sliver and china galore. Her lingerie is exquisite, all hand made with appliquéd lace etc.* ... I was excited for Joan. I decided that I must buy a new outfit for her wedding ... *I finally got a dress, (plain, straight-cut skirt with a perky little modified bustle in the back and umpteen little buttons for you to do up for me), ... it is a glorious wine color that just tones in beautifully with my "hearty" shoes and hat ...*

I had not sent a reply to the wedding invitation yet because I was unsure whether or not David would be able to make it down from Lindsay. Joan assured me it would be okay, even if David decided at the last minute—there would be a spot for him at my table. I wrote to David and told him that if he could make it, I would meet him at the noon bus, and I would have a new white shirt for him to change into. My mother graciously offered to drive him back to Lindsay on the Sunday. I mentioned to David that it would be a good opportunity to meet my father's partners, and ... *What would be really super would be if you could stay over Monday for my birthday and go to "Oklahoma" with us ...*

I had been running around so much in preparation for Joan's wedding that I had failed to make it to the Parliament buildings to pick up David's certificate. I decided to postpone that until a more convenient time—Simsie and I had a Saturday morning meeting at the church so that I could learn more about teaching Sunday school.

September was a busy month and the days were flying by—mostly. When the sun went down in the evenings, and I was home, alone in my room ... *I am missing you with a dull, painful ache. Between lectures I rush around trying to think up errands to do and people to phone so that somehow I can pass off those moments of complete desolation and loneliness...* I was finding that I needed David's encouragement—I counted on it to get me through my days. There were many moments that I found myself ... *lost in all the streets and corridors we trod together...*

My parents did their best to fill some of my evenings with entertainment. They took me to see Verdi's *la Traviata*, an Italian Tragedy performed by the Rome Opera Company at the International Cinema. The film was in Italian and had an English narrator. It ended in the usual Italian style ... *with the heroine expiring and everyone baring their souls ... I don't think I'll ever have any tears left for anything that happens to me after all I wept over the sorrows of Violetta...*

My lectures seemed dull and the office was unusually quiet. Mr. Wright lightened up every once in awhile and he even kidded me about trying to save Sandy McGregor from the clutches of the co-respondent he had served. Little moments like that made it bearable for me. I finally managed to get to the Parliament building to order David's Notorial certificate. They said it would be done in a week to ten days.

~

September was winding down. Mail from David was sparse and I hoped that was because he was busy. The early September sluggishness was gone—lectures, and the work that went with them, were being piled on steam-shovel style! Even the office had become a hive of activity ... *enough to do to keep me out of trouble for some time to come* ... I was putting the finishing touches on a new estate and Cookie kept me busy with gobs of odds and ends. I enjoyed working for him because he explained things in their simplest terms.

David's certificates finally came and I sent them to be framed ... *they should be done the beginning of next week if not by the weekend. If you are coming down perhaps I can speed them up so that you could take them back with you. I love you, I love you, I love you—you know who...*

~

My Aunt Flo and Uncle Grant were avid golfers. One Saturday they asked if I would caddie for them—it was great fun. While on the course, Uncle Grant told me a story about a minister friend of his who had been making him furious ... *The minister's favourite sport was picking up golf balls. Morning, noon and night he comes back with his pockets bulging ... his sermon last Sunday, "Praise God from Whom all Blessings Flow" ... we just heard tonight that he will return any balls to the owners who tell him what they lost ...*

~

September can still have some pretty warm days. I worried when David took the bus, especially if it was too hot out. Even my plan to go riding with Van fell through because she thought it was much too hot to ride. I decided to spend my Saturday shopping, and also picked up the family tickets for the Monday night performance of *Henry V*. Later in the evening, bored and thinking of David, so far from me ... *tonight I created an indecent little article of clothing by cutting my pink culottes down and making a bare midriff halter from the cuttings—I think you'll like it. I practiced swinging Mother's golf clubs out in the back yard and developed such a twist on my drive that I twisted my ankle out of joint, so I am hobbling around with it swathed in bandages now ... I hope you're having better golf weather up there than we are here. Be good to yourself—I love you, Thelma*

~

I was happy to hear news from David that things were beginning to pick up in Lindsay. He had been introduced at a church and the news in his letter sounded fruitful. I was beginning to be sure that our wedding was going to be *in the bag*. I was determined to speak to David about making our wedding reservations the next time I saw him. I missed him so much and felt that I just existed between our visits ... *All I do is go around missing you, especially when we usually had a rendezvous, like between lectures. The girls have taken pity on me, I look so forlorn ... they rush over and immediately start gossiping madly as soon as each lecture is over, but I haven't the heart to tell them that it only makes me miss you more ...*

~

The end of September finally arrived. Our first-year sup results were posted and most of them were pretty grim. Walton and

Prest did okay, Ena got three 50's and a 58, Joy got a 29 in Torts, and Lorna missed hers entirely. Out of the 115 students who wrote, only 41 passed! There were 152 students left, out of the original 320. I wrote to David that he should be thankful that he had left that kind of slaughter behind and was on to better things, even if he was only averaging one client a day!

~

Sidney, Joan Morris, Barb Duncan, and I were invited to the Toronto Ladies' Golf Club, as the dinner guests of Margaret Parney. It was a nice evening, in a quiet, dull sort of way. Margaret was entertaining, as usual, but Sidney and I spent most of the evening picking out the married couples. We thought the married ones were the ones who had happy, contented looks on their faces; the single ones were the ones with looks of desperate frustration. This just confirmed our expectations of how we would look once we had those wedding rings on our fingers! Sidney's man was supposed to be coming up to Toronto sometime in November and we were going to try to arrange a party at the Brant Inn.

On the way to our dinner we witnessed what we thought was just an example of reckless driving. A car coming toward us caused the car in front of us to swerve. We thought all was well, but slowed down, because the car in front of us had come pretty close to another car. We were about to joke about almost getting into an accident when we heard the crash—it was a terrible head-on collision! We girls decided that since we had witnessed the accident, it was our civic duty to give our names to the police. Later that night I wrote to David … *Won't it be something if the poor victim dies and four female lawyers are witnesses in the manslaughter trial? I had your card handy, but I wouldn't want to see you act for the drunk. He was too contemptible...*

~

I had not had much of a religious education at home, my father being an intellectual agnostic. My mother had been a very devout Anglican while growing up; but, she had fallen under the influence of my father and had lapsed in her commitment to the church. Everything mother did was to please father; she was an extremely devoted Victorian wife.

I felt that before I got married in a church that I should make some sort of commitment to it. I also wanted to be married in a *nice* church. Even though I had attended Timothy Eaton Memorial Church at one time, eventually, I settled on Grace Anglican Church. I was not in a position, personally, to give money to the church for my ceremony, so I felt that I should give of myself instead. Ignorant as I was of Bible teachings, the year before I was married I taught a girl's Bible study group. The girls in my group, mostly 12 year olds, were quite an interesting lot and they bore the names of some of the foremost families in Toronto. Of course, in the back of my mind was the thought that some of those connections might serve David and me well, once we began our law practice. Due to my lack of actual religious education I conducted the sessions as more of a study group, asking the girls how they would apply the lessons to their daily lives. We had some very interesting discussions in reference to the church and how we lived. I worked hard on the classes for these girls; what great fun they were. The girls were amazed when they discovered I was still in school—"I don't think she looks that old!" one of them said. Those girls certainly added an element to my life that I enjoyed very much!

I also went to Confirmation classes with the teenagers. Eventually, the Rector mentioned to me that I did not belong in that class. He asked me to come on Sunday evenings, after *Evensong*, to a group for young engaged couples. David managed to attend those classes a few times, as well. His father was part of the World Council of Churches and endorsed these sessions for young couples.

~

Thanksgiving would soon be upon us and I wrote to David asking about his plans. I felt I should be in Toronto for my Sunday school class because I did not want my girls to think that their teacher was not interested in them. I mentioned to David that I could take the Sunday a.m. train home in order to arrive on time to church. That way I would also be able to rest up before … *getting back to the grind … Already I have gobs of work to do. If you're looking for me Saturday afternoon, I'll be in the Great library under stacks of Wills, and Conflicts of Laws cases. But through it all, I love you just the same. Goodnight, my love, Thelma…*

October 1948

I was getting a sense from some of David's correspondence to me that he was feeling a bit low in spirit. I told him that he should be proud of the accomplishments he had already attained. I began to think that maybe I should not bother David so much with all of my little troubles, but then I wrote him ... *if you'll tell me your grief, I'll tell you mine and we'll still be the happiest couple we know yet (but wait til you see us married!)* ... Thanksgiving was just around the corner and I could not wait to see him!

I found myself constantly apologizing to David for not writing as often as I should, but I was finding that my life was so busy. Many nights, by the time I arrived home, I was just too beat to pick up a pen. Sometimes, when I was too tired to write, I would try calling, but David was not always there. That would depress me more, even though I knew he was probably out at some local function trying to drum up business for our office.

~

Mr. Dowker, the minister who was going to marry David and me, phoned me and mentioned that someone else wanted him to marry them on the same day we had picked—June 25, 1949. He asked if I would mind having our wedding either earlier, or later than three o'clock. I was not keen on a 2:30 start, feeling a later time would be more suitable.

I was constantly on the lookout for wedding things. I found a beautiful pair of brocade slippers to wear with my wedding dress. They were marked down to $13.50 from $22.95. My mother had the wedding fever too, and was busy checking out china patterns for me. She was also trying to get me an introduction to Cassidy's wholesale store where she had gotten her china.

There were times when I had so much reading to do for my Osgoode classes that I did not even get into the office. One week I was out of the office for two days ... *reading great gobs of law, for guess who, P.W. of course, for an opinion for an insurance company that wants to take an uncomfortable B.C. precedent to the Supreme Court ...*

Our Sup exams were right around the corner again and ... *I finally smartened up tonight and ploughed into my notes with the aid of the ones I inherited from you ... got a lot cleaned up without having to waste time getting books ... I find that Willis doesn't give up nearly as many cases as Caesar gave you in Wills. He just goes into one important case on each point in detail. He is really giving us a solid course on Succession Duties ... only 26 more weeks of school left ...*

On October 3, we celebrated my father's birthday. His presents consisted of a bow-tie from me, and a projector for coloured snap shots from my mother. This was all washed down with ... *the most scrumptious lobster dinner, topped off with rum cake. Don't you wish you were here? I do too ... What a feed! After dinner we saw our pictures twice through the new projector. Then I spent the rest of the night learning what my Sunday school class has already had, and what I am to teach them tomorrow. I think I am learning the most ...*

~

I was so proud of myself on the morning I closed five deals. Of course it was made even more possible by the fact that our firm had a sweet *racket* going—that of acting for vendor, purchaser, and first and second mortgages. Even I, the student, stood to make some money on those deals, as we charged for the longest description, and for the sub-search. Most of these were in the same book, which made the job easier. I made a whopping seventy-five cents!

Some of the lawyers I bumped into in the line-up were impressed with the wad of deeds and mortgages I turned in. While waiting to register my papers, I "accidentally-on-purpose" allowed a *Cunningham and Thomson* business card to fall out of my purse, with the hope that someone would pick it up and throw a little agency work David's way. I was willing to do anything it took to speed along the wedding plans!

~

Sometimes I would not hear from David for a few days, or even a week, and then I would receive two letters at the same time. That would always lift my spirits. I was dazzled with two that arrived in early October—the stationary was impressive, as were the facts and figures David had sent me regarding the business!

When David and I had talked on the phone about our Thanksgiving plans, he asked me about the car accident that I and my friends had witnessed. I told him not to worry—we girls had our stories down pat and we would not fall into the usual pitfalls that could catch ordinary witnesses ... *Besides I haven't seen a thing in the paper ... nor have the police contacted me. My guess is that the drunk was wealthy and influential enough to buy his way out of that jam ...*

Mother and Father continued to keep me occupied. We went to see *Good Sam* at the Nortown Theatre. Gary Cooper was his old, natural self. It was a film like, *Mr. Deeds Goes to Town*, and I told David he must see it ... *I laughed til the tears rolled down my cheeks; I always seem to end up crying at shows these days whether they're comedies or tragedies. That's what comes of not being with you. I love you, dearest, oxoxo Thelma oxoxo...*

~

Finally the second set of Sup results came out—only 12 of the 80 who wrote missed the mark. I hoped that was a good sign, that we had had our purge and that the rest of the year would be more reasonable for us. I actually did not even care what marks I had obtained ... *but if they were any good it will only go to show that I never should have had to re-write. Well, anyway I've learned my lesson now and I'm going to be mighty careful that it doesn't happen again next year ...*

~

Many were the weekends that I would head off to Lindsay, if David could not make it to Toronto. That way I could also keep in touch with what was going on in *our office*! I was thrilled to pieces when David shared with me the news of his plans to have a home built to suit us. I had thought it would be years before something like that would happen ... *You are some go-getter. And besides you're the sweetest fancy anyone ever had ... It just gives me goose pimples to think of you as my husband. But that's what you're going to be, that's for sure...*

~

My parents decided to purchase a new car—complete with air conditioning and seat covers to match the red paint! I wrote to David ... *I'll pick you up in it at the station on Friday night, if they'll trust me with it ... I've just been thinking about a car. Since you get on so well with your bank manager, couldn't we finance the purchase of a car through the bank, maybe on the D.V.A. arrangement so as to get better terms of payment and so that we won't have to pay interest on the amounts already paid off...*

~

Finally, my Bar admission pictures were finished. They turned out pretty nice. However, when my father refused to hang one in his office until I actually passed, I wondered at his faith in me. I went ahead anyway and handed out copies to the rest of the relatives. I figured, if everyone had a copy that would give me more incentive to make sure I passed! ... *I got your glossies too. My, our pictures make a handsome couple! I was showing them to the Kidd's last night and Mr. Kidd said that if he had the woman in my picture prosecuting him, he'd move for a change of venue, but if she was backed up by the other half he'd move out of the country! ...*

~

Simpson's was having a furniture sale; so, I thought to go over and take a look. The prices were positively *abortive*, to use one of David's favourite expressions. The cheapest Davenport was $49.50—and it was just a single. I did see a nice dining room suite that I fancied, but the matching china cabinet and buffet were $75.00 each. After seeing that price, I did not even check the price on the table and chairs! I noticed some nice leatherette chesterfields reduced from $244.00 to $116.00. I was beginning to realize how much it was going to cost David and me to set up house ... *Could you get some nail kegs for us to sit on?* ... I wrote to him—half serious—half not!

~

Dearest David:
Enclosed you will find a copy of an agreement that I had made for your precedent file. I think it should prove a very useful precedent if you ever get any real estate ... This was a case where the vendor could not find a place to live before the set closing date of a property, so decided not to close on the set date. Our firm issued a writ for the return of the $500 deposit, and $300 in damages for the loss of the bargain, solicitor's fees for the search, and for the cost of the survey. Both parties were happy with the agreement, however ... *our client may feel differently when, along with his $100, he gets our account for $88.90 and then has to pay for the survey out of the remainder. He'll make about $1.10 on the deal* ...

... *I was very happy to learn that you got some accounts out and that the ploughing match has brought all sorts of ruffians to town* ... I was sure with all the extra traffic in Lindsay that David would be able to drum up more business.

~

In mid-October I attended Elizabeth Newton's lecture on Wills. She dealt with the subject quite ably, and simply. She was very convincing in her cautioning against home-made wills, and even against *dying intestate*. There were nearly 300 women in attendance.

Bea Lyons, a surgeon, gave the closing remarks at the lecture, asking us what the difference was between a lawyer and a surgeon ... *"when a lawyer finishes his argument he asks himself if there is anything that he has left out, whereas on finishing our operation the question a surgeon asks himself is quite the contrary"*...

David's letters were sparse in October and I hoped that was because the town was in the throes of a post-holiday boom, or because he was busy with new clients that the ploughing match might have brought his way. My own office was a hubbub of excitement because of our fast approaching moving day. Some of the rugs and furniture were going to be discarded, so I thought to keep my eye on the situation, just in case there was anything I could salvage for David's and my office.

~

David did manage to make it to Toronto for Thanksgiving. It was wonderful not having to share him with too many other people; we even got some time to ourselves. It gave me a small glimpse of what our married life would be like ... *quiet evenings by the fire, planning and hoping. I'll love every one of them* ... I was worried about David returning to Lindsay, with all the extra holiday traffic, and I said a little prayer that he would arrive safely. After he left, I remembered about the Land Title forms ... *If you want to send them back through me I'll know what to do with them*...

Strange isn't it, how you can spend an entire weekend with someone and then, as soon as they leave, you remember some of the little things you forgot to mention. Well, not so little really ... *Mom got me a 1949 Calendar and the first thing I did was pick a date for our wedding—June 25th ... we can start counting the days, even if we have to change it. I want to have it set now somehow just to get my goal anchored ... my calendar says that there are just 255 days of spinsterhood left—Long engagement!*

~

I felt my lectures were getting grimmer and duller than ever, and that things in the office were just as tedious. Of course, I would try to put a plug in for David every time mention of a divorce case in Bracebridge was brought up. I even mentioned that the firm was wasting the plaintiff's money, by sending Cookie all the way there from Toronto ... *when you're half way there already. My admonitions may bear fruit yet ...*

... I had dinner tonight at the Savarin with Mom and Dad...they were going to see "The Mating of Millie" and I could not resist it ... It was really very humorous--you must see it ... I love you and miss you and want to be with you for ever and always ...

~

I was impressed when David showed me a letter from his father. It was nice to see how he was trying to support his son's endeavours to build a business in a county town. A lawyer friend of David's father had settled in the Minden area and they had exchanged business cards. I thought that was an excellent idea—the two firms could "help each other out"—so to speak.

I was continuing with my fast pace of life—attending lectures, working, and running around for supplies for David ... *I went to Dye and Durham right after lectures and brought back the Land Title's forms which they said were worth $1.20 a dozen—$3.60 for the lot ... the balance owing is $3.00 for the Will Backs, you will have a credit of sixty cents with them ...*

November 1948

I knew David was busy building the business, but there were moments, when I had not heard from him for a few days, that I would get in such a flap. I would phone him, and if there was no answer, I would start wondering what might be going on! I would pace and mumble ... *Will I have to read about it in the newspapers to find out what you are doing now?* ... I was aware that the *Jean McAllister* trial was going on—and the *Tory Hill* murder—I hoped David was getting in on some of that action!

I was keeping a scrapbook of David's accomplishments and I showed it to everyone I could ... *I do wish you could find the write-up on your speech to Rotary to fill it out properly ... I gotcha Christmas present today so you better be good between now and Christmas or I may resell it. If I can find a lawyer with the initials D.M.T. who wants to buy an initialled ... Oh! What, I nearly let it out! ...*

The move into the new McMillan, Binch offices was finally over, but the library was one unholy mess! I had no idea how the movers had managed to get the books so mixed up—reports, statutes, and texts had just been piled on the shelves. I was hoping it would not take too long to get them sorted out.

November was gearing up to be just as busy a month as October had been. I received the notice for the November 12th Convocation from Varsity, and I wrote to David saying how much I hoped he could make it. I was also excited because November meant that the Royal Winter Fair Horse Show would be in town ... *I would love to get us tickets for the Mounties' Musical Ride* ...

I began to feel that I was getting more solid work in the office too, which I hoped would equip me to be a better help to David. I was being groomed to take over the real estate department while Mrs. Lamey and Mr. Lynch were on holidays. Mrs. Lamey lectured me on how to create goodwill with clients, while steering them through the execution of their documents as speedily as possible. Besides all of that, I was suing on a contract for a farm case, and keeping records for Cookie. Being busy helped time pass more quickly.

David called me and hoped that I would come up for the weekend, but my work was piling up. There was nothing I would have liked better than to head off to Lindsay, but I had to get at my summarizing; and with Mrs. Lamey going on holidays for three weeks, I would be lucky to get any rest.

Somehow I did manage to squeeze in an interesting event ... *I went to hear Mr. Wright speak to the Osgoode Liberal Club last night. It was a very interesting philosophical talk and a stimulating discussion on Socialism* ... and there were still so many arrangements to set in place for my wedding ... *I am just counting the days ... praying that they go quickly ...*

~

In mid-November David came to Toronto and spent a lovely weekend with me. I missed him the minute he left ... *I miss you more every time we are torn apart. It was wonderful having you around this weekend* ... David was getting discouraged about how things were going in Lindsay, but I made it clear to him that I was not disheartened by his impecunious position ... *I am still convinced that we can make a go of it in Lindsay ... it's worth the extra slugging to make that dream come true* ... I assured David there was plenty of time for us to prove to my father that we could make a good living in a small town practice—just one big deal, like an Incorporation, or a housing project—that would do it! I told him to keep his chin up; I would be waiting for his phone call informing me that we had landed the deal that would answer our prayers!

... I saw Don Keith on the street today and asked him if I could bring Eleanor in to him to swear her affidavit—he readily agreed ... If nothing unforeseen happened, I would at least get the writ filed. Don used to take the odd trip to Lindsay and I asked that if he ever had room in his car, I would like to come along. He smiled and said: "No problem." I also wrote to David...*Would you please ask Mel where I am supposed to serve Laura—at the Pasadena Restaurant? That's the only location I have for her now ...*

Even though I worked late the odd night in the library, I was still hardly making a dent in my work load. I kept wishing that all this effort I was putting in was for the benefit of my future with David, instead of McMillan, Binch. But, I had to rationalize that in the long run, David and I would profit from my hard work ... *I kept at it until 12:30 last night. Woe is me. Our lights will be going out any minute now, so I'd better get in my concluding I love you and close. I love you—Thelma*

P.S. I got a nice note from Van thanking us for our cake knife and inviting us to drop in to see their home next time you are down.

~

I wrote to David that I had some info for him on the *Rodden* divorce case. I had phoned the Department of Reform Institutions to find out how I should describe her husband, the defendant. Their reply was: "Of the Industrial Farm of Bururash, in the District of Sudbury." I typed the new pages for the writs, accordingly. I also inquired about how to serve him and was advised to address our request c/o the Superintendent; one George Wright, Esq.—he would take care of the service by affidavit. I had been unable to find any precedent in the office in regards to a request for maintenance on behalf of the children in the Statement of Claim; so, I had to assume that David and Mel had done enough research of their own, and that the claim was okay as it stood.

~

The Wedding Bureau phoned to tell me that Wymilwood had a rule that only Victoria College brides could have their wedding reception there, plus they were closed by June 25th. My mother and I decided to try to arrange another location ... *we'll be sure to have some nice place. I think the next choice might be the Alexandra Palace. What do you think of that?* ...

Bookkeeping was definitely not one of my strengths and I found it difficult to solve the mysteries of adjusting and closing entries ... *Wilson gave us an exercise which he said would take us 3 hours, (in lieu of the 3 lectures we are missing). It has taken me 4 hours already and no doubt if I get Dad going on it tomorrow it will take all night again* ... If I had not had David's notebooks, I do not know how I would have managed!

~

McMillan, Binch decided to shorten the office hours and it was such a blessing only having to work until 4:00. I hoped that it would be a permanent feature for the balance of the year. I was still concerned about all the activities David was getting involved in up in Lindsay, but I also realized how valuable they were for business contacts. I wrote to David not to overdo things, for the sake of his health; and I encouraged him to get Mrs. Magahy in to do some of the typing ... *to save you too many late nights* ...

~

My excitement continued to build as I dreamed of what life would be like with David, once we were married. I mentioned to him that we could live in the flat next to the office. That way we would have no difficulty having our lunches at home every day. I had the place all furnished and decorated in my mind's eye—a dream of a love-nest with David there all the time. I even thought up a dozen of my best luncheon menus—ones that could be prepared quickly and efficiently, in order to allow time for *dessert*!

~

David was not the only one having a difficult time getting started as a lawyer. My friend, Vern Purcell, mentioned to me that his real estate business had fallen off quite badly and he was considering *hanging out a shingle* in East York. Vern mentioned that one of our other friends, Jimmy, was lecturing in Commercial Law at Varsity. It appeared that we were all trying to do whatever we could to make it in the world we had chosen!

~

November was ending well. David wrote me that business had picked up some, and that he had begun to negotiate for the flat next to the office. Work, at both school and office, was going well. I had closed three deals in one day, handling $20,000.00 in cheques and $85.00 in cash ... *Another day another $325.00 in fees for the firm, but the wrong firm!* ... I wrote to David.

I was happy that the firm decided to continue with the 4:00 closing time. I could get all my odd jobs done before supper and then settle down to studying. I was able to get through ... *great gobs of Constitutional Law this week that I thought I'd have to let cool off until this set of exams is over ... I miss you like everything* ...

December 1948

David may not always have been good at writing letters, but he called frequently. In many ways that was nicer because I got to hear his voice. I had to remind him, though, that he was to call collect ... *Dearest, you know Mom wants to pay for all our phone calls, for the cause of true love* ...

The church was gearing up for Christmas events. Outside of holiday planning, a group of us would get into some heavy discussions. One that particularly interested me was Alton Trueblood's *Alternative to Futility*, an excellent book. We ended up spending an entire day discussing that issue!

I was slowly getting through my Constitutional Law notes and was feeling much better with the state of my work, even though there was still a lot to be done ... *I am going to try to catch up by next weekend so I can take it completely off with you ... so don't panic if I don't write ... I love you, Thelma* ...

~

Once again, the joy of having had such a wonderful weekend with David quickly dissipated when he left for Lindsay. I was confused by my tumultuous emotions, finding it difficult to keep focused. When those moments hit me, I would flip through wedding magazines, and then write to David about the interesting things I had found ... *I discovered a smart design for a headboard in the January issue of "Charm" magazine—the pattern is obtainable at an address on Eglinton Avenue West ... So don't make one til we investigate this one. It has built-in night tables* ...

The pattern is also supposed to show you how to build the bed. There are even patterns for some interesting looking dining room tables...

I went to the Bank yesterday to deposit a dividend cheque in the LGMQ fund ... brought it up to $16.96! That should pay for something ... With the usual deluge of love— Thelma

~

It was sad that our good friend, Red (Mel) Walton, was so ill just before Christmas. He had been admitted to Sunnybrook Hospital with lumbar pneumonia. His wife, June, had phoned to tell me how worried she was. When I heard that he had an unprecedented majority of white corpuscles over red, I prayed it was not leukemia. June was hoping Red would be home for Christmas. I suggested to David if that was the case, we should pay him a visit.

Sidney was summoned to testify in the drunk-driving accident we girls had witnessed. When she arrived at court, the counsel for the accused requested a remand. The trial had been delayed so long because the police wanted to make sure they had all their evidence in place. I was just burned about the hardship to the poor victim, and was hoping that I would be summoned to appear too.

~

I attended the first meeting of the "Osgoode Liberal Club." Sidney had taken on the position of "Chair" and she filled it very ably indeed. Vern Singer was the president of the "Young Liberal Federation" and he gave us a bona fide pep talk ... *with a view to Federal elections in the fall of '49. To think I'll be out then and free to get interested in such things. Hopefully this will not make me an outcast in Lindsay* ... I even began to dream of David running for office one day, and pictured myself speaking on his behalf from the ... *back of hay ricks exhorting the farmers to vote for you, my husband!* ... *I slugged away at Conflicts all the rest of the day* ... *and I love you ever, ever so much—and I'll just be on tender-hooks until our re-union at Christmas...*

~

I also attended the "Women's Law" dinner at the Royal York in early December. David's friend, Judge Trelevan, was the speaker. The meal was wonderful: from the seafood cocktail, to the consommé roast duckling, to the frozen strawberry parfait. However, the speech was not brilliant. I overlooked that aspect of the evening, though, because Trelevan was such a sincere man, and he touched on a subject that interested me ... *"Words can be Beautiful", and recited poetry like Andy Clark did on his neighbourly News Broadcasts. I only got a chance to shake hands with him ... I didn't get a chance to chat with him and hear how wonderful he thinks you are. I hope I have my first jury trial before him* ... The highlight of the evening was the presentation of *Murder and Lilacs*. It was written by Janie Jansen and Margaret Campbell Beard, and had just been published in New York under the *nom de plume* of John Baird.

~

Despite the holidays coming up, David was still working hard up in Lindsay. He had planned a trip to Minden and I kept my fingers crossed—especially for the $330 fee he would earn if all went well. Mother was constantly *hawk-eyeing* the Toronto Press for news items from the Lindsay area. One article she clipped was of Premier Frost's home being robbed. I joked ... *One of your clients, I presume Mr. Thomson?* ... And I was not referring to the robbers!

I was happy to see Red back at lectures ... *He didn't look too bad. I must ask him next time I see him what edict Caesar issued for him* ... I also made a mental note to ask him what he and June were doing for New Years Eve.

I was so steeped in studying that I thought it would never end ... *I did Conflicts all this afternoon and tonight ... but I've just done barely 1/3 of my notes ... reading about Annulment Jurisdiction makes my longing for you more acute. I just can't fathom that wilful refusal to consummate business, can you? How different people can be!* ...

~

I was wondering how David could get some information on winding a company up, so I approached Mr. Corrigan, in the office. He said he had read an article by Cudney, in a recent C.B.R. (Canadian Bar Review) that had set out various ways to do it. He even suggested that once David decided which way he wanted to go, then their office could supply him with numerous precedents. He was very kind to discuss the matter with me.

... *P.W. was a different proposition this afternoon tho', he started out well by saying that he liked the memo on Law that I had prepared for his C.B.R. article, and that he appreciated my coming in to take charge of the Greek Ladies. He spoilt it all by keeping me late to fix up something he had forgotten* ...

I think we must have been born under clashing meteors or something. We just can't seem to do anything peacefully together ...

I forgot to tell you that I have been looking around for Reasons for Incorporation for you and Bailey. They aren't in Fraser or Palmer, but there is a good set in vol. 1 of the Refresher Course at page 136 that might do the trick to cinch the job for Bailey ...

I decided it was time to look into some sort of medical plan for David and myself. I found a plan that was just starting up, which seemed to be quite a bit less expensive than the Associate Medical Services. When combined with the hospital plan, after a ten month period, David and I would have almost 100% coverage on maternity. The catch was that you had to be seeing a doctor who was enrolled with them ... *It occurred to me that it would be a good idea to find out if there is a doctor in Lindsay under the Plan, and if so, is he one we would want to go to ...*

... I tried again at Mrs. Bart's and her Grandmother's to get Laura and didn't. Should I advertise in the Personal Column for her, or note the pleadings closed and get her struck off as a defendant? Please ask Mel and tell me ... I will keep after Mrs. Bart until she hears from her, but so far she hasn't. Its too bad she's holding things up like this as I could set the action down 21 days after serving her, couldn't I? ...

~

On December 10th, I got my 1949 calendar out and started to calculate the number of days I had left of school—130! Our lectures, for December ended on the 22nd, and did not resume until January 17th. I had to write my Bookkeeping exam on the 23rd, Conflicts on January 5th, and Practice on January 11th. I went over David's Bookkeeping paper, trying to make sense of it. Dad refused to help me any more—his reasoning being that I would not learn if he kept doing things for me.

I could hardly wait for Christmas, when I would be free enough to be able to share some fun and relaxed times with David. He had cajoled several times during early December, trying to get me to say what I wanted for Christmas. I wrote in one of my letters ... *I am very sorry that I can't help you much with hints, direct or otherwise, as to what you could give me for Christmas ... in keeping with your budget ... What about a nice little china cream and sugar, or crystal salt and peppers ... The new car came this afternoon and Dad came home from the office to take us for a drive! ... I got a nice note from Grace on her Xmas card giving us a very pressing invitation and telling me that Lonny has big beautiful dark eyes like his Uncle David! That child I must see ...*

~

The Christmas season was wonderful. I survived the Sunday school Christmas party with 53 children running everywhere, decimating the food like a plague of locusts. I wished I had longer with David—but such was life. January loomed around the corner—so did work and studies.

January 1949

*I had a little party tea
My guests were only three
I, myself, and me
T'was I ate all the strawberries
And drank all the tea
And it was I who ate the pie
And passed the cake to me*

The New Year started out on a high note ... *Your wonderful news of the BIG deal came today and I like to think that that puts our wedding in the bag ... Dare we talk figures? Even apart from the benefits to be derived from those deals alone, the association with Mutual Canada & Sun Life will be very valuable for future reference too. I am only sorry that you went thru such an ordeal before the Town Council. I wish I could have been there to help you, or at least smooth your furrowed brow afterwards ...*

~

I finally found a suitable place for David's and my wedding reception—the Yorktown Inn on Yonge Street North. It was a very large, colonial-style house with two-story pillars at the front and lots of grounds surrounding it. The price was right and they were available for June 25th! My mother and I decided to check them out by having dinner there. Mother was so into my wedding—that was all we talked about at our meals together.

David was always trying to give me extra confidence when I got a bit discouraged, sometimes I would think ... *why should I* worry about passing when such a wonderful barrister, solicitor, commissioner for oaths, notary public., is willing to marry me, even if don't pass? ...

While I was trying to learn all about wills, and things, business in Lindsay was really picking up. David and Mel were working hard.

There was a big upheaval at the office—it was quite shocking. I had thought that Mrs. Lamey would be promoted to a private office, but instead she was put in the "bull pen" with the students. Two former members of the Aylesworth firm joined McMillan, Binch—J. A. Head and Hamilton J. Stuart. They brought with them their clients, The Royal Bank and the Austin Motor Car Company; plus loads of files and furniture.

February 1949

Dearest:
... I do think however that we should try to get a car if our financial position warrants it even if we have to get it on time ... Failing that, I think we might get a cottage for the month of July perhaps in Haliburton and spend the last few days of June after our wedding in some luxurious place where we can just frolic and have our meals brought up to us ... and then spend the rest of our honeymoon just being ruggedly lazy ... We had a Conant speak to us in our Practice lecture today ... what a windbag of a political mouthpiece he turned out to be. Please get me out of this superficial disillusioning city quick, Dear ...

~

Valentines Day was around the corner and I had to send David a note apologizing for not being such a good Valentine. I had hunted high and low, and could not find one anywhere—possibly because I had left it to the last minute ... *But you'll get yours whenever it turns up ... probably in Evidence or something ... still have gobs of notes to copy ... heavy day at the office today ... hope you had as much business ... So long for now, Dearest—I love you and want you for my Valentines forever—Valentine or not—More Love, Thelma*

I felt even worse for my procrastination when David's beautiful Valentine remembrance arrived at my house. I wrote to him that it was the most expressive one I had ever received!

~

I finally heard from Laura, the woman I had been chasing, to serve with Court papers. She phoned me to tell me off for bothering her grandmother's landlady with my phone calls! That did it for me ... *I am going to serve her tomorrow at the drugstore where she works ... and I'll try to set it down as soon as possible (21 days from tomorrow, I see by the Rules) ...*

~

The origin of the office furniture that David and I managed to buy has an interesting story behind it. While serving as an articling student, I had ridden in the elevator with a disbarred New York lawyer known as "One-share Sweeny." He had "made a killing" buying one share in a number of companies, and then he would peruse the shareholders, and the company books. At the shareholders' meeting he would make such a ruckus over the way the company was being managed that they would buy him off! For these shenanigans, he was disbarred from the New York Bar. He endeavoured to start the same enterprise in Toronto. He even attempted to enlist me. I am sure that his offer had something to do with the fact that the head office of the Victoria Grey Trust Company was in Lindsay, where David had set up our practice. During an elevator ride Sweeny had talked about the fact that the shareholders' meetings for the Trust Company were held in Lindsay, and he suggested we might have an interesting collaboration if I would provide him with a list of the shareholders. Of course, that was something I would never dream of doing!

Sweeny was a persistent man though ... *I met our friend, "One Share", on the street today, and he was most insistent that I have dinner with him in his suite at the King Eddy. I was most insistent that we postpone the date until you were down and could join us. He didn't seem to go for that idea at all. It can't be that he balks at the price of another meal. I don't think his interest in me is as paternal as would become his years. He was more rascally than ever today, with a flower in his button hole and all. He says that he has some business to send you, but I don't know whether that is just come-on stuff for me, or not. Anyway I don't want to go see him ...* Even though Sweeny withdrew the dinner invitation, I guess he still liked me well enough that he offered to sell me and David all his office furniture when he went out of business. It was in pretty good shape—just a little beat up. So, that is the story of how we bought "One-

Share Sweeny's" used office furniture! A friend, from Branksome, had married a fellow whose family were in the coal business, so we solicited him to take the furniture to Lindsay on one of his flatbed trucks.

March 1949

I finally decided on some furniture that I had found at Eaton's and Simpson's. I tried to negotiate to buy it on credit, but was refused because I did not earn enough money. That meant that I would have to send the credit applications to David ... *I was thinking of pledging your credit as your wife but I balked at forging "name to be" as it could be so detrimental professionally if there were any repercussions ... I'm sorry, but that's the best I can do at this time ... I gave both Eaton's and Simpson's the necessary down payments...*

~

I sent David a copy of the will of an old lady who must have been on her death-bed at the time of writing it. The will was written on a scruffy-looking scrap of notepaper; I assumed the lawyer who witnessed it had been called in the middle of the night. Such was the way things were done in those days.

Both David and I were worried about Mel Walton's health—he was to be David's best man. I got an up-date from June—Mel was making progress, despite having caught a bad cold.

14 WEEKS BEFORE GRADUATION

I received some very shocking news—my friend Simsie (Marjorie Ann Sims) and her fiancé, Pete, broke off their engagement, just four weeks before the wedding. I was devastated for her. I knew—well, I hoped, that would not happen to David and me ... *Only 14 more weeks of school left ... then a lifetime of loving. And how I love you...* I wanted to reassure David—and myself!

April 1949

... Mom talked me into going to see the show, "John loves Mary!" You should see it too ... reminded me of some the stormier stages of our romance.

... I was talking to Bart in the library yesterday ... He had a problem to interpret a will and in desperation asked me where he could find anything on it ... I got a kick out of the episode thinking how hard it must have been on him to admit that a female could tell him the answer ...
Re: Rodden v Rodden
I have not yet received the Affidavit of Service of the Notice of Trial from Burwash. I guess I'd better go down to the office tomorrow to see if it's kicking around there ... I am a little concerned as the 10 days for service were up today ...
... Believe it or not my summary has just caught up with my current notes on Constitutional Law. I have come to the end of the printed notes you gave me—just three more pages of Syllabus to go. Your notes have been a big help Darling. Thanks ever so much, especially the Evidence ones, they have saved me a month of nights in the library. If I make the grade, I'll owe it to you ... I'm trying for you ...

~

My parents changed their minds about spending Easter weekend in Chicago; however, they did spend a few days there, prior to Easter. Mother was still checking out the newspapers for leads for David. She wrote him a letter from the Hilton Hotel that she and Father were staying in ... *I noticed in the Chicago paper this morning where one of my favourite hotels was sold for $600,000. Edgewater Beach, I wish I could swing this deal to your office* ... I was pleased, when David showed me the letter, to also read that my mother felt that I was a most reliable, capable girl.

Eaton's finally broke down and sent Mother their catalogue. I decided on the dining table from them, as it was less expensive—only $29.95. However, the matching chairs were $10.50 each. The cutlery was made in Canada and was 1/3 the price of the Swedish pieces I had been waiting for. I noticed that Eaton's also had an unfinished chest for only $13.95 ... *couldn't we please get 2 of them now?*

~

I was thrilled to learn that David had landed a rape case—not thrilled someone had been raped, but that the case would earn us $200. I was anxious to do what I could to help out. I wrote to David that I had talked to Sidney about it. She said, if he was pleading consent, she could lend him a memo on it that she had spent six months preparing.

David was gaining a good reputation in Lindsay. Other lawyers even started to throw work his way … *Mary knows a lawyer in Port Hope who was grousing about having to go to Lindsay for a case, so Mary suggested that he get you to take it; he said that he'd like to, remembering his early days in practice … Ann Halstead has also reminded Ross Dunn that he'd better start sending his agency work to you instead of to Stinson as he has been doing … I'll just think of June 25 and you and beam. I love you. Mush 'n stuff—T. K.*

… Dearest David:
We enjoyed the drive back last night. The colours displayed by the sunset were glorious. Best of all was the impression that the office and the town had made on Mom and Dad. I actually got Dad to admit that he was impressed. It took some badgering but he did finally admit it without reservation…

Time was flying by—work was good, but I was anxious to finish my schooling and start my married life. My letters were filled with my busy days and with how I wished the work I was doing was to benefit David and me … *Today I sent out reporting letters and accounts for the two deals I handled for Mr. Berry at $165.00 and $175.00 respectively! How I wish those fees were going to Cunningham and Thomson! One reporting letter is my masterpiece --the longest one I have ever dreamt up. I asked Carol to make a copy of it for our precedent file … Wish you were here. Miss you like all get out. Be good to yourself…*

~

Sidney finally testified at the drunk-driving trial and she was the perfect witness … *So was Miss Vincent … the boy got ten days, no option. His lawyer was practically hopeless. He must have put half an hour's preparation on the case. He had a glimmer of a defence now and then, but never carried his points through to the punch line and yet just before he was led away to jail the boy peeled off a roll of about $30.00 to him. This profession we are in can be a sweet racket for some people …*

… I shall await your arrival Saturday a.m. in the Students' Library at Osgoode. I'll be on tender-hooks anyway but I might as well be sitting with a book in front of me in case your bus is late. Will you please bring the schedule for our

honeymoon so that we can at least try to get reservations for the Saguenay trip and find out more definitely what it will cost? I'll try to make some preliminary inquiries this week...

... I am sorry but I haven't had a chance to mail my letter to you until today ... I'll phone you right after the exam and we can make our plans from there. The exam is just incidental ... I must admit I'm fed up with it anyway. Monday will be the day of reckoning ...

... The Mortimer Sneed like character who sat beside me was originally from Lindsay but the lure of the big money in the city got him and he is working as a cook at the Old Mill for $40.00 per week. He had been up to see his mother who is dying in the Lindsay hospital and he said that he got Stinson to come out there to make her will this afternoon ... I told him that two smart young lawyers were setting up in town and he asked me where you were located so you may see him yet ...

GRADUATING FROM OSGOODE

David

Thelma

ONLY WOMAN to be called was Mrs. David Thomson, who is congratulated by husband. New dean of school, Prof. C. E. Smalley-Baker was among those called to bar

~ A Twentieth Century "Portia" – Bio of Thelma Bernice Kerr-Thomson ~

UNIVERSITY OF TORONTO
FACULTY OF ARTS

B. A.

NAME Thelma Bernice Kerr
DATE AND PLACE OF BIRTH Sept 27, 1922 - Toronto
HOME ADDRESS 17 E Glenmore Drive, Toronto
PARENT OR GUARDIAN V.J.C. Kerr
FATHER'S OCCUPATION AND NATIONALITY Chartered Accountant - British
MOTHER'S NATIONALITY British
RELIGIOUS DENOMINATION United Church
SCHOOLS Allenby P.S., Forest Hill Village S.S., Branksome Hall

DATE	PLACE	CERTIF-ICATE	ENG. COMP.	ENG. LIT.	CAN. HIST	ANC. HIST.	MUSIC	MOD. HIST.	ALGEBRA	GEOM.	TRIG.	PHYSICS	CHEMISTRY	AGRIC. I.	AGRIC. II.	BOTANY	ZOOLOGY	LAT. AUTH.	LAT. COMP.	FR. AUTH.	FR. COMP.	GER. AUTH.	GER. COMP.	GREEK AUTH.	GREEK COMP.	ITAL. AUTH.	ITAL. COMP.	SPAN. AUTH.	SPAN. COMP.

ADMITTED TO N. Scene   CONDITION IF ANY

ACADEMIC YEAR	SESSION	COLLEGE	ACADEMIC YEAR	SESSION	COLLEGE
First	1941-42	Univ.	Third	1944-45	U.C.
Second	1943-44	Univ.	Fourth	1945-46	U.C.

~ 139 ~

Thelma Bernice Kerr

I Year May 1941 Bedard	I Year May 1943 Bedard	I Year May 1944 Featman	III Year May 1945	IV Year May 1946
French 14 36 80 C	French 1 36 85 A	English 2 C 54 74 C	Eng & Rom. Hist. 33/13 B	Uk & Rom. Hist. 46 37 70 B
English 1 & 11 68 65 B	Phys. Tr. P			
Phys. Tr. P				
	Law	Law	Law	Law
House Econ.	Economics 61 III	Lat 66 III 10	62 III	64 III
Biology 61 III	Philosophy 61 III	Civics 63 III	Comp. & R.tt. Law 66 IV	Comp. Cicotl. Law 65 III
Chem. II 62 IV	Legal Science 62 IV	Law of Prop. I 74 I	Admin. Law 53 B1	Can. Const. Law 68 I
House Ec. 62 II	Hist. of Eng. Law 62 II	Commercial Law 64 III	Property II 65 III	Juris. Intnat. & Priv. 58 BL
Physics 66 III	Contracts 66 III	Can. Comm. Law 60 III	Rom-Canquelaw 60 VIII	Private Law 58 BL
	Constitl Law 80 I	Philosophy 80 I	Comme. Law II 63 III	Jurisprudence 64 III
	Leg & Pol. Bibling 66 IV	Psychology 66 IV	Pub. Intrn. Law 50 BL	Philosophy 65 III
			Phil.Sci. 66 IV	Pol. Science 70 IV
			Pol. Sci. 61 IV	
			Psychol. 75 II	

William D. [signature]

OCT 12 1977

~ A Twentieth Century "Portia" – Bio of Thelma Bernice Kerr-Thomson ~

FACULTY OF LAW, UNIVERSITY OF TORONTO, Toronto 5, Canada

Name: KERR, Thelma Bernice
Home Address: 17 Elderwood Drive, Toronto 10, Ontario
Student No.: ....
LL.B. Degree: 1948

Date and Place of Birth: September 27, 1922 – Toronto, Ontario
Admission Record: B.A. (Honour Law) – University of Toronto

Key to Grading: Honours: 75% or more; Pass (Class I): 66%–74%; Pass (Class II): 61%–65%; Pass: 58% and 50 in each paper; Grades: A: 75–100; B: 65–74; C: 55–64; D: 50–54; F: Failure; S: Supplemental; Aeg.: Aegrotat.

SUBJECTS	GRADE	MARK	SUBJECTS	GRADE	MARK
Fifth Year of the combined B.A. (Honour Law) – LL.B. course (discontinued in 1949)					
1946–1947					
Family Law	B				
Local Government	C				
1947–1948					
Trade Regulation	B				
Comparative Common & Civil Law	B				

Certified Correct: D.K. Clark
Secretary
Date: October 11, 1977

After graduating from U of T with my BA in Law, followed by the three years at Osgoode Hall, combined with articling at the law firm, I was finally going to receive my papers stating *I was a lawyer*! It was an evening ceremony and I was so tired from writing exams, and articling at the law office that I just wanted to get it over with. I do not think it was a stellar occasion, not like the 1946 U of T graduation, despite its low key atmosphere due to the war ending.

I studied hard for my Bar exams, preparing a *précis* for each of the subjects in which I had to write an exam, and then going over and over each *précis*. Bar exams consisted of a great deal of memory work—remembering the surnames of litigants, or Latin phrases encompassing the meanings of landmark legal decisions.

Once the exams were completed, there was no real ceremony. You were called to the Bar and given a role of credentials, and then a Chief Justice would give a talk. It was boring, to say the least! I was exhausted and just wanted to sleep! But, I got a nice piece of parchment that said I was qualified to offer my services to the public, as a barrister/solicitor, notary public and commissioner for oaths. I received a certificate stating that I was qualified to practice before the Supreme Court of Canada.

My principle emotion when I passed the Bar was one of relief––I had finally made it—I had gotten through that gruelling, gritty period of endless hours of studying and articling. My father's health was failing, so there was no celebration afterward. I was happy that David managed to make it down for the ceremony.

There were ten girls in my first year class at Osgoode Hall; of those, only five were called to the Bar.

Graduating Class—Osgoode Hall

Thelma—front row—4th from left

Note: the ten female students grouped together in the front row

New Dean Among 60 Called to Bar at Special Convocation

One of the 60 persons called to the bar of Ontario at a special convocation in Osgoode Hall yesterday was Stewart Douglas Turner (Doug Turner (left) of the 1948 Argo football club), who left Toronto last night to practice law and play football in Calgary. He is shown (left) with his parents, Mr. and Mrs. H. E. Turner. Only woman in the group was Mrs. Thelma Kerr Thomson, Toronto (right).

SOUPSTAINS BAD, LAWYERS WARNED BY CHIEF JUSTICE

RHODES SCHOLAR B. J. MACKINNON
Vankleek Hill Resident to Practise in Ottawa

School's out today for Osgoode Hall's newest crop of law grads. Yesterday, before breaking class for the last time, the 60 budding lawyers were witness at convocation exercises as Hon. J. C. McRuer stepped down from his role of chief justice of Ontario's high court to dispense a few facts of life on court etiquette in the manner of a confiding father giving fireside advice to a wayward son.

The chief justice counselled them to be cautious of "clean linen, a clean tie, a clean shirt—a white shirt is in good taste." Soup stains may not be a sign of a poor lawyer, but certainly of a careless one.

He cautioned those who are likely to be among the star counsel of tomorrow to show the same sportsmanship, in defeat and victory, as on the gridiron or hockey ice. "Don't be overly elated when you win, or unduly depressed when you lose," he said. "Maintain your dignity at all times."

Urges Higher Standard

Chief Justice McRuer, in a brief critical mood, hurled a challenge to these legal lights of tomorrow to help raise the standards of their profession, because in Ontario "we haven't reached the same standards, in freedom of the bar, as in Britain."

Bibles clutched in their hands, the graduates stood and swore to three oaths, the loyalty oath, the solicitor's oath and the barrister's oath.

The graduating class included one woman, Mrs. David Thomson, daughter of Mr. and Mrs. Frank L. Kerr, Elderwood Drive, who went through the exercises under the proud eye of her lawyer-husband, an Osgoode Hall grad of a year ago. They are to practise in partnership in Lindsay.

Was Rhodes Scholar

Another grad was B. J. MacKinnon of Vankleek Hill, Ont., who won a Rhodes scholarship from McMaster university and returned a month ago from Oxford armed with the degrees of B.A., M.A. and B.C.L., as well as a B.A. from McMaster. He plans to practice in Ottawa.

The bar call was answered by Osgoode's new dean, Prof. C. E. Smalley-Baker, a native New Brunswicker, who comes to Osgoode from 20 years at the University of Birmingham, where he was dean.

The precious parchments, which go with the bar call, were received by Doug Turner, Calgary Stampeder football star, and Paul McNamara, a director of the Toronto Baseball club; by a retired army officer, Lieut.-Col. J. F. Swayze, Niagara Falls, and Terrence Murphy, of Elmsley Place, Toronto, at 22 the youngest member of the graduating class.

← Thelma

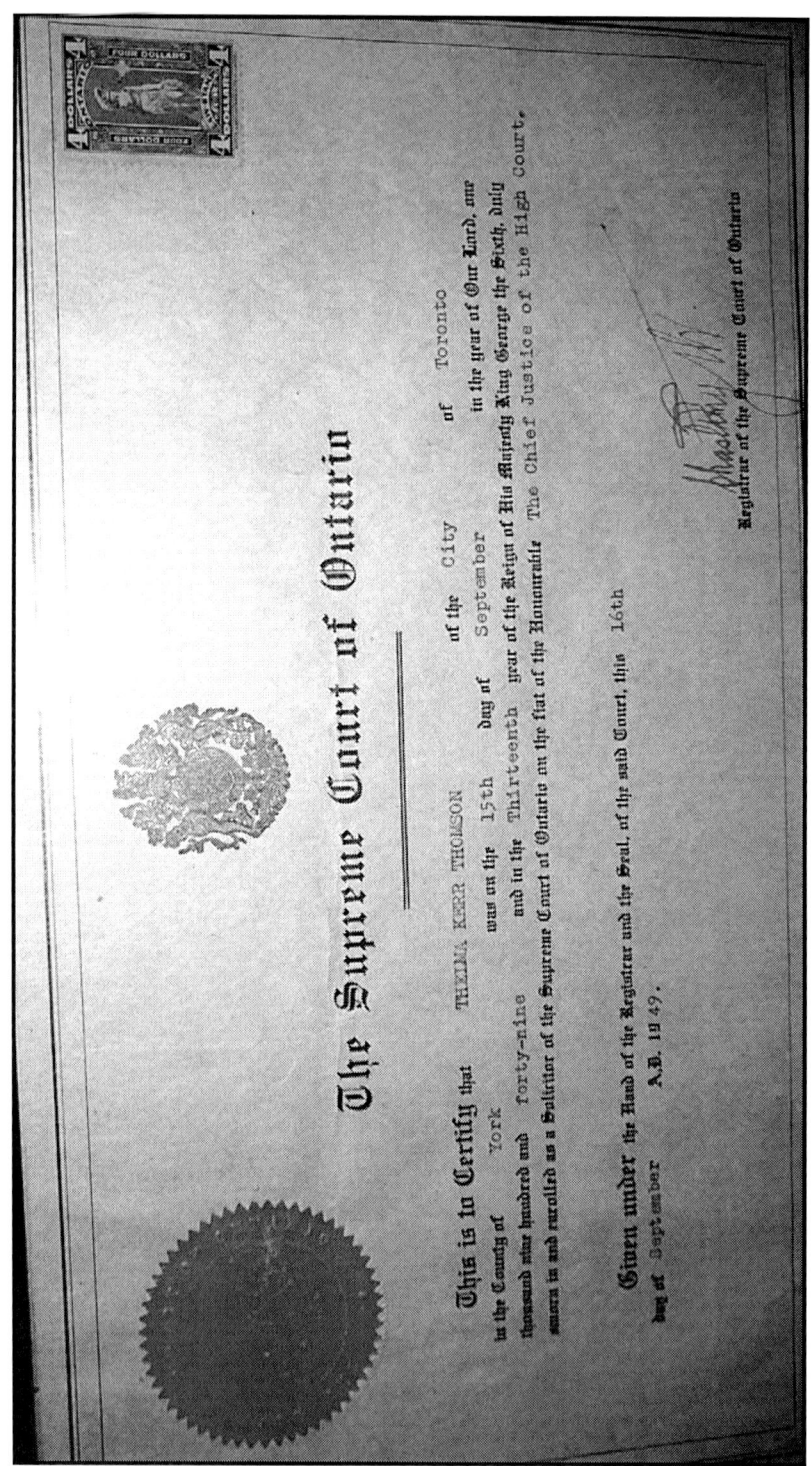

MAY 1949—26 DAYS TO GO...

Dearest:

Please excuse me for not writing sooner. You have no idea how hectic it has been around here these past few days. People have been phoning trying to sell me everything from washing machines to pianos... Yesterday being wash day I did my housewifely duty then went to keep my appointment with Dr. Brooke. He appeared only long enough to tell me that he had been trying to get me just as I left home to tell me that he had to appear in Court. However I went down again to-day and he gave me lots of good sound fatherly advice-and arranged for me to go to a gynaecologist for the works on the 10th. He seemed most concerned about either of us being frigid-and told me to send you to see him if you were-and advised me to be natural and relax and try to enjoy it! I thought he knew me better than that. My professional manner must have deceived him.

I phoned Nancy yesterday to find out when you were going to meet Aunt Margaret. But they had gone out and I have not heard anything from her. So I am wondering what happened...

Mrs. Blair phoned Mom and told her that she is going to have a shower for me. Isn't that wonderful of her? I really have not seen much of her for years-She certainly is very kind. Mom has been working like a beaver on a list of people for her to invite. I thought weddings were romantic and sentimental, but now I'm seeing a lot of mercenary rank commercialism on the inside.

Ryries phoned me today to tell me that they had received an order from the <u>Directors</u> of the John F. Ritchie Co. in Quebec, which Dad audits, to send me a place setting in my sterling silver. Isn't that wonderful of them? They were all very kind to me when I was down in Quebec.

Mother got some tables sent up on which to display our stuff-Just wait til you see it all spread out all over the den. It's unbelievable.

I got to cook the dinner tonight, for practice-and Dad, my pal, said he wouldn't have known that Mom didn't cook it ...

THE WEDDING

Grace Church on-the-Hill
TORONTO

Bride's Name: Thelma Bernice Kerr
Groom's Name: David Moffatt Thomson
Date: June 25, 1949
Ceremony At: Grace Church on the Hill
Officiated By: Father Thomson & Cannon Dowker
Attendants: Grace Duncombe –
Megan Nicholl
Melville Halton
Bert McComiskey
Wallace A. Scott
Ewart O. Bridges
Melvin J. Cunningham

Miss Thelma B. Kerr, Daughter of Mr. and Mrs. Frank Lester Kerr, whose marriage to Mr. David Moffatt Thomson, son of Rev. J. B. Thomson and Mrs. Thomson, will take place this afternoon in Grace Church on-the-Hill.

NEWLYWEDS TO FORM LINDSAY LEGAL FIRM

Grace Church on-the-Hill was the setting for the marriage of Thelma Bernice Kerr, daughter of Mr. and Mrs. Frank L. Kerr, to David Moffat Thomson, of Lindsay, son of Rev. J. B. Thomson, Toronto. The groom's father, assisted Rev. G. H. Dowker, who officiated. Given in marriage by her father, the bride wore white faille, designed on classical lines, with a floral pattern. A headdress of lilly-of-the-valley caught her veil of Belgian lace with a scalloped edge, and she carried a prayer book and pink roses. The bridal attendants, both sisters of the groom, were Mrs. Raymond N. Duncombe, of Waterford, wearing pink marquisette with blue flowers, and Mrs. Hugh T. Nichol, of Haliburton, wearing blue with pink flowers. They wore matching bonnets. Melville R. Walton was best man, while Melvin J. Cunningham, Albert J. McComiskey, Wallace Scott and Ewart Bridges were ushers. The couple will live in Lindsay where they will practise law together.

When it was confirmed that David and I were to be married, I wanted to make sure that I would still be able to bear children. I had had some terrible tumbles off of horses, one of which had landed me astride a jump fence! I was stunned. I remember sitting there for some time before the instructor's gales of laughter ceased. I feared that after such a fall, my ability to bear children may have been compromised. My mother made an appointment for me with the family doctor, who in turn referred me to a gynaecologist. The doctor did not find any cause for concern. I believe my mother also hoped that the appointment would ease some of my concerns in regards to my wedding night, having gone through the terrifying experience that she had on hers.

~

My father, unbeknownst to me, had phoned the Rector and asked about the traditional donation for a wedding. The Rector said it was not necessary because I had taught a class at the Church, but my father insisted because he appreciated the fact that I was going to have a nice wedding in the main chancel of the Church. David and I had wanted a small, quiet family wedding in the little chapel just off to the side. Father was against that idea—I was his only daughter. His friends and colleagues expected him to give me a proper send off!

~

Finally, my wedding day arrived. David and I were married on June 25th, 1949. By the time I walked down the aisle, my girlfriends from Branksome were all pregnant—some with their second child. In those times you did not have pregnant bridesmaids, so David's two sisters, Grace and Megan, were my attendants.

When I awoke on my wedding morning, it was terribly humid. I had my hair done and then dressed in my beautiful moiré silk gown. Because of its long sleeves, I was quite hot, already!

Breaking away from the tradition of having the bride and groom photos taken after the ceremony, prior to heading to the church I had the photographer come to my house for my pictures with David, while we were still fresh.

David's father assisted the Anglican Rector with the service. I am sure he would have been honoured to have performed the whole ceremony, but the Rector said it was his church and that he had to be the Official on the books. Father Thomson said a nice prayer over us after the marriage vows were exchanged.

I remember walking down the aisle and seeing all of our favourite friends in the pews. Many of my father's partners and their wives, and some of the lawyers and their wives, from the law firm where I had articled were there. The thing that I remember most, as I walked down the aisle on my father's arm, was how happy and content I felt that it was David waiting for me at the altar.

I was astounded at some of the gifts we received—silver and Royal Dalton figurines—things that were appreciated, but that would be very much out of place for the humble lifestyle that David and I would be living.

David's best man, Red Walton, was a childhood friend who had been a *Spitfire* pilot during the war. He had been stationed in Malta, but after the war he would not talk much about his experiences, other than they had been very trying for him. He was never really well after the war either, but that did not stop him from being a bit of a prankster. Maybe that comes with having red hair! We were afraid he was going to do something to decorate David's father's car, which we were going away in after the wedding, so we hid the *carat* at the churchyard down the street. Unfortunately that precaution was unnecessary because, Red, on the day of our wedding, experienced a malaria attack. He had been subject to them during the war. At our wedding he was perspiring profusely, and in such a weakened condition that he was unable to pull off any of the pranks we had feared!

We had a lovely wedding, with around 100 guests in attendance at the Church. We ended up holding our reception at the University of Toronto's Women's Club, on St. George Street. I was particularly touched by the toast to the bride that my brother-in-law, the Reverend Ross Thomson gave, as he kindly welcomed me into the family. I could not have been happier—David had such a kind, loving family, which was a delight for me, since my own home had always had a very reserved atmosphere.

Lawyers Wed In Grace Church

Mr. and Mrs. David Moffatt Thomson sign the register.
Ballard of Eaton's

Marriage and a career will combine for Thelma Bernice Kerr and David Moffatt Thomson who were married in Grace Church-on-the-Hill. Both are graduates of the University of Toronto Law School and Osgoode Hall and are planning to practise law together. The bride is the daughter of Mr. and Mrs. Frank Lester Kerr and the groom is the son of Rev. James Blackstock Thomson. The service was conducted in a setting of standards of white flowers and Rev. G. Hasted Dowker officiated, assisted by the groom's father. Miss Christina McLean was at the organ and the boys' choir sang.

The bride, given in marriage by her father, chose a gown of white faille in floral pattern styled on classical lines. Her scalloped veil of Belgian lace was caught with a coronet of lily of the valley and she carried pink roses and stephanotis in a spray on her prayer book. Attending the bride were Mrs. Raymond Duncombe, of Waterford, and Mrs. Hugh T. Nichol, of Haliburton. Their gowns were of sheer marquisette with lace with matching flower trimmed bonnets. Mrs. Duncombe was in pink with blue flowers, and Mrs. Nicholson was in blue with pink flowers. Melville R. Walton was best man and ushers were Melvin J. Cunningham, Albert J. McComiskey, Wallace A. Scott and Ewart Bridges.

A reception followed at the University Women's Club and then the couple went to Temagami for their honeymoon. They will live in Lindsay.

~ A Twentieth Century "Portia" – Bio of Thelma Bernice Kerr-Thomson ~

WEDDING BELLS...

Married In Toronto

THOMSON — KERR

A very pretty wedding took place at Grace Church-on-the-Hill, Toronto, Saturday June 25th at 3 p.m. when Thelma Bernice Kerr daughter of Mr. and Mrs. Frank Lester Kerr, Toronto was united in marriage to Mr. David Moffatt Thomson son of Rev. Jas Blackstock Thomson of Toronto. The Rev. G Hasted Dowker, rector, performed the ceremony assisted by the father of the groom.

The bride was given in marriage by her father and wore an original gown of pure white faille, traced with a delicate floral design on princess lines, with a sweetheart neckline and a circular train. Her veil of Belgium lace was caught with a coronet of lily-of-the-valley. She also wore an antique gold filagree necklace set with pearls and sapphires, the gift of the groom. The bride was attended by Mrs. Raymond N. Duncombe of Waterburg and Mrs. Hugh T. Nichol of Haliburton sisters of the groom. They were gowned in sheer marquisette with square neckline outlined in lace, lace midriff and mittens. Mrs Duncombe in pink and Mrs. Nichol in blue, each with matching flower trimmed bonnets. Mrs. Duncombe carried a bouquet of pink sweetheart roses surrounded by blue carnations and Mrs. Nichol blue carnations in the centre of a wreath of pink roses. The church was decorated with tall white standards and pew bows centered with pink roses. The choir boys provided the music Mr. Melville R. Walton of Toronto acted as best man and the ushers were Mr. Melvin J. Cunningham Mr. Ewart Bridges, Mr. Wallace Scott and Mr. Albert McComiskey.

The reception was held at the University Women's Club where the bride's mother received in powder blue crepe with matching tulle hat and a corsage of pink sweetheart roses and the groom's stepmother in mauve lace with a pink milan hat and a corsage of sweet peas and pink roses. For travelling the bride wore a pure silk jacket dress of turquoise blue, while milan hat and white accessories.

On their return Mr. and Mrs. Thomson will take up residence in Lindsay, the groom being a member of the law firm of Cunningham and Thomson.

REEDS — FALLIS

Cambridge St. Baptist Church, was the setting for the marriage of Alice Marguerite Fallis, daughter of Mr. and Mrs. Vyrtle A. Fallis Lindsay, to Lloyd George Reeds son of Mr. and Mrs. Thos H. Reeds of Reaboro.

MR. AND MRS. DAVID THOMSON

HONEYMOON

Dear David

Just received your welcome letter of the 18th and glad to know you are better set to leave the note of the 29th. The train should arrive at Temagami between 9 and 10 a.m., and the boat leaves around 10:30 ... I expect you will get up there around 1 or 2 ... Hubre wrote and said he would be on hand to take you over on his boat; he always takes care of the keys. Hubre said he'd have everything in order for you and if you want anything ask him to stop by on his way up to his Island. Don't forget to get kerosene for the lamps—he will be able to get it for you from camp. Do you suppose you could send a money order in American money? Oh well, don't worry about it now, I'll get it sometime. The weather here is terrific, wish it would rain. Well, David I wish you both the very best good health, wealth and happiness. Hope you have a wonderful holiday. Sincerely, Mary

~

We spent the first night of our honeymoon at the Guild Inn on Lake Ontario, just east of Toronto. From there we took a train up to North Bay. We had rented a cottage in Temagami, from David's stepmother's sister, for our honeymoon. The cottage was on an island and the only way to get to it was via a ferry boat. The native fellow, Hubres Brown, who ran the ferry, knew that we were just married and he decided to pull a little joke on David. David had noticed a place that was selling fishing bait, so he had run off to get some. I began to panic when Hubres started to pull away from the dock. I was thinking that I was going to be all alone on my honeymoon! Hubres was grinning as he watched my bridegroom running along the dock in order to get to the boat. What a tease, Hubre was. We all had a good laugh, afterward!

When I walked through the door of the cottage it looked like it had not been cleaned for years. A duck must have somehow gotten down the chimney and he had messed up the entire place. So, I started out my honeymoon learning how to scrub a floor—something I had never done before. Once David and I got the cottage cleaned up, it was not too bad and we stayed a full month. We had a box of canned goods with us and we fished for our meat. We ate a lot of fish!

One day I had a hankering for something other than fish. The nearest Hudson Bay Post was 18 miles away. There was a canoe at the cottage for us to use, so we paddled to Bear Island. We bought ourselves a little roast beef, some slabs of ice to keep the meat cold, and headed back to the cottage. It was a hot day and by the time we got back to our island, the ice had melted so we had to cook the roast right away—over a fire because there was no woodstove.

Not only was there no woodstove, there were no modern conveniences! Our bathroom was an outhouse behind the cottage. Every morning I would have to skirt around the neighbourhood porcupine that had taken up residence close by our bathroom facilities. Another wildlife adventure we were faced with was a moose that had somehow made it to the island from the mainland. He was a giant fellow—so big in fact that he shook our cottage when he came near. David fetched the wood axe and kept it close by us—just in case—we were really scared!

Hubres invited us to his place for supper one night. His mother was an excellent cook. He mentioned that he knew of a *secret* lake where there was excellent trout fishing and that he would take us there if we wanted. Of course, a good fishing hole was something that David and I could not turn down!

Despite the lack of amenities, David and I had a wonderful time, but all good things must come to an end. I still had to finish my articling work at McMillan, Binch. They had been kind enough to give me the month of July off for my honeymoon, but I had to return to Toronto in August. I did not actually move to Lindsay until after my call to the Bar in September 1949.

~ A Twentieth Century "Portia" – Bio of Thelma Bernice Kerr-Thomson ~

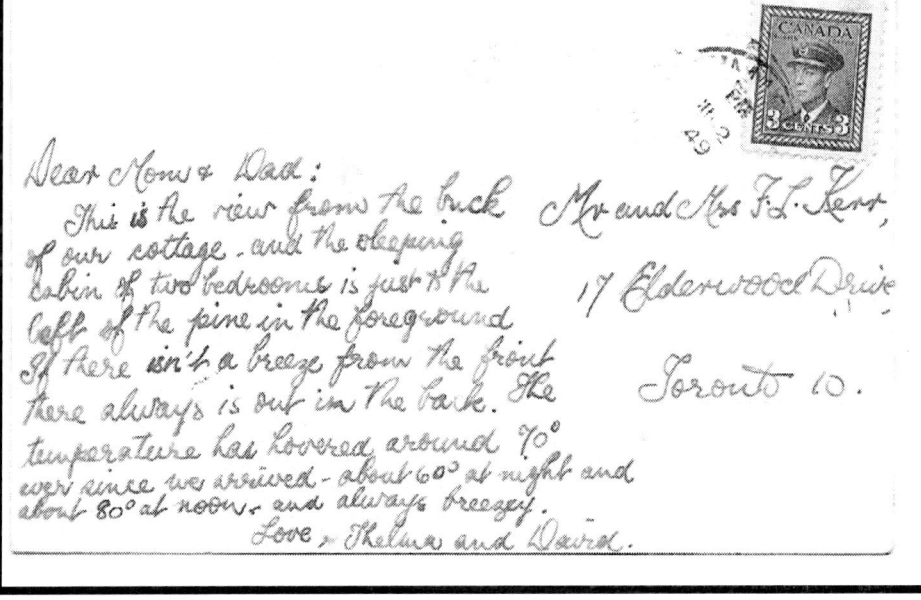

Standing by David's father's car upon the return from our honeymoon

LETTER AFTER HONEYMOON

Dearest <u>Husband</u>:

It is still a big thrill for me to call you that—and always will be. This is the first time that I have ever had to write to you as such —and I certainly hope it won't be often. I thought being married meant being together always—that's what it means to me and that's the way I want it.

Last night I took everything there was in the house for respiratory ailments, including C.B.Q's and some of the tablets the Dr gave Mom for her allergy, which contain a mild dose of penicillin. Today I have hardly a trace of a cold left. Now I don't know which remedy to give the credit for the cure so as to stock up on it for the next time. Mom got me a little box of her prescription to take back <u>home</u> with me. I also got some other things—so be ready for me…

I also have lined up to bring back: 2 tennis racquets, 2 golf bags with numerous balls and tees, and the family's camping equipment, complete with tent, sleeping bags, beds and stove—and maybe the table (if they don't want it for picnics). They would rather not sell it to us as they would like to feel free to borrow it back from us should the occasion arise.

I phoned Eleanor Rodden today and explained all to her—I tried to get Walton tonight, but OX3949 is suspended so I'll get him at Frank Kelly's tomorrow. I turned the collars on your shirts and I phoned Alphie at Osgoode. She said that Constitutional Law will be Sept the third, and Practice the 8th, so I still have plenty of time.

I phoned to see how Minxie**was tonight as Mom offered to drive me out to get her on the way down to get Dad, and they told me that in trying to fix the horn they had broken part of the steering apparatus and had to send for a part, but they expect her to be done tomorrow. Would you like me to get back Thurs a.m. so that you can take her to Fenelon Falls? If you would, please phone me and I'll come.

I got a notice that there is a gift in the U.S. Customs from California for us--I hope it's good ... See you soon (the sooner the quicker), Your ever-loving wife—Thelma

** Minxie was a little Hillmen Minx car

Kerr Coat of Arms

Thomson Coat of Arms

Kent Street
Lindsay
Ontario, Canada

LINDSAY

Dear Partners:— circa Nov/75

This is a quick impression I did a long time ago in art class of our firms second location near the theatre & old post office & clock as shown in this card. It might as well stay here as one of our mementos of our early days here.

Wishing you all the best
Thelma.

LETTERS OF CONGRATULATIONS

> **SCHOOL OF LAW**
> **UNIVERSITY OF TORONTO**
>
> Oct. 4, 1949
>
> Dear Mrs. Thomson:
>
> I was delighted indeed to receive an announcement that you are joining your husband's firm. I have heard it said that while a woman may have trouble managing one man, she has none at all in managing two or more. My best wishes for your success and for the continued success of the firm. Please give my regards to your partners.
>
> Yours sincerely,
> Bora Laskin

Translation of above letter…October 4, 1949…Dear Mrs. Thomson: I was delighted indeed to receive an announcement that you are joining your husband's firm. I have heard it said that while a woman may have trouble managing one man, she has none at all with managing two or more. My best wishes for your success and for the continued success of the firm. Please give my regards to your partners.
Yours sincerely, Bora Laskin

```
SUITE 209                                                    BRANCH
156 YONGE STREET                                   545A ST. CLAIR AVE. WEST
WA. 9121                                                    ME. 8824
```

KASSIRER AND CADSBY
BARRISTERS AND SOLICITORS
TORONTO

BRYANT M. KASSIRER
MILTON A. CADSBY

WRITTEN AT 156 Yonge Street.

Cunningham, Thomson & Thomson,
Barristers, Etc.,
14 Williams St. N.,
Lindsay, Ontario.

Dear Mel, David & Thelma:

      Congratulations and best wishes and let's hope a woman's touch is the lucky touch.

                    Sincerely,

                    Bryant.

BMK/MVG

```
HOLMESTED, SUTTON, HILL & KEMP          TELEPHONE ELGIN 9317
    BARRISTERS & SOLICITORS              CABLE ADDRESS "HOSTED"

A.W. HOLMESTED, K.C.   L.V SUTTON, K.C.   1809 ROYAL BANK BUILDING
G. E. HILL             C. H. KEMP            KING & YONGE STREETS
D. L. CAMPBELL         A.R. MacDONALD
```

TORONTO-1

September 28th, 1949.

Mrs. Thelma Kerr Thomson,
Messrs. Cunningham & Thomson,
Barristers,
14 William Street North,
LINDSAY, Ontario.

Dear Mrs. Thomson:

      I was very happy to receive the announcement of your new firm.

      May I wish you and your firm every success.

      With kind regards.

      Yours sincerely,

[signature: Leonard V. Sutton]

LVS:PT

PAUL A. COPELAND, Q.C.
BARRISTER, SOLICITOR & NOTARY PUBLIC
ORILLIA, ONTARIO

REC'D APR 5 1954

April 2, 1954.

Miss Thelma K. Thomson,
Barrister, etc.,
Suites 17-25,
Greg Mac Building,
Lindsay, Ontario.

Dear Miss Thomson:

    I am enclosing your speech on Wills and I want to thank you very much for the use of the speech.

    Once again I wish to thank you for your co-operation in this matter.

Yours very truly,

Paul A Copeland

PAC:JES
ENCL.

JUDGE'S CHAMBERS
LINDSAY, ONTARIO

Sept. 30th, 1949.

Messrs Cunningham, Thomson & Thomson,
Barristers etc.,
William St. N.,
LINDSAY.

Dear Sirs:-

    Your card announcing the acquisition of a new member of the firm has been received, and it looks to me now that you are going to have too many Thomsons in the business unless Cunningham gets busy and takes unto himself a Junior partner like the other member of the firm has been so successful in doing.

    May I on my own behalf, and on behalf of my family, and also for the members of the Bar of Victoria County, convey to you my congratulations, and wish you all prosperity and good luck with the new firm in the practice of law in this County.

Yours very truly,

J. A. McGibbon

JAMc/OC.   (J.A. McGibbon)

JUDGE.

McMILLAN, BINCH, WILKINSON, STUART, BERRY & WRIGHT

GORDON MCMILLAN, K.C.
HAMILTON STUART, K.C.
WILFRED R. BINCH, K.C.
FRANK WILKINSON, K.C.
NIXON T. BERRY, K.C.
PETER WRIGHT
EWART R. LYNCH
ROSS J. DUNN
J. H. CORRIGAN
W. G. C. HOWLAND
WM. T. COOK
JOHN A. HEAD

COUNSEL
D. L. MCCARTHY, K.C.

BARRISTERS & SOLICITORS
50 KING STREET WEST
TORONTO 1

CABLE ADDRESS "WARDRITE"
TELEPHONE ELGIN 5121

September 28, 1949

Messrs. Cunningham, Thomson & Thomson,
Barristers, etc.,
14 William Street North,
Lindsay, Ontario.

Dear Madam & Sirs:

    The announcement that you have added another illustrious member to your already famous firm has been received with great joy here and on behalf of the female members of our establishment (we now number fifteen with two spares helping out) we wish to extend congratulations to all parties. To the gentlemen we say (no one dissenting) you have done well by yourselves; to the female member, Mrs. Thelma Kerr Thomson, we say be your own sweet self and don't let those male members push you around.

    Several copies were purchased of the Globe & Mail with a first showing of a very lovely "picture" of the newest member of the firm on the occasion of her call to the bar. This picture is being treasured by many of the girls, including the writer of this epistle.

    All nonsense aside, our heartiest good wishes for your success and we will follow your trials and tribulations, all mere incidents in a law office, with the greatest interest.

    Remember there is always the open door here and you will be welcomed whenever you care to honour us with a visit.

Hastily but sincerely yours,

Isabel Clement

THE BEGINNINGS

> **Thomson & Thomson**
> Barristers, Solicitors, Notaries
>
> David M. Thomson, Q.C., B.A., LL.B.
> Thelma K. Thomson, B.A., LL.B.
>
> Telephone
> Area Code 416
> 324-3577
>
> 145 Kent St. West
> Lindsay, Ont.

David and I began our law practice, together, in August of 1949, a month after our wedding (even though I did not move to Lindsay permanently until September, as noted previously). I was so pleased with all the best wishes for David and me. However, my mother would most likely have had a stroke had she seen what a mess I was moving into. David and I had chosen to live in two of the rooms in the apartment; we converted the rest into our office.

It was a hot summer, permeated with the aroma of "Lynn's" cooking. He was a former Navy cook and he made the best chilli in town. Unfortunately, we could not afford it and had to be satisfied with savouring the smell wafting through the floorboards. I guess he did not feel sorry for us because he never once considered sending us some—maybe he never had any leftovers. Actually, we could not even afford to go for a coffee to his place! I remember having to work over the same old tea bags, day after day.

Those early beginnings were difficult and I managed to do a lot of creative cooking. I even learned to cook organ meats, something I had never done before. David and I also used to get payment for our services in some very strange ways. One lady, who owed us money, used to sell eggs—we ate a lot of eggs, and old hens past their prime!

We did not have a refrigerator when we were first married. In the cooler weather, we would just put our food outside the window. David had purchased a ticket from the Kiwanians, who had a boat with an outboard motor up for a draw. Upon our return from our honeymoon, we found out that David had won. We decided that we needed a refrigerator more than a boat, so David sold the boat. It was tough to get appliances right after the war because so many of the plants had been making war-related products. My mother's cousin was married to a director of GE (General Electric), so we had gotten our stove through GE—I think the local GE dealer was mad we got our stove before he got his. He had a waiting list of customers. We had to wait for our fridge, though, because he did not have any in stock.

    I found that the crates that oranges were shipped in made very useful furniture in those early years. Our bedside tables were a pair of orange crates that I camouflaged with some remnant material. When we moved to our first apartment they were put in the guest room. The rest of our furniture was not extravagant either, as I had obtained most of it from the scratch and dent department at Eaton's Annex store, which was behind the old Toronto City Hall. I remember complaining to David, in one of my letters, that I had to pay $49.50 for a studio couch. That couch turned out to be a good investment, though—over the years many people slept on it! Mary Eugenia Charles visited us when we were in our first apartment—what an honour, the woman who became the Prime Minister of Dominica sleeping on our $49.50 studio couch!

    Lindsay was very much dominated by the Conservative party––it was still the "old boy's club." Lesley M. Frost, who was Ontario's Premier for 25 years, was from Lindsay, so it was *Frost* country. Frost had supporters that were very loyal to him—David and I tried to avoid any political acknowledgement, but that was not always easy in a small town—they called you out.

    Then there was the time we had a Liberal political meeting, which actually drew a crowd in "conservative Frost country." George James McIlraith (July 29, 1908 - August 19, 1992) who, at the time, was the Parliamentary Assistant to the Minister of Defence, (1951 - 1953) came to speak at this meeting. He had a hotel room reserved in the *Crummy Corner* commercial hotel on the main drag. We had invited the executive of the local Liberal party association to our apartment for some libation, and to meet George. He enjoyed meeting with that group so much that he did not want to go back to his hotel room. He ended up sleeping on my $49.50 couch, in the guestroom with the orange crate bedside tables! That was a great joke to our friend, the editor of the local weekly newspaper!

~

    As I mentioned earlier, David had set up our practice with a partner, Mel Cunningham. As far as I was concerned, Mel was a scholar and a gentleman, but unbeknownst to us he had Tourette's syndrome. In those days, not even the medical profession knew much about that neurological condition. Mel had articled with me, and had also been in David's class of 1948. His behaviour started to become very erratic and difficult to deal with, which we eventually came to realize could have been an aspect of Tourette's.

Mel had been in the Navy and had gone through some traumatic events. He had also decided to *come out of the closet* and announced that he was a homosexual. This proclamation did not go over too well in Lindsay in the early 1950's—small-town Ontario was not ready for a homosexual lawyer. Most people in those days thought it was evil—always a matter of choice, but David and I thought homosexuality was something that could be overcome with the right counselling. Mel was a Roman Catholic, so we suggested he attend a church retreat. David went to see the Monsignor of the Roman Catholic Church in the area and asked if he could help our partner sort out his life-style decision. His reply to David—"We got too many of those already in the church; he better find somewhere else to sort himself out." Eventually, Mel left our firm—it really was a sad time for David and me because we cared deeply for our friend. He passed away at 40, from a cerebral haemorrhage.

One thing I will attest to, though—Mel always treated me as an equal in the office. David did as well. I give my husband credit for his ability to do that in times where it was not so common a practice. His sisters told me that their mother had been the brains of the family; their father was a dear, kindly preacher, easy to love, but not the greatest leader within the family unit. I think I owe David's mother the credit for the respect my husband had for a woman with a good mind. He had been, and continued to be, encouraging and supportive of my efforts.

~

In the beginning we could not afford a secretary; we did our typing after office hours, on an old second-hand manual typewriter. Eventually, we hired a typist who owed us for handling the bankruptcy of the beverage bottling company she and her husband had owned.

~

Even though I was a lawyer, I received a very mixed reception from the women's groups to which I spoke—women were just too used to hearing "words of wisdom" from males. However, this is where I should pay tribute to a British woman doctor, Agnes Jamieson, who had pioneered in Coboconk, to the north of Lindsay.

She was the first professional woman to practice medicine in that area, and had done such a stellar service that I think she was really responsible for helping to pave the way for the community's acceptance of me. I heard stories of her delivering babies under extraordinary circumstances, including on an Indian reserve, where there was nothing but newspapers in which to wrap a newborn baby. She coped magnificently under very difficult circumstances. There is a memorial to her in an art gallery in Haliburton.

It was not easy building a clientele, but I did everything I possibly could to assist David. I was not actually a fan of women's groups, but I joined every one that I could, so that I could get known. I made myself available to speak on wills, our legal system, or government departments—anything a group wanted. I began by speaking to women's institutes, homemakers groups, farm wives, and service clubs—anyone who needed a fill-in, even if for only half an hour. My usual payment or honorarium for these presentations was a nice china teacup. I talked about the desirability of a woman making a will because at that time women did not think they needed one. They assumed their husbands would look after them in their wills, but that was not the reality. Many women were left destitute when their husband died *intestate* (without a will)—it was terrible!

I got myself on the Speakers Committee for the Professional Women's Club, when jury service for women was introduced in the 1950's. When the bill was first brought forward there were numerous *outs* that women could take—they were allowed abundant excuses. Many women were shy and diffident about participating in public life. I took it upon myself to encourage them to do their public duty by participating in our justice system. I was an advocate for women at a time when countless numbers of them did not assert themselves.

One area that I was very passionate about was promoting women to protect their interests through a will. As previously mentioned, I spoke to several of the farm women's groups, because so many old farmers left the farm to the eldest son that had stayed home to help run the farm. The farmer's wife was thrown back on the *Intestate Law,* which at that time only provided her with a one-third dower interest in the farm. If she did not get along with the daughter-in-law, that one-third interest amounted to a miserable existence of occupying a single room in the farmhouse.

Eventually, many of these women started listening to me; some even consulted with me to draw up their wills. I wrote numerous handwritten wills at deathbeds, because many old farmers would wait until they were sure they were dying before they would spring the money for a will. Back then, we usually charged $25 for a house call, even if it was way out in the country. At that time, taxation was a big issue, too, because there was both the *Dominion Estates Tax,* and the *Ontario Succession Duties.* Now it is all on the "Death of a Taxpayer" under the *Income Tax Act.*

I have included an excerpt from a Readers Digest article, plus a speech I made on wills to the Service Clubs and Woman's Groups…

~
Don't Postpone Making Your Will –
<u>*Readers Digest September 1952*</u>

SPEAKS ON WILLS

Mrs. D. Thomson, Lindsay's only lady lawyer was the guest speaker at the Rotary Luncheon on Monday where she gave an interesting and informative address on Wills, stressing the importance of competent legal advice in preparing these important documents

Mrs. Thomson was introduced by Rotarian Mel Cunningham and the vote of thanks extended by Rotarian Frank Creighton.

The Privilege of making a will is in danger of being lost in two ways; firstly— practically because income taxes and high prices even now leave us little chance of saving anything for our wills to operate upon, and succession duties pounce upon a large percentage of what does escape. Any increase in social services and the taxes to provide them would be likely to take the balance. Secondly— theoretically, if the theory that private property is entirely wrong should prevail and private ownership is forbidden to us during our lifetime, the right to will is gone. And what do we get in exchange? Security from the cradle to cremation. Not the cemetery because the family plot will disappear as the family unit gives place to support and direction by the State and as individuality goes, there will be no separate graves with distinguishing headstones. It will be cremation … Probably some good use will be found for our ashes—to make soap or better still a fertilizer …

Excerpts from my speech on Wills and Dominion Estate Tax

It is indeed a great pleasure for me to be with you tonight ... to meet those of my neighbours whom I have not yet had the occasion to meet. I especially appreciate the kind invitation extended to me by your Mrs. Gillis, inviting me to speak to you on Wills and Estates, Ontario Succession Duties, with some particular reference to the new Dominion Estates Tax Amending Act.

I would like to speak to you briefly about wills in general. I find there is a great deal of misinformation ... I feel that in discussing the terms of a person's will with them, you get great insight into all the things that they have found most worthwhile in their lives, and which they want most to be remembered for after they have departed this life ... The order of importance of things to them is very often shaped by the variety of experiences and relationships which they have had in their lives ... you may see a wealthy father still trying to benefit and protect his children by setting up trusts for them ... placing terms and conditions upon their inheritance ... It is also quite common especially in the earlier days (Family Compact) in this Province, to see marriage settlements made so that daughters might be protected from having spendthrift sons-in-laws encroach on the inheritance their fathers left them.

We frequently find a sense of humour in wills, such as the merchant who provided in his will as follows—"Fix it so that my over-draft at the bank goes to my wife, she can explain it, my equity in my car goes to my son, he will then have to work to keep up the payments. Give my good will to the supply houses, they took some awful chances on me and are entitled to something. My equipment you can give to the Junkman, he has had his eye on it for some time and—I want six of my creditors for pall bearers, they have carried me so long that they might as well finish the job"

... another will which is recorded as having been probated, provided that the human remains of the Testator "be composted for fertilizer to contribute to the growth of an elm to be planted in some rural thoroughfare so that the weary wayfarer may rest and innocent children may play beneath its umbrageous branches made luxuriant by my remains"

Even the practical joker may have the last laugh through the medium of his will, as in the story of the wealthy old eccentric whose relatives had gathered from far and near to hear the reading of the will, each with high hopes ... Their hopes were soon dashed, the will was short—"*being of sound mind I spent every last cent on high living—there is nothing left for my relatives to squabble over after I am gone.*"

Seriously though, it is the concern of every normal person who has loved ones, and who has acquired something of this worlds' goods in his lifetime, to try to leave them to the best advantage of those whom he wishes most to benefit, with a minimum of tax and handling costs ... let me caution you against buying a Will form to make your own will. The wording of wills has been the subject of judicial interpretation for hundreds of years, so they have acquired very special meanings—I caution you to consult someone who is trained in the use of these words to draw your will for you. You might save a small fee, but leave your estate open to a very expensive application to the Court for the interpretation of words which you may unwittingly have used ... it is really worthwhile to get expert advice for your estate's planning ...

... also, to do it while you are well and in possession of all your faculties ... give the terms of your wills the consideration they deserve. <u>Death-bed Wills</u> are never the most satisfactory solution to estates planning, but they are better than no will at all. If you do not have a will, your property is disposed of in accordance with the terms of the <u>Devolution of Estates Act</u>, which treats all the nearest blood relatives as having an equal right to inherit your estate. Not all people would treat their relatives with the same equal consideration as that embodied in the Devolution of Estates Act ... Under its terms the widow or widower has a claim to the first twenty thousand dollars, with the residue over and above that amount being shared with the children of the deceased ... if the children are under the age of twenty-one, the Ontario Provincial Guardian's Department will step in to take charge of the children's share ... Another additional expense encountered when there is no will is that the nearest next of kin, who has first right, must post a bond with the Court to guarantee their due administration for the estate ... a bond from a Commercial Surety Company costs the estate a fee of $4.00 per thousand on the first ten thousand dollars worth of the estate, with a reducing amount on a sliding scale above that. The bond has to be renewed annually with the Court, until the estate has been fully administered, or until children's amount is settled ...

The formalities for a properly executed Will in the province of Ontario are, that it should be accurately dated, proof of last and effective will; and be signed by the Testator in the presence of two witnesses ... The witnessing is the first guarantee that our law sets up against influence or coercion, a safeguard that the Testator has testamentary capacity. It is considered that if the two witnesses see each other, and the testator signs the will, this is prima facie evidence that the testator has not been coerced ... The law then presumes soundness of mind and lack of undue influence. The witnesses must be persons who do not benefit by the will ...

Some questions most frequently asked—can my will be broken, or do I leave my no-good son $1.00? ... Briefly a will can only be set aside by a dependant of the testator, who at the time of his or her death was deprived of any benefit and advantage up to the amount that he or she could claim if the testator had died intestate ...

A person who has no blood relatives, or next of kin, has even more reason for making a will, even if only to benefit his favourite charity, because in the absence of a will, or blood relative, the estate escheats to the Crown ... I caution you—it is just as necessary for a wife to make a will as it is for her husband ... in the case of a common disaster which took both husband and wife and it is decided that she was the younger of the two and that by law she would have been presumed to have survived longer ... If she has not made a will, it will then go according to the laws of intestate succession ... this frequently results in the wife's relatives acquiring the property if there are no children of the marriage ... it is our practice, when we draw wills, to provide for such common disaster, by including in a will what we call the survivorship clause ... that the wife inherits from the husband and vice versa on the condition that she survives him by a certain number of days, usually thirty or sixty days ... This provision saves the expenses of a double probate...minimizing legal expenses ... Lawyers don't draw wills to line their own pockets ...

Over the years we have devised many ways of avoiding attracting succession duties and estate taxes, where an estate is sufficiently large to make it dutiable. There has been a great deal of discussion about the new Dominion Estate Tax Law lately ... However, the new Estate Tax Amending Act makes obsolete some of our favourite loopholes for minimizing the estate tax levied by the Dominion Government ... now we will have to think up new ones ...

The new Amending Act also makes obsolete some of the devices which we have been using in the past, by way of lifetime gifts in order to reduce the value of a testator's estate taxable by Dominion Government ... The new Act contains the provision to make prior to death gifts cumulative, so that any gifts made by the deceased during his lifetime, after October 22nd, 1968 ... are included in the taxable value of the estate…also contains some relief by way of deferred instalment payments of the estate tax to the maximum of six equal annual instalments including the prescribed interest …

The final message I want to leave with you is not to be afraid to trust your lawyer with the facts and figures relative to your estate. A lawyer cannot be forced to disclose them to the Income Tax department because communications between solicitor and client are absolutely privileged in law—no Court can compel a solicitor to disclose any information revealed to him in confidence by his client …

I hope you are not disappointed that I have not told you how to go home and draw up your own wills … But, I hope I have convinced you to go to your lawyer and make a full disclosure of your affairs, including the extent of your assets, how they are held, and what encumbrances there are against them; the particulars of your Insurance policies, and any family difficulties you may have … Let your lawyer help you arrange your affairs so as to attract the minimum amount of taxation. It is an offence to avoid taxation, once the status of your affairs has attracted it. But it is no offence to avoid attracting taxation in the first instance by rearranging your affairs … the saving of taxation can be offset by the fee that you are charged for professional advice …

No doubt it was a cynical, disgruntled man who said it was a women's world … they ask a man how is his mother; when he marries, people exclaim what a lovely bride; when he dies they inquire how much did he leave her … I would add to this—how he did leave it, how thoughtfully and carefully did he provide for those who are most deserving of his care.

… in the end, our will is the last act of our stewardship, our last opportunity to deal wisely with the talents with which we were entrusted … this is more important than how much is left!

MEDIA SUPPORT—NOT!

Media advertising, as I pointed out earlier in my memoir, was geared to women being *happy little homemakers*. Their happiness was based on the shiny new modern appliances that were being manufactured in the post-war times. Ads showing women in heels and fancy dresses, pushing a vacuum cleaner, were pictured in magazines, and on the new media of television. One program started out with: "Hello out there in vacuum land!" I used to think that the vacuum was between their ears!

Ironically, some people thought that because I was a woman they could get me to do their work for a cheaper rate—I refused to cheapen myself—many of those potential clients turned on their heel and left.

FIRST FEW YEARS

The law practice was our *baby* for the first six years of our marriage. The county law library was in terrible shape. Most of the senior members of the Bar in Lindsay were World War I veterans that had been fast-tracked through an 18-month law school course that the profession had set for them. We found such individuals weak in the matters of law, plus they had not bothered to maintain the county law library. With our respect for legal research, David and I were determined to have a good law library, making that our first mission.

We were able to buy some of the annual series through a second-hand law book salesman, and from estates of lawyers who had died. We had a nice bookcase built on the cold north wall, and we filled it with these books. Eventually, we had the most up-to-date, state-of-the-art law library in town. Many of our contemporaries would borrow our books when researching their cases.

Unfortunately, since I was a woman, I was expendable as to time because my clientele was very, very slow in developing. The locals assumed I was just helping out in my husband's office; I had a tough time convincing them that I was equally qualified to practice law. Occasionally, David would try to pass off some of the more time-consuming clients to me, telling them that I was the "real brains of the firm." I remember some of them looking around, totally disinterested, as I would be explaining the issues to them. David's office was right next to mine. Frequently, I heard him yell out: "Just tell them that I will take care of their problems!" That seemed to be what the clients wanted to hear!

To build my clientele, I had to take all kinds of cases in Police Court and Small Claims Court, in order to get my name in the newspaper so that people would realize that I was fully qualified. Thankfully, the editor of the weekly newspaper entrusted some of his work to me; he became one of my first clients. He trusted me with collections, and of course I had plenty of time to send threatening letters to non-payers. I actually got better results than the collection agency he had previously used! He would publish very kind comments about the cases I had, with headlines like, "Lady Lawyer Wins Again!"

As the first and only female lawyer in general practice in Victoria, Peterborough County, and Haliburton, I enjoyed the consternation I could create amongst the policemen whom I appeared with in the courtrooms. They had been taught to call the defence lawyers *Sir,* and they had no idea what they should call me. The Captain of the O.P.P. (Ontario Provincial Police) decided to call me *Madam,* to which I replied that I was not that kind of a *Madam* (a term used for brothel operators). The O.P.P. Captain was David's friend. David had advised him on the training of new officers for court appearances. It was fun for me to *josh* them off base when they made their spiel, and it always seemed to help my case!

Haliburton did not have their own court services; they used the higher courts in Lindsay for any such services that might be needed. There was a Small Claims Court held in Haliburton, in a hall with a pot-belly stove, like the one in Fenelon Falls, where I had also appeared. If the bailiff did not arrive on time to get the pot-belly stove stoked up, to warm the room before court started, it would be so cold that we would have to plead our cases in our overshoes, mitts and winter coats!

One day I had a case against a lawyer from Toronto; it was a precedent he needed to set, and he had lowered himself to appear in our little, outlying Small Claims Court. When we walked into the court room, it was freezing! The judge dangled his hearing aid over the bench, and then said, "Speak up, my dear, speak up!" It was all most undignified! He batted the hearing aid a few times, and then said, "I want to see you in my chambers!" His chamber was a back room off of the courtroom. Protocol demanded that he should have invited the other lawyer in as well, in case he had anything confidential to say. I said to the other lawyer: "I'll tell you what's on his mind." When I went into the back room, the judge said: "I left my hearing aid in my car all night and it's so frozen that it doesn't work. We'll have to adjourn this case." The Toronto lawyer was absolutely outraged, having driven all the way up from Toronto for this case, then to have it end that way!

~ A Twentieth Century "Portia" – Bio of Thelma Bernice Kerr-Thomson ~

An Ad, for the Crown and Anchor Game at the local fair, that David put in the Local Lindsay Post to help build our law following.

A BRUSH WITH THE *LAWLESS?*

David and I had been married for three years when the infamous *Boyd Gang* made a prison break. They were gentleman bank robbers who left a chivalrous impression on the bank clerks they robbed. (I had the privilege to meet the female lawyer who defended the Boyd Gang.)

David and I were remodelling our former living space, to expand our office, so we rented a cottage on Sturgeon Lake. David was away much of the time, doing trial work in various criminal courts in the other counties and towns. He was gaining quite a reputation and had picked up a substantial amount of criminal work that other lawyers in Lindsay would refer to him.

The police figured the Boyd gang might be heading to Lindsay because Edwin Boyd's mother had passed away—she lived in the Lindsay area. Our cottage was about ten miles out of town and I was there, alone, a lot of the time. There was an old hardwood tree that had branches that scraped on the roof at night, and every time I heard them scrape I figured somebody was trying to break into the cottage. My imagination ran rampant—I would begin thinking that maybe it was somebody with a grudge against the prosecutor, or worse yet, the Boyd gang was looking for an empty cottage to hide out in. One morning, on my way to work, I was stopped at a road block; an OPP officer got out of a Silverwood's Dairy truck. He had been watching the road for the Boyd's! Eventually, they were caught in the Toronto area.

BIRTH OF OUR FIRST SON

Six years after David and I began our practice we were expecting our first son, Cameron. We also decided that it was time to have a real home, having gone from the apartment above the stores, to another apartment. David obtained a veterans' loan and we built a three bedroom home on a lot on the most northerly boundary of town, just south of Pottinger Street. There were open fields all around. We gave up our apartment and rented a cottage on the southern tip of Sturgeon Lake, while the house was being built. We lived there until our house was ready in November. That cottage was really cold in October and November. David and I used to wait until we got to the office so that we could wash up in the warm water in our office washroom, before opening up for business.

David and I had not had to hire anyone to replace our first partner, Mel, in the office up until this point. However, now, with me expecting a baby, and with the sudden impact of David's ill health, we were forced to look at hiring someone to help out while my husband was recuperating. He had been diagnosed with pericarditis, an inflammation of the fibrous sac surrounding the heart. Later, when a nuclear diagnosis was performed at London University Hospital, we learned that he had actually had a cardiac infarction—commonly known as a heart attack. We did not have a cardiologist in town, at the time, so David was looked after by his fishing buddy, who was an internist. He decreed that my husband should have three weeks of total rest, followed by a period of half days at work. David did not abide by all these restrictions and we did not publicize the fact he was recovering from a cardiac incident either—that would have been bad for business.

I tried to carry on, but I definitely needed help. I was fortunate to be able to hire David Logan, the son of a highly respected surgeon. I was put in touch with the young man by a friend of his family who said to me: "You better grab this boy to help you out in your law practice; he's going to be good." I hoped that the respect within the community that that family held would hopefully rub off on our practice. I had heard that David Logan was in his last year of the Bar admission course, so I contacted him and asked if he would join us upon his graduation. I actually hired him before he was called to the Bar because I needed someone at the office to *hold the fort*—keep us in business and make it look as though we were still busy. David Logan became a vital part of the firm.

In the summertime we hired an articling law student to help our new recruit, and we managed to maintain the appearance of an active law office. We were building a loyal staff too, having hired some superb country girls that were not "clock watchers." We had asked the head of the high school's Business department to refer any of his top students to us, to be trained as legal stenographers. I did most of their training, as I was still not in as much demand as my male colleagues. The stigma of being a female lawyer still hung over my head. When the girls got good, my male partners took them on.

We were very fortunate in the choice of our first junior partner. David Logan turned out to be tremendously loyal to us—professionally and personally. I was aware that another lawyer tried to tempt him to his practice—David categorically refused the offer, stating that we had been a big help to him in his start as a lawyer. Knowing that my husband was ordered to only work part-time for about three months, I offered to split any income earned, during that time frame, with David Logan. I also mentioned to him that if he needed to pursue employment with another law firm, with better prospects than we were able to offer at the time, then that was okay—I would understand.

David Logan was married, and had two children. We afforded his family accommodations in the four-plex we had bought from a client who had gone bankrupt. We gave David the apartment for a nominal "token rent," in exchange for his looking after the building management and janitorial services. I discovered that people who have been committed to preparing for the Bar do not always acquire much in the way of carpentry skills, but we all managed. The main thing was that we were able to keep up the appearances of having a busy law practice until my husband was able to return—which he did much sooner than he should have.

~

Many of the older women in Lindsay were appalled that I was still working so close to my due date. I appeared in the Court of Appeal three weeks before Cam was born. I did not have my own gown because they cost $150, so I borrowed Premier Les Frost's gown to cover my rotund belly. When the judge called me, "Miss," I turned and showed him my side view, and informed him that I was not a "Miss"—I was "Mrs. Thomson!" The case was over a used car sale. The car was not worth much, but apparently the Used Car Dealers Association was interested in the results of this case. The car had been found smashed before it was fully paid for. The case established what a used car dealer ought to do under those circumstances. I lost the case, but the Dealers Association got the decision they were looking for. My car dealer friend, Ed Duggan, sent me the biggest box of chocolates I had ever seen. I was nursing Cam at the time, so I could not eat them. I have a soft spot in my heart for that car dealer, till this day! He also sold David my first car, and painted it for my birthday gift.

~

Three weeks prior to Cam's birth I spent most of my time in the Lindsay hospital, at David's bedside. I ate my meals with the student nurses. The local doctor, who had seen me through all of my prenatal care, was as new in medicine as David and I were at the Bar. He ordered an x-ray, which established that I was carrying a posterior-breech baby. He wanted to refer me to a specialist. My parents wanted me to go to the specialist, Doctor McArthur, to whom all their friends' daughters went. Lecturing in OB/GYN at U of T Medical School, he was very renowned in his field. My father said he "drank cocktails with the right people." That's how we got referred to him.

My parents and I did not have a happy relationship at this point in my life. I had planned to stay with them while I was pleading my case in the Ontario Court of Appeals, and I was in court when I had my first labour pains. My poor father had to take me to the Toronto General Hospital. That was a Wednesday night; my son was not born until Monday morning. My mother's lack of support for my situation was hard on me. She thought we should have done better family planning. Maybe she thought she was too young to be a grandmother. Or, maybe she harboured some resentment about the path I had chosen in life, when I decided to go for the Bar and not become a socialite—something that would be a credit to her family. She also questioned the way I had spent so much of the family resources. I believe my decision to become a lawyer might have been a cause of contention between her and my father, as well—my mother was ambiguous about it and frequently questioned the wisdom of me pursuing a legal career—as did my father's partners!

David's family was not a lot of support for me either. His mother had died when he was 20. She was a diabetic and he had told me that sometimes when he came home from school he would find her in a diabetic coma. He would give her something to eat to restore her blood sugar. His father remarried at the age of 69, to a younger woman who had stayed home to look after her parents. She felt she had been cheated of a lot of life's pleasures, and she was determined to make up for lost time, gadding around with poor old Father Thomson, visiting all his relatives out West. The family felt she was making demands on him that he was not fit for, or had the means to provide. My husband and his sisters were constantly comparing her with their mother, who had been a model preacher's wife.

So, this was a difficult time for me. I was very much on my own, with my husband convalescing at the Dahl's summer cottage. I had no extended family support. David did manage to come to Toronto when he got the news that the baby was born. He stayed with his father and stepmother. Unfortunately, my mother treated him badly, as though he were responsible for all the trouble I was having with this breech birth.

Cameron was born on July 11, 1955—he was born *blue*. There had been another famous case, during this time, of a baby born blue, with an upside-down heart. That baby had been operated on by Dr. Fraser-Mustard and had been saved by the heart surgery performed soon after birth. It was in all the newspapers.

When Cam was born the obstetrician asked: "Who is your paediatrician?"

"This is my first baby," I replied; "I don't have a paediatrician!"

"Well, your baby is blue; you better get one! I don't know enough about babies, I'm just an obstetrician and gynaecologist." I was referred to a paediatrician who kept rushing Cam in and out of Sick Kid's Hospital. Apparently he had ingested a great amount of the amniotic fluid during his passage through the birth canal and his lungs needed to be pumped out. He was also kept in an incubator for his breathing problems.

Because Cam was in and out of "Sick Kids" so much, I only got random chances to nurse him. I was afraid he was not going to survive. I spent ten days in a "Mother-crafted hospital," a place where new mothers were taught how to look after their babies. I sure needed that! I was very weak after the long painful delivery, and great loss of blood. I learned how to bathe a baby, but it took all morning the way they taught the procedure. To make sure I was giving my baby enough milk, I learned how to keep track of the baby's weight before and after breastfeeding.

Many of the skills that I learned at the Mother-craft hospital were not critical to keeping a baby alive, as I later realized with the birth of my second child; but, we were all afraid that Cam was a very delicate baby, and not likely to survive the first year without such special precautions. I was told to bring him back to the paediatrician at six months, and at a one year. Fortunately, when Cam was a year old he was pronounced as a healthy baby; he did not have any *blue baby* complications. But, that whole year had been very trying for us!

BIRTH OF SECOND CHILD AND FATHER'S PASSING

Our second child, Bruce, was born on February 8, 1957, just nineteen months after Cam. The "accountant's daughter" was figuring out the financial scenario, rationalizing that if I had to hire a babysitter/housekeeper I would get the process over with quickly by having my children close together—I wanted at least one sibling for Cam. Plus, I wanted the children to grow up together and not be lonely, as I had been as a child. I was 35—in the 1950's that was considered old to be having children. I rationalized that if I had the children close together, that one housekeeper would do when I returned to work; I would not have to have a succession. However, I did not realize, with having the boys that close that I would end up with two children in diapers at the same time!

Bruce was a posterior-breech birth, as well. The family doctor that had given me my prenatal care was not able to attend me when I went into labour, because his father was dying at the time. He recommended I go to Peterborough, to a classmate of his who had specialized in obstetrics. David was too nervous to drive me there, so Bill Dahl took me. He covered the backseat with blankets and away we went.

People sometimes do not consider all the circumstances that others might be facing. I was inundated with a tremendous amount of flack from the local people, they were upset that, even though I had been on the board of the local hospital, I had gone to Toronto to have my first baby, and then to Peterborough to have my second one. They did not understand that the kind of obstetric care I required needed more expertise than we had in our local hospital at the time. Lindsay had not been able to attract, or keep ambitious young doctors who wanted to be specialists—there was not enough demand for them, nor the equipment for them to develop their expertise.

~

It was during my pregnancy with Bruce that my father's health began to fail rapidly. Father had emphysema. Today they have portable oxygen tanks; however, that was not the case in the 1950's. Father did not have oxygen and he lingered unwell at home for some time. He had to take early retirement and he felt he got the short end of the stick from his firm, when negotiating the terms of his departure. He deemed the firm was not abiding by his original partnership agreement; they'd had too many partners retire on those favourable terms before his turn came.

My parents did get to Arizona when I was expecting Bruce. They thought the Arizona atmosphere would be beneficial to my father's health. When Bruce was born in February, they returned home. I think Mother resented that; she thought Dad would have been better if they could have stayed in Arizona. She gave me the impression that it was very inconsiderate of me to have a second baby at such a time. Once again, she was not very supportive. Of course, she was preoccupied with my father's illness. Dad's health continued to worsen.

I contracted a bad dose of the flu when I got home from the hospital with Bruce. I tried to hire back the woman who had helped me when I had Cam, but I think the neighbour had slipped her an extra wad to go to their place instead of mine. She did try to help me while she was babysitting the kids next door, but that did not work out too well. Because of the difficult birth, followed by the flu, I was not doing well nursing Bruce. To top it all off, my mother phoned me in August and demanded that I come to Toronto and help her nurse Dad at home!

I certainly felt my father could have been far better cared for in the hospital, but Mother thought I would know what to do because I had worked in a hospital during the war years. As exhausted as I

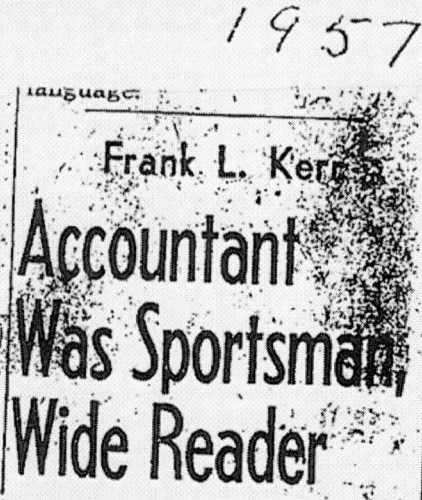

1957

Frank L. Kerr

Accountant Was Sportsman, Wide Reader

Frank Lester Kerr, a partner in the firm of Thorn, Mulholland, Howson and McPherson, chartered accountants, died at his home, 17 Elderwood Dr., Sunday.

Mr. Kerr, of an old Empire Loyalist family, was born in Newcastle, N.B., and was educated at Brantford, N.B., and at McGill University.

He studied accountancy in Ottawa, and was admitted to the Institute of Chartered Accountants of Ontario in 1917.

He was a member of the Caledon Mountain Trout Club, and the Toronto Cricket, Skating and Curling Club.

His interests had included hunting, fishing and riding. He also was an extensive reader of history and economics.

He leaves his wife, the former Madeleine Courtney; a daughter, Mrs. David Thomson, a lawyer living in Lindsay; two grandsons, Cameron David and Bruce Kerr Thomson; his mother, Mrs. Hugh Kerr, a sister, Mrs. Sidney Violet, both of Vancouver, and a brother, Ralph Kerr of Toronto.

was, I surrendered to her wishes. Reluctantly, I hired a housekeeper, Mrs. Macintosh, a wonderful country woman, to come and look after my boys while I was in Toronto. The boys loved Mrs. Mac, and she loved them, always wanting to take them home with her.

Mother did not make it easy for me—it was a bad scene. She had nursed her father and her brother; she thought she knew what was best. She was trying to force gruel into Dad's mouth, but he was incontinent and excreting it almost as soon as it went down his throat—it was a horrific situation. I arranged for a VON nurse to come in everyday, to help bathe Dad, and turn him over in his bed because he had bedsores. Mother would cry out: "Oh don't move him, it hurts!" Of course, I realized that sometimes when looking after someone you might have to do some things that would hurt them. Thank goodness for the VON nurse!

My Dad died on September 15, 1957, in the midst of a terrible thunderstorm. That was a scene I want to forget. It seems like a long time ago to me now, but I still miss him. He was very wise in human nature, as well as business matters.

Despite all the difficulties I had experienced, I enjoyed motherhood. Of course I had hovered over Cameron to make sure he made it through that first year, and I enjoyed Bruce too, albeit he was a totally different personality than his brother. Cam was a very calm, quiet baby—Bruce was just the opposite, always in trouble, always exploring, escaping the crib, the playpen—getting into everything—my impish little mischief. If he had been the first child he might have been an only child!

As much as I enjoyed my boys, I began to miss adult conversations. My husband was making a name for himself as a litigation counsel. It turned out that he had a real gift for it—as a trial lawyer he could preach to a jury the way his father could preach to a congregation! David had real powers of persuasion. He was working numerous different sessions of the Supreme Court in county towns around the lakeshore—like Cobourg and Bellville, to name a couple. This meant that David was away a lot, and I must admit that I agreed with Nancy White when she sang the song she composed about the *babbling* getting to her—it was getting to me too!

I had been the only lawyer on the hospital board, and I continued to do that until Bruce was born. I had also maintained some of the office bookkeeping—continuing to manage and issue our partners' cheques, but that was not the same as working in the office.

Cameron and Bruce

By the time Bruce was born, my husband's health was improving. David Logan was still helping us out. Eventually, he became our first partner. Three more partners came along as the business grew, about ten years apart. The second one was Bruce Glass, whose father was the manager of Lindsay's Zeller's store. He turned out tremendously, a common sense boy, and exceedingly loyal to us. Like David Logan's father, Bruce's father had died when he was in high school; my husband was like a surrogate father and mentor to both of those young men.

I thought it would be a good idea to start a daycare in the basement of the house in order to have my boys close by, and to give them other children to play with. With my E.C.E. training during the war years, along the help of my friend, Gwen Scott, who had her E.C.E. certificate, we opened our centre. Strangely, I found that easier than being home alone with just my two boys. My original plan had been to return to the office when Cam started school, but I went back when Bruce was about two, in order to help cope with office overload. We moved the daycare to downtown Lindsay, to a space above Gwen's family's paint and wallpaper store. She took over the running of it.

We continued hiring articling students in the summer, because we were swamped with summer cottage real estate deals, which were a big part of our business. We used these students for title searching. The summer property business was what we needed to capitalize on in order to expand. David and I rarely took summer holidays, usually just a day before and after a long holiday weekend.

We did find the time to build a cottage on Sturgeon Lake, just a few doors from the cottage we had rented while we were building our first house. The rich people were over on the bays, on the windy, east side of the lake. Our lot cost $500; it was on a swampy shoreline on Betty's Bay, on the west side of the lake. We did not get as much of a breeze in the hot weather. We did all of the building ourselves. I remember the first load of lumber we bought cost us $800—so, our initial investment in the cottage was $1,300, plus the price of a keg of nails.

We borrowed tools from a contractor friend. He would come over every evening to inspect what we had done that day—we referred to those visits as our "evening critiques." He would pick up his level and go around to all the studding and framing to check that we were keeping everything plumb. I think he came over so much because he felt sure that we would eventually break down and let him finish the job for us. But we made it—even put the roof on ourselves. I will never forget how hot it was that summer. My parents came up to visit and thought we were absolutely crazy not to have a home in town. The cabin was originally intended to be used during hunting and fishing season, but as the boys came along it became a family cottage.

AN UNFORTUNATE EXPERIENCE—"W" 1967

Things were moving along. David Logan and Bruce Glass, were working out well and they were entirely comfortable treating me as an equal in the office. Unfortunately, David had a second heart attack in 1964. David's workload had increased and I felt that we needed a senior man to take more responsibility in the office. In 1967 I called a former classmate of David's (I am going to refer to this individual as "W") and asked him if he would be interested in joining us. Unbeknownst to me, he had been relatively unsuccessful as a Danforth Avenue real estate lawyer. He had always exclaimed that he was going to be a litigation counsel, so I thought "W" could take some of the litigations burden from David's shoulders. When the drug problem became prominent in the area, it was a very heavy responsibility being in charge of the Federal prosecutions in such a geographically large area.

"W" was the first partner to give me a hard time—another bully to encounter. He had a booming voice, which he used to intimidate. He expected me to withdraw from the practice. I had referred a number of my litigation clients to him, but many of them came back to me, not having liked his approach to things. We had some tumultuous firm meetings, dealing with the discord of "W" not being able accept a female as an equal partner. One of his ridiculous proposals was that we treat the firm like a *three-family business*. I believe he wanted to take over all of David's litigation practice and cut me out completely. Over the course of the first year, I billed far more billable hours than he did. I think "W" was jealous of the clientele that I had developed by doing community service, and that he was expecting me to hand it all over to him, and then stay at home with my children! During some of those meetings it was pointed out to him that he was expected to build up his own clientele, just as each one of us had done!

Thankfully, David Logan and Bruce Glass backed me up. They realized that, as a pioneer in the firm, I had done, and was still doing, a great deal of unpaid billable hours to build up the practice—they accepted me as an equal partner. They were going the extra mile for the firm, too. David reacted quite strongly to "W's" attitude and finally spoke to him at a meeting that I was not present at. I remember that night well—David had come home steaming mad!

The upside of "W" not accepting me was that he finally left our office. He was extremely tall, about 6'4, and when he had first joined us I had purchased an office chair for him to *fit to his specifications*—and that chair was the only thing he asked for when he left! Well, aside from trying to get David Logan to go with him. "W" was not a team player and that was a most unfortunate experience for David and me.

NEW PARTNERS

Rodney Farn, our third partner, worked for us as a student. When he was admitted to the Bar, we asked him to join our firm. Ivan Reynolds became our fourth partner. Ivan was the nephew of a family that was prominent in local municipal politics; I believe his uncle was the county Reeve. Ivan was a good pick for expanding the practice into the rural community. Lindsay only had a population of about 10,000 when we started out, but with the rural community and the resort areas that we served, including Haliburton, there were about 26,000 people in the immediate area.

Rodney and Ivan joined the partnership after "W" left; neither one had a problem treating me as an equal. I turned a great deal of my practice over to them, plus they got involved in some of our real estate work. We also hired an experienced, older lawyer, Rex Thomas, whom I referred to as, *Sexy Rexy*. He took over as the head of our real estate department, so that I could concentrate more on wills and estates.

Rex knew a great deal about real estate because he had been a manager for the Victoria Grey Trust Company, which had the lion's share of farm mortgages in the area. When they were bought out by Grey and Bruce, Rex was let go because they assumed he was not up on the latest developments in the mortgage business. However, David realized the knowledge that Rex would bring to our firm—he was a wonderful boon to us. He even trained one of our clerks to assistant him with Title searches, and to be his legs for closing the real estate deals. We definitely got full value for our dollar!

Rex was still with the office when David and I left in 1974, but he had slowed down quite a bit by that time. He lived a block away from the office and was allowed to come and go as he pleased. He was still keeping on top of the real estate work, though, with the help of the girl he had trained.

THE NEW OFFICE—1967—OUR CENTENNIAL PROJECT

Our office staff attended a number of Bar conventions because we firmly believed in constant improvement. We would all sign up for different lectures; David and I believed that our greatest strength as a law office would be in each of us having a specialty. One of the lectures I attended was given by an accountant from Deloitte and Touche. He discussed what the ideal county town law firm should be––five was considered the perfect number for a town the size of Lindsay, which had a population of about 15,000 in 1967. I guess David and I were right on track to having a perfect model law office.

In 1967, the same year "W" had joined our firm, David and I decided it was time to build our own office; so, with the recent lecture fresh in my mind, we built a building just the right size for five lawyers. It was located on the edge of a residential area. Half the lot was zoned commercial, the other half, residential. We went through a difficult process to get half of the lot zoned commercial, running into some unexpected opposition from the neighbours that thought we were going to disturb their quiet neighbourhood by increasing the traffic in the area. To top that off—another hurdle—one of the other law firms in town dreamt up reasons to oppose us. But, despite all the difficulties, we prevailed and built a very striking, modern law office.

I furnished the office quite attractively. The library boardroom was across the front section, David was in the big, front corner office; I was in the office next to him. I used to watch the widows and divorcees come in, all perfumed and gussied up as they marched into my husband's office. He was such a considerate person; I think they all had a crush on him. He had something of his father's compassionate manner with people who were going through a stressful time in their lives.

DEER HUNTING ADVENTURES

David's sister, Grace, re-married to a man who loved hunting, fishing and trapping in Algonquin Park. Rex only had three years of formal elementary school, but he was a remarkable man and knew his way around the forests. In later years, he operated commercial deer hunts from a lodge in Haliburton. The road to the lodge was not passable, so Rex had brought in some equipment and started to make a road. The big hunt usually took place at the beginning of November, with about 12-20 men paying a fee. A special group patronized his lodge year after year and it became customary for him to invite us up for a family hunt before the commercial hunters arrived.

The family hunt amounted to cleaning the lodge for the arrival of the paying clients. I remember the first time we were invited—Rex showed me where David and I could sleep—on a couch in the living room. I had asked: "Now, which end shall I put my head so the sun doesn't wake me up?" Rex had replied: "Oh don't worry! You'll be up before the sun is up!"

That's the way it was at the deer lodge. We cleaned the lodge and prepared the kitchen for the gargantuan meals to be served to the hunters. A couple of local women came in to prepare the wood stove—they even cut the wood!

It was great fun being in on the hunt, too! Rex had a pack of deer hounds he always took up to the camp; he towed them on a barge behind his motor launch. With my fondness for dogs, I volunteered to ride on the scout he towed the hounds on, to make sure none of them fell off or got into trouble on the trip up the lake.

By the first week of November, there was usually a bit of snow, already, which was a good thing because that made it easier to follow the deer tracks. Having been raised in the city, I could not believe the seriousness with which the northern community took these deer hunts. Most stores on the main street of Lindsay were closed during deer hunting season, the local merchants closing their business to take at least a week off to go deer hunting!

One group that came to the lodge was Italian—how they loved music and dancing in the evenings. The two cooks, Grace, and I were the only women to dance with, and we had a blast—these fellows were a fun bunch. They brought their own wine, but never got tidally; Rex was very careful about that, anyway. On the rainy days when we could not hunt, Rex would plan activities in the lodge. Besides card games, he had an old player piano that we would wind up and sing around.

I did not actually get out on a hunt until after David had had his second heart attack—then I thought I should go with him. Rex planned that we could take a deer watch close enough to the lodge that I could drive my *Mustang* to the spot. On the first day we went out, we drove to the place designated as the deer watch and the fellows that were handling the hounds tried to steer the deer our way so that I could get a deer. We had to stay very quiet and still. David and I had gotten hungry and we were toasting some cheese sandwiches over a fire when I looked up and saw a little face looking over the top of the hill. It looked like a goat to me, but it was a deer that the men had chased our way. And there we sat, eating, our guns leaning against the tree! The deer ran between me and my *Mustang*! I realized that if I did shoot at the deer I would probably hit my *Mustang*! And that would never do! I loved that car so much that I drove it for eight years and had it painted gold!

FINDING MY WAY IN A MAN'S WORLD—

THE WAY IT WAS FOR ME THROUGHOUT THE YEARS IN THE LAST BASTION OF THE "OLD BOYS' CLUB"

I was constantly referred to as "Portia" by the local Crown Counsel when I was representing a first-time offender. "Here comes Portia with her pitch for mercy," he would say as I entered the courtroom!

Until David and I hired our junior partners, we were doing everything it took to build our practice. I had had enough of real estate work as a student; however, in our new situation, searching titles revealed interesting local history. Besides, real estate deals helped to pay the rent! As we hired the junior partners, I found myself leaning more toward wills, estates, and estate taxation. Many women were starting to contribute to the household income at the time and I felt an urgency to educate them in these areas, in order to protect their rights. I found that the accounting training my father had given me had left me capable of understanding balance sheets; therefore, I fell quite readily into the position of covering the wills and estates department in our firm. I organized the other work and passed it on to the junior partners. I also looked forward to being able to practice part-time after we bought the farm.

As I mentioned before, I reached out to the women in the area, speaking to as many women's groups as I could. I also did my share of the Duty Council work in the Family and Juvenile Courts. I felt I could be more effective there than in Criminal Court because I had a difficult time handling pathological liars. Many were the cases when I would sit with a client in my office while they would tell me their story; then, they would come up with a different account in court. When that happened, I used to wish they would drop through a trap door! The $18.50 an hour for this legal aid work was not worth it!

I began to remember the Big Sister work I had done after graduating from Branksome—I thought that maybe I could make a difference with some of the young people in the area that were having a *brush with the law*. I was particularly concerned about the affect on the children of dysfunctional families, feeling strongly that it was not the direct fault of these children when they got into trouble. Some of the issues that came before the Court were typical teenage behaviours, such as boys pushing over outhouses—actions that did not warrant jail time—just a firm lecture!

I had an excellent rapport with the Crown Attorney, Lorne Jordan. He was sympathetic to my desire to keep first-time offenders from acquiring a criminal record that would blight their future opportunities. We had the understanding, between us, to give first-time offenders a good scare so that they would not come back! Many of these young people expected to be led away to jail—instead they were given probation. Lorne and I felt that was a much better solution for children from dysfunctional homes. Of course, there was a Probation Officer or a Social Worker helping these children to follow through with their plans to change their ways!

As a result of the work I was doing with the young people in the community, when the local presiding judge had a heart attack, I was called upon to take over as *Pro-temp* (for the time being) while he recuperated. I sat on the Bench for three months. The pay at the time was $125 a day. I believe that was the first time in the history of Lindsay's *law facilities* that the toilet seat was put down! Horsehair chairs, which I had to sit on while presiding over Court, made me itchy, despite the heavy robe I wore.

I must say that experience was very demanding and interesting. Many were the times I would reserve judgment. Then I would burn the midnight oil, considering all of the facts before writing my conclusions to be presented at the next appearance. I was confronted with more than one situation where there was one boy who was the ringleader, the others just his followers. I would give the ringleader a scary tongue-lashing, with the hope that I would not see him back again! Then, I would turn to the ones I considered to be *the followers* and let them know just how close they had come to putting a big blotch on their futures!

~

There is one case I oversaw in Family Court that I felt badly about. It concerned a young farm girl whose parents had her sleeping in the loft of the farm house, with only a curtain between her and the hired man. Eventually, the girl ran away with the man; the parents were upset with their daughter. It was a most unfortunate situation. The hired man was not such a nice guy. He had gotten her into drugs and alcohol, and goodness knows what else. The police picked the girl up in the Toronto drug district.

The parents asked me to see what I could do to help their daughter, after she was sent to a girls' Correction school. I visited her there and discovered that she was an amazing artist, and was excelling in the school program. I thought it would be in her best interest to stay where she was, but her parents wanted me to try and appeal their daughter's case—they wanted her back working on the farm. I felt that was contrary to the girl's best interest, and told them so. They hired another lawyer. I have never forgotten that girl; I do not know what happened to her, but her face and drawings haunt me to this day.

~

Occasionally I took on a Domestic case. Some people felt I was gifted in that area. One notorious case, which stands out in my mind, was the divorce of a very attractive European lady who had been married to a railroader. When he passed away, she remarried a successful, local widower. She lost her railway pass, which she had used to visit her children. Unfortunately, her new husband had just been looking for a cheap housekeeper for his nice new home, plus he turned out to be parsimonious. He was so mean that he even cut her off from visiting her children! As a result of his demands, the relationship turned into quite an unhappy situation. He was not even thrilled with the lovely European meals she would cook for him—he preferred meat and mashed potatoes! There was a compassionate family doctor that was trying to help them with their situation, but in the end, the unsatisfied husband sued for a divorce. Plus, he charged his wife with adultery!

She came to me to oppose the grounds of adultery, stating quite adamantly that she had not ever stepped outside of the marriage! One had to be circumspective—especially in a small town. I decided to counter-sue for the dissolution of the marriage. Fortunately, for our case, the family doctor came forward with some significant evidence for our defence, and the case was put on the Court list. The court room was filled with curious locals wanting to hear *the dirt*! The doctor stated that he had found the man to be impotent! Upon hearing the revelation of such an insult to his manhood, especially in open court, the man became outraged! The Judge awarded the order for dissolution. The man stood up and protested loudly, babbling on about what she had cost him—even to the point of declaring that he had paid $800 for the ring she was still wearing! She took the ring from her finger and threw it at him. To make matters worse for the husband, the Judge awarded my client a cash settlement for her housekeeping services, plus damages for the manner in which she had been treated.

The thing that I found strange was that the locals who attended the court hearing were divided into two camps. Many of the men were outraged at the outcome—even some of the women. I heard rumours that many thought the woman was nothing more than a *gold digger*.

~

Many were the bedside wills I wrote, at all hours, in the early days of my practice. House calls, visits to nursing homes to make wills, and trips into the farming community were all in a day's work. As previously mentioned, many cost-conscious farmers would not *spring* a fee for a will until they were sure they were dying. There were numerous nights I would be called upon to make wills for these last minute characters—definitely not an ideal situation for me, or them!

In order to speed the process along, I drafted a form to be filled in at the bedside. The tricky part was trying to have the document signed and witnessed by other than a family member. Plus, there were times when I had some horrific night calls—"third red barn on the right, can't miss it;" or, I would just have to look out for the farm house with the lights all-a-blazing. The nursing experience I had had during the war years helped me to cope with some of the dire physical situations I was faced with on many of these visits.

~

In the early 1950's, in order to serve the farming community better, I started a branch office in Fenelon Falls, which was about 20 minutes from Lindsay. I rented an upstairs space in an insurance/real estate office and traveled there once a week in order to meet with my clients. The insurance receptionist handled my appointments and phone calls, and also drummed up some business for me. She was well known within the surrounding communities. In turn for her help, I did some wills and estate planning for her family.

The only heat in this building was a potbelly stove in the waiting room. Since my office was upstairs, in the back of the building, no heat ever seemed to reach it! If a client wanted a confidential hearing with me, we had to close the door; in the winter months it could get pretty frigid! This location expanded our clientele because so many of the people who lived on the outlying farms would not drive to Lindsay to do business. I remember one old client whose daughters took him to Lindsay, for the first time, for his seventieth birthday! That is just the way things were back then.

~

One of my favourite clients was Eddy Wong; he owned a Chinese café. He had such a sad life and I was anxious to help him. He had an ongoing battle with the local Medical Health Officer, with regard to his septic tank. There were a lot of septic tanks in the area that were not up to the code of the by-laws, but for some reason the Officer was making an example of this poor man. The local newspaper editor was upset about one of the streams that was becoming like a sewer because of the leaking septic tanks.

This poor Chinese man had sent to China for his childhood sweetheart. There were numerous restrictions in those days, so I assisted him with the paper work. Finally, she arrived and they had a little boy. The boy turned out to be a fine young man. He stayed on with his father, helping to run the café, until he was drowned when his fishing boat capsized just below the falls. The Chinese man's wife had returned to China because she did not like Canada. He was so lonely. He would phone me up, just to talk, over a free cup of coffee and a piece of pie. He sure made good pies!

~

Another area I worked in was the Small Claims Court. We were always short of judges—there was never a full roster on the Bench. I was asked to sit in as acting Judge, a number of times. It was not big money for this position, though. When we moved to the Windsor area, the list for small claims was full and the hearings were tedious. It was not unusual to have an interpreter on each side of the case, when a party was not fluent enough in English to give evidence. I remember one case where a daughter was interpreting for her father—I knew enough French that I could tell she was doing a substantial amount of embellishing on the statements her father was making on the witness stand.

Several difficult cases that I dealt with involved Pakistani landlords who were renting *slum apartments* to students. The students' parents came before the Court, complaining about the inadequate lighting and heating in those apartments—as a result, they were withholding the rent. The landlords were trying to collect the rent through the Court, but the parents and students felt that the lease conditions were not being met and that the spaces were not safe.

I would hear about 25 Small Claims cases before 4 p.m. in one day, after which the Courthouse staff would receive overtime pay. There were always some cases where a solution could not be reached, but I did my best to settle as many as possible. I was very conscious of the fact that some of these people had taken a day off work to attend court. I found these proceedings to be tedious, and I was not paid well—a mere $125 a day. I did quite a few sittings for Bruce Macdonald, a local judge who had been hurt in an auto accident.

When I first started the Small Claims Court work, I did not realize the entire proceedings were being taped and could be heard in the stenographer's office. One day, when I went back to the office, the stenographers were all chuckling about something I had said about a very disgruntled individual. When this person complained about my decision, I had blurted out that we could not send all our customers away happy!

~

During those early years I did face a lot of resentment because I was the first professional woman in the area to have my own car, plus I had a housekeeper! At one point I had even been approached and asked to run as a candidate for the local Provincial Liberal Party. I was no fool, though—I lived in *Frost Country*! I believed women would be envious and would not vote for me because many of them felt I would be neglecting my children to pursue my own personal ambition. Little did they know that I was actually more interested in Federal Affairs—my original ambition before deciding to proceed with law. The local affairs seemed petty to me. When I had been a Counsel for a client, I had had to attend some local town county Council meetings where I had observed way too much tedious, menial bickering!

~

One unfortunate situation that I was able to bring to a solution was when a couple of neighbours, sharing a mutual driveway, were constantly feuding about blocking access. They even resorted to throwing rocks at each other! I looked up the title and found that the property had never actually been properly surveyed. I suggested that both parties engage a surveyor to do a proper survey. It turned out that the driveway was wide enough at the back to park both cars. I was awarded with a fancy silver cocktail shaker for my part in solving this situation! And this was during a time when David and I could not afford to put anything in it!

~

While at Law school I had joined the Elizabeth Fry Society. Did I ever need an education on the *seedy side* of life! I remember going down to Toronto's Don Jail, determined to encourage prostitutes that there was another, more desirable way of life that they could pursue. Well, I admit, these women had a good laugh, at my expense!

~

One summer, I was given the agency job to search the titles on 700 township lots in Haliburton for a German lumber company that was buying them. A German classmate of mine, Deter Bernhardt, had been asked to negotiate the purchase of the properties and because I lived near the area, he had contacted me to search the titles. I was to make sure there were no limitations on mineral rights, or other existing rights on the lots. I commuted every day, in my 1967 Mustang, which I had just purchased for $3,000, from a fellow who had gone bankrupt. The Minden registry saw a lot of me that summer. Rod Farn, who eventually became a senior partner in our firm, accompanied me to learn how to search property titles. Deter was very pleased with the thorough job I did, going right back to the Crown grants. There were not many conveyances between the Crown grants and existing vendors of the lots and islands involved in this sale.

Trio Convicted Of Stealing Chickens Escape Jail Term

Three of the four Lindsay men charged with the theft of eight chickens and one rooster from Cecil Carew, Elgin Street, Lindsay pleaded guilty to the charge. The fourth man pleaded not guilty and the charge was subsequently dismissed by Magistrate Gee.

The four, a 17-year-old Cambray lad, living in Lindsay, a 19-year-old Lindsay man, a 25-year-old Lindsay man, father of three, and a 29-year-old trapper, all elected trial before Magistrate Gee. All but the 29-year-old trapper pleaded guilty. The 17-year-old lad was defended by Mrs. Thomson. Crown Attorney Jordan said that in view of the plea, the cases involving the three who pleaded guilty would be tried first and the case involving the man who pleaded not guilty would be tried separately.

Cecil Carew, owner of the fowl, said that on the night of the theft (Monday night) he and his family had attended the theatre. He had returned home about 11.30 p.m. and had not inspected the chicken house. He noticed the eight hens and rooster gone when he went out in the morning to feed the fowl. He valued the birds, which he said were laying remarkably well, at $5 each.

Howard Lynch, a nightwatchman at the Toronto Construction Co. Job at Colborne Street at the bank of the Scugog, told the Court that the four accused had arrived at his office about 11 p.m. to borrow one gallon of gas. He said that he gave them the fuel and when he was getting a band-aid from his car to apply to one of the accused's hands, a pair of rubber boots disappeared from the shack. Later he said he saw the 25-year-old accused heading in direction of the boots. Lynch said that he saw the boots then and got them before the accused reached them. He said that a row started and he was later to call the police.

James Stone told Magistrate Gee that he had been in the company of the two oldest accused and had been drinking beer and wine with them. He said that he had later gone to a shack on the river bank and had become ill because of a bout with the wine. He recalled wakening at 1 a.m. to find the 29-year-old accused lying on the bed sleeping and the 25-year-old accused cooking something which later turned out to be chicken. He was given a piece of chicken and went home. Constable Mark came up to

suspended sentence of one year. old man's car and had found a live chicken. This chicken had subsequently been identified with the rest of the flock.

The 17-year-old lad's attorney said that the youth had never been in trouble before and had picked the wrong company. She said that the accused was ready to make restitution for two birds and would suggested a suspended sentence. Crown Attorney Jordan agreed.

In the case of the other two, said Mr. Jordan, he could not agree to a suspended sentence. He pointed out that the 19-year-old accused had been convicted of shopbreaking in Lindsay in August, 1949. He was given one year's suspended sentence. In March of 1950, the accused was again convicted of a similar offense and was put on two year's suspended sentence and was still on suspended sentence at the time of this most recent offense. He said that in August, 1950, this accused was also convicted of a theft of gasoline and was given 15 days.

The 25-year-old accused, said Mr. Jordan, had been convicted in October, 1949 of creating a disturbance. In January of this year, he had been convicted of a theft of liquor and had been placed on

(Continued On Page 4)

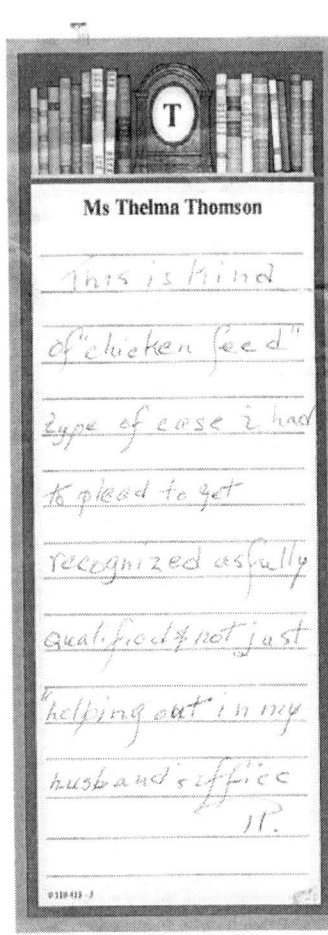

Ms Thelma Thomson

This is kind of "chicken feed" type of case I had to plead to get recognized as fully qualified & not just helping out in my husband's office 11.

Lady Lawyer Addresses B & P Women

Members of the Lindsay Business and Professional Women's Club held their first dinner meeting in St. Paul's Parish Hall on Monday evening with 50 in attendance. President Harriet Bate was in the chair.

The guest speaker was one of the club's own number in the person of Mrs. David Thomson, Lindsay's first lady lawyer who chose as her subject, "Law as a Career for Women".

During the evening a "Mystery Draw" was made for two guest passes to the local theatres, the gift of Mr. G. K. Garbig. Proceeds for this draw are to be used towards the purchase of the club's project, a refrigerator for the Baby Formulae at the Ross Memorial Hospital.

Mrs. D. Thomson Addresses West Ops Institute

The February meeting of West Ops Institute was held at Moose Hall. The meeting opened with Ode after which the Lord's prayer was repeated. Thank you cards were read from Kenney's School and Mrs. White. It was moved by Mrs. Stewart and seconded by Mr. Cornforth that we give $10.00 towards Girls Cereal Club for trip to Peterboro. It was moved by Mrs. H. Walden that we continue our euchres the next to be held on Feb. 17 with Mrs. Wallace as convenor and Mrs. Stewart, Mrs. Rowntree and Mrs. Traynor her helpers.

The current events were ably given by Mrs. Tyner. The roll call was answered by "A Notable Event of the Year". A lovely solo was rendered by Mrs. Shier accompanied by Mrs. Bailey on piano.

Our guest speaker for the afternoon was Mrs. Dave Thomson, Lindsay's Lady Lawyer, who gave us an interesting talk about wills. She impressed on us how important it was for each person to make his or her will. The meeting closed with the King. A lovely lunch was served by the hostesses Mrs. White, Mrs. Tyner and Mrs. Cayley.

Landlord Asks For Eviction Of Tenant

Claiming that he wanted his Mariposa house for his own use, John H. Cooper, 75 Lawlor Ave., Toronto, laid a charge of malicious damage against his tenant, an arsenal employee here. When the case was brought to court today, the malicious damage was said to consist of removing approximately 20 inches a twindow trim from the house, the disappearance of a quantity of cedar fence rails, and the removal of two "bricks" from the insul brick sided house.

According to Cooper's story, the defendant had written him asking the rental of the five-room partly furnished house. He advised him the price was $15 a month, with six months' rent payable in advance. Subsequently, another letter was received from the defendant, asking whether he would accept $75 for the six-month period, and Cooper had advised him that the price had not been changed and that references were required. Then on March 28, said Cooper, he received a money order for $90, but no references, and promptly returned it. Cooper visited his property on Good Friday, to find that the defendant, his wife, and his nine children had already moved in. As they had not obtained a key to the house, said Cooper, entry was gained by removing the trim from a window and slipping the window catch. Both front and rear doors, he said were equipped with Yale locks, and the piece of trim was still missing.

Mr. D. Thompson, acting for the defendant, moved for dismissal of the case, on the grounds that it was properly a civil action, as it might be termed a case of offer and acceptance. In the first instance, he argued, there had been no mention of references.

Landlord
(Continued From Page 1)

"In all my experience, I have never seen a case where the tenant made no attempt to get a key from his landlord," was Crown Attorney Jordan's reply. "In my opinion this was a contemptible and high-handed action. If I had been the landlord, they wouldn't have been there very long. I'm only sorry that under the circumstances the accused couldn't be charged with breaking and entry!"

Judgement in the case was reserved for two weeks, during which time the defendant was ordered to leave the premises.

Finds Place For Family

The case of a Mariposa Township father of ten, who is alleged to have secured possession of a house by the unorthodox means of removing a window sash rather than waiting for a key from his landlord was adjourned for a further week in police court here today.

D. Thomson, counsel for the accused, told the court that other living quarters had been found for his client, who would be moving into them in a few days' time.

The landlord laid a complaint when he discovered that the accused had moved into his house without his knowledge or consent. At an earlier hearing of the case, evidence showed that the accused had paid six months rent in advance by money order, as requested in correspondence with the landlord, who had also asked for references. The landlord said he had returned the money order, and that this was in the mail while the tenant and his family were moving into the house.

Who Can Or Cannot Prepare Your Income Tax Returns?

A story, regarding income tax returns, appeared in a Peterboro newspaper, to the effect that only a licensed accountant was now permitted to make out these returns for others. This was allegedly according to a new Accountancy Act, effective August, 1st.

According to the Peterborough story, the ruling would not prevent a man from preparing his own income tax form, but would prevent anyone from preparing another man's tax form if he is not a licensed accountant. It points out that businesses and businessmen almost invariably have accountants prepare their tax returns, but do not always hire a licensed accountant. In some cases lawyers have undertaken this work for their clients.

Asked to comment on this, Mr. D. Thomson, of the Lindsay legal firm of Cunningham, Thomson and Thomson said that he had not yet had the opportunity to read a copy of the legislation in question. He later was successful in contacting a member of an accountants' association, who told him what had been proposed was a clause preventing persons other than licensed public accountants from carrying on the business of a public accountant.

Mr. Thomson says the question now becomes, "Is the business of preparing income tax returns carrying on the business of a public accountant?"

Mrs. Harry Hickson Hostess To Reaboro Womens Institute

The regular meeting of the Reaboro Women's Institute was held at the home of Mrs. Harry Hickson.

The meeting opened by singing the Ode and the Lord's Prayer repeated in unison.

The minutes of the June meeting were read by the Secretary, Mrs. Thurston and were adopted by Mrs. If Fleming who acted as president in the absence of Mrs. Bruce McKavin who was on the sick list.

The correspondence was read and dealt with.

A card of thanks was read from Mrs. Elmer Mahood.

The roll call was answered by home remedies.

There was a good attendance of members and a number of visitors present including some of the members of West Ops. W.I.

It was decided to hold a White Elephant Sale at the October meeting to raise some money.

The current events were given by Mrs. Lloyd Reids.

Mrs. Clayton Smith gave an excellent paper on House Economics. Norma Jean Sloan rendered two pleasing solos.

Sparks of Wisdom was enjoyed by all.

A musical quiz was conducted by Mrs. Clayton Smith and was won by Mrs. E. Mahood.

Mrs. Hickson then introduced the speaker Mrs. Thompson, the young barrister from Lindsay who brought a very instructive address on Wills.

The meeting closed with the Creed and singing "God Save The King".

A dainty lunch was served by the hostess, Mrs. Harry Hickson and her helpers, Mrs. Lorne Thurston, and Mrs. Ken Thorne and a social time was spent by all present.

The September meeting will be held at the home of Mrs. Clayton Smith.

Leniency Shown Lads Convicted Of Thefts

The three Haliburton lads who were involved in the eight breaking and entering charges heard last week were sentenced in Police Court this morning.

Before sentence was passed, Col. R. I. Moore, defense attorney for two of the 16-year-olds, asked the Court for a suspended sentence for the boys. He stated that the boys had been convicted of crimes that would warrant severe jail penalties for adults but since the boys were just in their middle teens, some leniency should be shown. Mrs. Thompson, attorney for the third lad, suggested a suspended sentence since it was the lad's first offense. Her client had since found a position in a lumber camp some 25 miles out of Haliburton and would be separated from his former associates.

Crown Attorney Jordan stated that $208. had been taken in the raids and $34.52 had been taken in goods. $101.50 damage had been done to cash registers in two garages and this should be paid. Defense explained that $225.60 had been paid to the parties from whom the money and goods had been taken.

The Crown then went on to say that the onus for the moral responsibilities rested on the parents and the parents had been made suffer enough, both having to make up the restitution and because of the humiliation their sons had brought on their heads. He said that the boys, while being remanded in custody for a few days, had had a mild taste of what incarceration meant and he would be satisfied with a suspended sentence.

Magistrate Gee said that the boys should be sent to a Reformatory and learn some useful trade but he would be very lenient this time and suspend sentence for two years and imposed court costs of $14 on each of the boys.

Eight Charges Face Youths

Three Haliburton youths appeared in court this morning to answer charges of breaking and entering in the Haliburton area. There are eight separate charges but the three youths are not all involved in each case.

The Crown asked for another remand of a week and bail was set at $1000 each.

A fourth boy was also implicated but was under 16 years and will be tried in a juvenile court.

12 THE GLOBE AND MAIL, WEDNESDAY, OCTOBER 31, 1973

AFTER A FASHION
Of tapes and law

By ZENA CHERRY

Lorraine Gotlib, a lawyer with McMillan, Binch, is chairman of a committee that has prepared 13 videotapes on legal subjects. They're in color, each is one hour long and it took almost a year to complete them.

Their purpose is to educate and help the lay public.

All the participants are lawyers.

Said Miss Gotlib, "Lots of brainy people can't talk, so we picked panellists for their eloquence. We did not tackle heavygoing corporate material, but subjects in which most people are involved at one time or another."

The tape on Family Law (custody, separation agreements) is moderated by John R. R. Jennings. Panellists are Sanford World and Malcolm C. Kronby.

James T. Robson is moderator of Wills and Estates, with Thelma Kerr Thompson of Lindsay, Ronald G. Burrows and Stanley Taube.

The one on Buying and Selling a House has Alan Bennett, Marion Kelly, John P. Hamilton, David H. Millman of Port Credit and James J. Wardlaw of Orangeville.

Other Toronto lawyers on these tapes include Owen Shime, Jeffrey Sack, Raymond Koskie, Peter F. M. Jones, W. Ian C. Binnie, Alastair Paterson, Moira L. Caswell, Samuel G. M. Grange, Donald H. Lamont.

The tapes will be shown on various cable systems. Also if you would like a list of the subjects and then would like to borrow any of the tapes to show to your own group or in your home, please contact John Griner, Administrator Ontario Branch, Canadian Bar Association, 67 Richmond St. West.

To mention a few more Toronto lawyers in this—Donald J. Donahue, C. Alicia Forgie, Leonard Fine, Samuel N. Filer, Marie C. Corbett and Rosalie S. Abella.

Victoria-Haliburton Liberal stalwarts, left to right: David Thomson, his wife, Thelma, guest speaker, Miss Judy La-Marsh, and riding candidate Cliff Benson posing for a picture before the Lindsay party rally.

Cliff Benson, Liberal Candidate; Walter Gordon, Minister of Finance; and David—Gordon had come to speak in Lindsay

THE FARM—1969

Cam had a menagerie of pets in the basement of our three-bedroom house that we were living in. He had created a number of mazes for his white mice so that he could perform some very interesting experiments with them. We were sure Cam was destined to be a vet. My mother refused to stay with us anymore, especially after Cam came to the dinner table with a white mouse peeking out of his vest pocket. After that incident, she stayed in a B&B when she came to visit. The house was becoming too small for the menagerie—and for the family! Plus, the neighbourhood was getting too built up; it was no longer as attractive to us as it had once been.

David was also having further cardiac problems and had been advised to change his lifestyle, and not to engage in such strenuous hunting expeditions as he usually ventured out on. It was at this time that David had the heart attack while deer hunting in northern Quebec. His friends had to get him out of the hunting camp as quickly as possible. They drove him to Gray Rocks and chartered a float plane to fly him to a lodge on Sturgeon Lake. His fishing buddy, the Internist, and I, drove out to get him.

David's litigation work and active community life was catching up with him. I used to say we were ships that passed in the hallway at night. He was chairman of the area high school board when they closed all the country schools, and he had the dream of transforming that local high school into a dual-purpose school. They developed a wonderful tech department, teaching motor mechanics, plumbing, and carpentry; plus other trades, as well as the academics required for university entrance. That was David's dream and he was in the process of accomplishing it the year he had that heart attack. He was also the founding president of the Chamber of Commerce, and was president during the famous *bull fight* we had in Lindsay. In short, my husband had undertaken a weighty load of community service, on top of maintaining a very busy litigation and law practice.

In truth, both David and I were heavily involved in community service, feeling it was a good way to build our practice. This was something, "W," our "misguided partner" had not understood. His idea of community service had been to go to hockey games and yell at the people he thought were wrong, and then invite them to go *fist-of-cuffs* in the laneway behind the arena, a behaviour that did not win him many friends! That was no way to build a clientele—especially in a small county town like Lindsay.

I had to appear before the Town Council while I was on the VON (Victorian Order of Nurses) Board, to ask for our annual grant. This was a part of my community service that was near and dear to my heart. I felt that there was a real lack of appreciation for some of the farm wives in the community. They had a hard row to hoe, because many times the farm would be left to the eldest son. It was taken for granted that the farmer's widow would remain cared for, and be part of the family. In a few cases, when the daughter-in-law and widow did not get along, the widow was left in a wretched situation. I felt that she should be provided for adequately. VON services also helped the women who had just given birth, if they had other children at home to look after. The husband would have to take time off work if the family could not afford to hire someone to help out. My main function on the VON board was to go to the town council every year and plead for the money to subsidize our nursing services. I would argue that if we did not get the funding, the town councillors, many of who were employers in town, would be losing man-days at work if the men had to stay home and look after their wives and other children, when they had a newborn in the family.

I was also in the IODE—Imperial Order of Daughters of the Empire. At the time we had a citizenship court in Lindsay, and the IODE members undertook to help new citizens prepare for the exams they had to pass before being granted citizenship. They were expected to prove that they understood our provincial and federal government services, and what they were voting for. I am very proud of the work the IODE did to help new citizens settle in.

There were some wonderful Dutch people who immigrated to our area because they admired the Canadian soldiers that had liberated Holland from the Nazis at the end of the war. They were hard-working people, and it certainly did not hurt our practice any that my husband gave them some free legal aid when they bought their properties, plus a piece of land to build a church on. They kept bringing family and friends over from the old country; I helped many of them with their citizenship papers. They were well-informed, superb farmers—a great asset to our area. I had great respect for them.

~

With everything that was going on in our lives, we decided to buy a one-hundred acre farm just outside of Lindsay. We bought the property from a son of Francis Eddy, who had purchased it after searching for a place where he might get some relief for his asthma. The farm was 800 feet above sea level, which would help his condition. He had married an American woman and was living in the United States; but, with his failing health he began to worry about the effect on his estate taxation if he were to die in the United States. He had decided, at that time, to return to Canada.

The old farmhouse had beautiful interior woodwork—the wood paneling extended halfway up the dining room walls. I was enthralled with the elaborate wood-paneled doors that had been refurbished. Good woodwork was something Francis Eddy knew and admired. Simply said, that old farm house was breathtakingly beautiful—a real family home, just like the one I had grown up in!

The decision to buy the farm was based on the fact we had to change our lifestyle, and give up some of our community service. We had done our bit; it was time for younger people to take their turn. That same year, Larry Parnell had approached David about accepting a position on the Bench. David turned the offer down—because we had just purchased the farm, and because of his health. As for me—I was ecstatic because this would be an opportunity for me to indulge in my love of horses for the first time since David and I were married. I bought my first horse when I was 47 years old!

Upon giving up his strenuous hunting trips, David became quite depressed. I suggested: "Well if you can get a horse to carry you through the woods, it won't be so strenuous for you, and you don't have to give up all the good things that you love in life, just because you can't go crashing through the woods on your own two feet."

~

Unfortunately the soil had been neglected by a previous owner, so it was not a good farm for growing crops. We actually rented much of the land out as pasture to the neighbouring farmers. It was also those good neighbours who taught us, *Farming 101*!

Gratton Moore was the warden of the county. We knew him from business connections. He had looked to our office for advice; now he was returning the favour. His brother lived on the other side of us. Those two families took us under their wings, and we learned a lot as they nursed us through our education period of becoming *wannabe farmers*. We sent soil samples from each field to Guelph Agricultural College, for analysis, to determine what fields could be restored, and what it would require. Our neighbour frequently stopped by to check on the restoration process.

There was an income tax angle here too—we managed to lose enough money on the farm that we could write off income losses against our professional income. It was a tricky loophole that we used to navigate, by restoring some of the fields for horse feed, and then renting the rough land to Gratton, who pastured his livestock on our farm for a rental that accommodated our income tax juggling.

~

Those days on the farm were some of the happiest days of my life. My first interest in having pasture land was to buy a horse of my own, at long last. I had begged my father for one all the years I was at home, to no avail. There was a livery stable nearby that David and I frequented; I wanted to make sure the family were all in accord with me *getting into* horses. David was somewhat reluctant. Although he was tremendously athletic and well coordinated, the adjustment to moving with the rhythm of a horse was a bit of a challenge for him, so I thought it best that we practice on rental horses first. And, of course, I started looking for a horse to buy. I had waited 47 years, now I had the perfect place where I could keep one—my own farm!

One day we went to the stable to ride and they were trying to put a saddle on a fine looking horse that was rearing up and being difficult. Right away I saw this was my challenge. I used to volunteer at a livery stable in Bayview, just to be near horses and horsy people, and they had let me ride for free on the new horses. I was to get them accustomed to the area, and calm them down so they could be rented out to the customers.

I looked this horse over and noticed that it had an injury on its hind leg. I put a $100 deposit on him and told them that I would buy him when our vet checked him over and ensured he could be nursed back to health. The wound on the hind leg looked like something I could cope with—I had also looked after injured horses at the Bayview stable.

So it was that I took on this horse, under the guidance of the vet. He said there was nothing wrong with the horse that could not be cured with some TLC on the leg, and putting 100 pounds on him, which I proceeded to do. When I was grooming him I thought he had all the attributes of a Thoroughbred, so I rolled back his lip—sure enough, he had the identifying tattoo. I wrote to Scott Young, a sports writer. He researched the tattoo number and told me my horse's registered name was *Munsy Boy*. He was a beautiful copper color. I felt at home; just grooming a horse was so relaxing to me. I treated his leg with an iodine salve, and fed him a good grain mix to build him back up. He thrived under my care and became quite frisky.

I rode him around the farm, to make sure he would settle down to being a lady's saddle horse. My husband was afraid the horse was too much for me, so he used to follow me around in an old Ford truck that a client had written off. David's original notion for the truck had been to have our boys learn to drive in it. Eventually, though, once the horse was back to good health, he proved to be too much horse for me. I was not the rider I had been 20 years before. Our family doctor was just getting into horses himself; on one of his visits to the farm he had taken a liking to the horse. He took him off my hands for what I had paid for him. That horse proved to be accident prone, though; he kept getting into trouble at the doctor's farm.

The next horse I bought was another $100 horse from the livery stable. He was rearing up when they slapped the big western saddle on him; I thought my little pony club saddle would be much more comfortable for him. It proved true. He had an amiable disposition. I was having a wonderful time riding him throughout the winter, even in the deep snow. When I figured out he was only two years old, something you can tell from a horse's teeth, I realized he was too young to be ridden. By the spring, when the snow had all melted, he was also too tall for me to mount without a snow drift to stand on. He had grown an entire hand on the good feed we had fed him over the winter months! David named him Ignoramus, Amos, for short. Amos was never really trained properly.

The boys, after having ridden at the livery stables with me, also took to riding, Cam more so than Bruce. Bruce was seriously dyslexic and needed help with his studies that the local schools could not provide for him, so we sent him to Lakefield College School after we bought the farm. Lakefield could offer him extra help with his hand-eye coordination. Apparently both of his brain hemispheres were equally developed and he had difficulty deciding which hand to write with. When one hand got tired he would use the other, so he was completely ambidextrous. Later in life Bruce became a computer whiz—if he could have written his high school exams on a computer, he would have done very well. So, in all fairness, Bruce did not have as much opportunity to ride as Cameron did, because he boarded at the school.

Cameron turned out to have a natural inclination for riding. He started a local 4-H horse club and we had monthly horse show events during the summer months. Our office sponsored some of the event prizes at those shows, and at the county fairs we attended.

I was in my glory! I wanted a larger family—what better way to get one than by breeding horses and dogs. When we had some success, I considered it was because of the knowledge that Cameron had gained through the 4-H club. He said, "Look, it doesn't cost anymore to feed a papered horse, why don't we get into some good papered horses?" We settled on American Quarter Horses, which were very practical for a family operation. They did not require as much care and attention as the Arabians, I preferred; or the Thoroughbreds that were too much for me to handle. We started off by breeding American Quarter Horse mares to a Thoroughbred stallion. The stallion was the grandson of *War Admiral,* the famous race horse, a good bloodline to mix with our Quarter Horse mares.

We put in an Olympic-sized Dressage ring with four inches of sand, to offer riding for the disabled. This was one of our favourite projects. An old Austrian Cavalryman, Joe Bauer, who had recovered from injuries suffered in a riding accident, would come out on the weekends to run the program for us. He was one of the originators of the "riding for the disabled" program in North America. This was one of the most rewarding things that we did.

Joe had been conscripted by the Nazis and had been sent to be an officer for a troupe of Cossacks in World War II. He told great stories around our campfires at night, when he stayed with us on the weekends. These stories were even more of an education than the riding lessons he gave our boys! We learned a great deal from Joe—he taught us all how to ride better, and how to train our young foals.

~

Cam and I had a lot of fun going around to horse auctions and horse dealers, looking for the ideal broodmares. We enjoyed some success in breeding, producing some good foals, which we showed at local county fairs and horse shows. Unfortunately, one of them broke out of the pasture where she was boarded, after we had sold the farm—she was hit by a car. Cam had been hoping to keep her for himself. This tragic event happened when he had moved back from U of T for the summer. David and I were in Windsor at the time. The OPP officer handed Cam his sidearm and said, "You know what you have to do." The horse was bleeding from the mouth and obviously in agony. She had been the best one we had produced, winning several ribbons at the local fairs.

My family and our menagerie of animals, in front of our farm house.

Saturday was our day for stable cleaning, fence mending and any other necessary farm chores. We hired the same man, Alvin, whom the previous owner had had working for him. Alvin was a middle-aged man who was developmentally challenged; he had worked as a farm labourer all of his life. During his school years everyone referred to him as *retarded*. Maybe so, according to society, but I can testify to one thing, he was pretty sharp about farming. He loved working with our boys; we all learned a lot from Alvin.

There was a big market garden area on the property and we tried desperately to maintain it. We would start out very ambitiously every spring; I used to call it our "string garden." We would put strings up to guide us in our planting, but when things began to grow we did not know the difference between the young plants and the weeds. We relied on Alvin to show us. We would draw straws to see which one of us had to work along with him to do the weeding and hoeing, because he would go home if he had to work alone. One day it became my turn—I admit that I was absolutely hopeless at the job!

After I had asked Alvin, several times, "Is this a weed or a plant?" he turned to me and said, "You're pretty ignorant, aren't you?" I had no alternative other than to agree. In his eyes I was pretty stupid—when it came to gardening, at least.

David was not a great help on the farm throughout the week—he was more of a Saturday farmer. One of the jokes around the neighbourhood was how David loved farm machinery. When he was in high school he had worked for Massey-Harris in the summers, in the reaper/thresher department. He had been a *chaser* to chase the parts that went into a reaper/thresher. So, David was familiar with that particular Massey-Harris machine, and he seemed to be fascinated with all old farm equipment when we went to the local farm fairs.

When we bought the farm, it came with an old 1939 Ford tractor. It was a wonderful old tractor; I loved to drive it. I wish I had a picture of it pulling our Toyota out of the ditch—what a scene that was! We had Toyota's answer to the Land Rover, a wonderful vehicle, but when we got stuck in the ditch one day, that poor old tractor was not powerful enough to pull it out! David used to use the front attachment on the tractor for clearing snow out of the farm laneway. This old Ford sometimes bucked on him when he got a big load of snow in the scoop. Finally, he went out and bought himself a big powerful blue diesel tractor—it became the joke of the neighbourhood that "Lawyer Thomson" had the best tractor in the neighbourhood! Of course everyone wanted to borrow it—I believe the neighbours got more use out of it then we did.

Even though farm life kept us all occupied, sometimes, throughout the week when David came home from the office, he would pick up the newspaper, pour himself a drink, and then sit down in the living room, while I scurried around in the kitchen to feed two hungry boys—and David. I believe there might have been the odd time, when I was tired from my long day at the office that I might have harboured a bit of resentment.

~

I liked to take walks along the road when it was either too hot to take one of the horses out for a ride, or inclement in some other way. The goat that we had purchased to keep the horses company would walk with me when I walked our Golden Retrievers. She was very friendly. We called her Ermetrude—Emmy for short. David was very clever in coming up with names and cute nicknames for our critters. One day a farmer stopped and said, "I'll help you catch your goat ma'am." I replied: "Oh no, she always walks with me." The locals must have thought I was pretty strange.

~

We learned a lot from our farm experience, not only from Alvin, but from some of our neighbours. I had one very special friend, Olive (Moore) Gratton. Knowing Olive, Ollie as we called her, and her family was a great learning experience for me. As I had been an only child, I really knew nothing of the fun a big family could have together. David had given me some inkling of it, being the youngest of five. Growing up, he used to have to do a lot of the *joe-jobs* around the house, but David had a gift for making work fun by the way he approached it.

Ollie's attitude to chores was similar to David's. She was very active in the farm women's institute, teaching the local girls the homemaking arts, at which she was quite accomplished. Ollie was also a member of the Powles Women's Institute. She took courses in Guelph, learning the latest on good homemaking. She was a wonderful seamstress and made entire outfits for bridal parties. Ollie was active in the women's agricultural group, so I was asked to speak at many of their meetings, which helped me to develop a new appreciation of the home and family life that came with life on a family farm.

~

There is a funny little story about the Powles family that I would like to tell here—"Powles Corners" was named after an old pioneer family. There was a "Y" in the road that went to Coboconk to the east and Rosedale to the west. The family had a property there, which at one time had been a large farm. The last surviving relative of that family was a business man who lived in Chicago; so, when the one relative who had remained on the property died, we got a call from this Chicago business man.

"Just call in an auctioneer," he instructed us. "Sell the farm; sell everything on it. I can't afford to take the time away to deal with it."

We arranged an auction sale for the household contents—everything sold. About five o'clock, just when the auction was winding up, a Cadillac came roaring into the farm yard and this big, bustling man got out.

"Have you sold that urn that was over the fireplace?" he hollered.

To which we replied: "Oh yes, it went some time ago; it was quite an attractive piece."

"Who bought it?" the man demanded.

The auctioneer looked through his records and said it had been a cash sale; there was no record of who actually purchased it.

"Oh dear! Uncle *so-and-so's* ashes were in that urn!"

Our firm did not handle the actual will on this estate—that was most likely looked after by the elderly lawyer who travelled up to Fenelon Falls once a week. We had probably ended up with the estate work, because this Chicago heir's firm would have contacted a Toronto firm to find out who worked in our area. David and I were very fortunate that some of our former Toronto associates referred a lot of that kind of work to us.

~

Back to Ollie Moore—we were fortunate that she lived to one side of us and was married to Gratton Moore. Ollie hosted great family parties, to which she invited us. She showed me a side of life on the farm that I had never known before and she made it possible for me to have a cozy farm home, and a law practice. Ollie came over three mornings a week and kept our house in order. She even took my ironing home with her. David wore a white shirt to the office everyday, and when we moved away from the Chinese laundry I was having a struggle finding the time to iron those white shirts in my evening hours. Even though I put in the same hours at the office as David did, there was no question that he would iron his own shirts! When I finished at the office, I still had a few more hours of work to keep up the household, the boys, and the animals!

Ollie knew more about horses then I did, too, because her father had farmed with horses. She would come over and maintain the home while I would go out and check on the horses before I left for work. If I had a problem with a fractious horse, or if something was amiss in the stable, I would fetch Ollie—she would know what to do. Her husband was a wonderful horseman too.

Ollie's husband ran a cow/calf operation. It was on his advice that we got fertilizer for some of the depleted fields, to restore them to productive acreages. Then he rented them from us to pasture his livestock. This gave me the opportunity to learn something about cattle, especially when they broke through the fence and got into our garden! I had some other great adventures too, when our horses broke through the fence and ended up down at our neighbour's farms. I would get home from work, still in my high heels, silk stockings and skirt, and some local farmer would phone and say, "Your darn horses are over here eating my cattle feed again." So I would have to grab a bucket of oats and try to retrieve the wayward horses. I must have looked ridiculous, dressed as I was, walking along the concession road, rattling the oat bucket in front of the horses to keep them following me—like the Pied Piper.

~

We had hired a British legal secretary, Olga Simons. She was an exceptional secretary. Before coming to Canada, Olga had married a Canadian soldier, Stan Simons. He was a fine character, and one of our closest friends. Stan worked with the "Department of Land and Forest." With his wartime weapons experience, he was designated the instructor for the game wardens who carried guns.

He taught David and me how to handle a gun. We had 22 calibre rifles to knock off the groundhogs that were always making holes in our pastures. Cam and Bruce learned to shoot when they were 13 and 12. We also used shotguns for ducks and partridges. There were a lot of partridges in our woods and when they would burst out of the tall grass at the edge of the wooded area, they spooked our horses. One of our horse friends suggested we get a Banty rooster and some hens in our stable so that the horses would get used to birds fluttering their wings. I remember many a cold night when I would check on things out in the barn—the Banties would be on the horses' backs, their feet tucked into their coats, to keep warm.

Back to Olga—she was the daughter of journalists and her brother was with Scotland Yard. We found out later that she had been an *undercover agent* for the British Secret Service during the war. Before the war she had worked undercover as a secretary for the head of the Communist Party in Britain, and her boss had sent her to India on a mission for him. From India, Olga wrote letters to her brother in Scotland Yard, about "sightseeing" in India, and between the lines of these letters she used invisible ink to tell him the mission she was on for the Communist Party. She was a very interesting and intelligent woman, and apparently she had been very beautiful in her espionage days—a definite advantage in that line of work.

Olga was a great asset to our office, but sometimes she found conditions at her home hard to tolerate. She and Stan stayed with his parents who lived out in the country. She would work overtime in the office just so she would not have to go home early. Not only was Canadian life different for Olga, she found that hers and Stan's backgrounds were very dissimilar—she felt that his family was uneducated and backward compared to her well educated family, and she was having a difficult time adjusting. She made frequent trips back to England. But, Olga loved Stan enough to keep returning to him. They had a daughter, and then one summer when she was in England she arranged a private adoption of a little boy. She was hoping a boy would help cement the marriage—because Stan would have a son he could take hunting. It must have worked because despite all their differences they remained together.

~

We hired Joan Humphries when she was in her mid-twenties. She had completed the Bell telephone course for a switchboard operator. In those early days the switchboard we had, for just three lawyers, would light up like a Christmas tree, sometimes. There was a light for each line and she not only managed that beautifully, but she *mother-henned* everybody who was sitting in the waiting room. Joan knew that vicinity like the back of her hand, having grown up on a local farm—she was connected by either blood or marriage to half the people in the county! She was also very helpful in advising us who might not pay so promptly, and that we would be wise to get a retainer from them before doing too much work!

I enjoyed a great friendship with Joan; she taught me a lot about country people. When I retired, after David died, I wanted to return to Lindsay because I had always enjoyed the summers and activities there. I sold the house we had bought in the retirement community on Pigeon Lake and bought a condominium within walking distance of Joan's home. She was still working at our old office, but when she took her morning walk, she would drop in to see me. She would catch me up on the office news, and bring me produce from the garden she and her husband maintained.

One of the things I did with Joan during my retirement was to enter the Heart and Stroke Car Rally. I owned a little Honda Civic, which was quite handy for touring around, and for going out to lunch with my friends at local resorts around the lake. I became an active member of The Heart and Stroke Foundation after my bypass surgery. I wanted to give confidence to people that they could survive such an experience and still have a relatively full life afterward.

Every year our local Heart and Stroke chapter ran a Road Rally, which involved a tour of the countryside. We had to visit certain checkpoints indicated on the map, and then do whatever was required at those checkpoints. Joan knew the countryside like the back of her hand; I had a real ringer in asking her to be my co-pilot in these rallies! The first year, we came third; the second year, second—finally, in June 1992, we won!

A BIG CASE

The Federal Government had appointed David as the Senior Crown Counsel for the Pineridge region, because he had distinguished himself as an exceptional litigation counsel. When drug offences became a big problem in our vicinity, David became very busy with the RCMP (Royal Canadian Mounted Police) drug squad. The Mounted Police stations we worked with covered quite a large area—as far south as Oshawa, Brechin on Lake Simcoe, Beaverton, and Coboconk. We enjoyed a great relationship with the Mounties we worked with. We were so busy in the office that we did not have the time to prepare them for the cross-examination they would have from the Defence counsel at a trial, so we used to invite them for barbeques at the farm, after work. After the meal, we would go over the details of what to expect when being cross-examined.

I really admired the Mounties; they were very dedicated men. Many, who had been assigned to lengthy periods of undercover work, had lost their homes and families. They were lonely men, so we tried to fill some of that void when they were working with us. I remember the girls at the senior high school, which was located across from our office, would *go crazy* when they saw the Mounties, dressed in their *pinks*, coming and going from our building.

One story I must tell is when one of them kept bragging that he was the best rider in the troupe at the Regina training centre. Mounties had to undergo horseback riding as part of their initial training. Well, this fellow was looking forward to getting out to our farm so he could ride one of our horses. We brought out David's horse and led him up to the mounting block. This fellow rushed at the horse from the rear, vaulted over his croup, and hit the saddle! Well, the horse was not used to being mounted that way and before the Mountie knew what was happening, he was flying through the air!

Unfortunately, the Mountie suffered a dislocated shoulder in the fall and David had to take him to the hospital. The Emergency department was on guard because some tourists in the region had been abusing their OHIP numbers by trying to get benefits without proper identification. When David attempted to pass the Mountie off as his nephew, the Emergency receptionist gave him quite a gruelling about identifying himself, and proving that he was entitled to OHIP! This was a very sticky situation because the Mountie had been working *undercover* for quite some time and had absolutely no personal identification on him. Also, because he had been working on the drug importing operation, he could not identify himself, especially since he was a key witness in a trial that involved the importation of large quantities of hashish. It was all very embarrassing—eventually he had to blow his cover to get his dislocated shoulder treated. That episode put a ringer in our trial.

David was the Crown prosecutor on this case. It was one of the biggest drug importing trials that Canada had seen, to date. An importing ring discovered that they were being recognized at Malton Airport—now known as Pearson Airport—they decided to move their operation to an airport where they would not be so easily identified. They picked Oshawa, which was in our Pineridge district, so we had the burden of carrying that trial. The operation was huge, well financed, and oh so clever! The Mounties knew who the underdogs (mules) in the ring were, but they had never been able to identify the main brains behind the operation. This was what we were working on.

The drugs were imported in window and door frames that had been hollowed out and filled with hashish from India. Upon arrival, the hashish was removed from the frames and then transported to the northern part of Haliburton for distribution. We were trying to trace the movements of this operation.

In the course of this trial my son, Cam, who was going to Fenelon Falls High School, noticed there was a black car following the school bus every day when he went to school. When he got off the school bus, when he came home, that same black car was there. I too had noticed a black car parked down at the bottom of the hill, when I was out riding. It was apparent that someone was observing our farm. David reported this to the RCMP officer that was in charge of the case we were working on.

"Oh no, it's us!" he exclaimed. "We knew that your family was being threatened by this ring; you were getting too close to the top in the investigation, and you had evidence of some of the top guns involved. These people were threatening to knock off some of your family to try to stop further investigation." Then he added: "We gotta do a better job of looking after your boys."

Bruce was still at Lakefield College, so the RCMP put a Mountie on him, too. Bruce said he felt disadvantaged because *Randy Andy*, Prince Andrew, was studying at Lakefield at that time, and he had two Mounties looking after him!

I was quite involved in the trials, as well. One trial involved the distribution of marijuana, by some young counsellors in a wealthy Jewish summer camp to the north of us. A trio of experienced counsel from Toronto were defending the young camp counsellors that had been charged with distribution. We definitely had a strong defence team to contend with. One of the Defence lawyers was Norman Born, who was very famous at that time, and Austin Cooper, another high-ranking counsel on the team. However, we had quite a display of exhibits that the Mounties had identified, all very carefully labelled as to where they were found, and how they were handled.

I was given the opportunity to be *junior counsel* to David. One of the big guns from Toronto asked the Bench to remove the instructing officer from the prosecution counsel table. They were objecting that the officer was having some input into evidence that was not being sworn in, in the witness box. David made a frantic call to the office, requesting that I "please" come and help keep the evidence organized for him. I had done a lot of quick court appearances when doing agency work for Toronto firms, so I kept my gown and a pair of black patent pumps in my office, ready to take a quick trip to the courthouse whenever called upon. It sure was exciting, even as harassing as it was going up against those *big guns*! We were over extended, but we got through it. We obtained a number of convictions, which unfortunately involved some children of several very prominent Jewish families from Toronto. In the end, those well-known Toronto criminal defence lawyers, despite how good they were, lost! Unfortunately, the top guys in the drug ring were not on trial in our courtroom—they were dealt with in the *Indian Importing Trial*, which was held in Toronto. We had just prosecuted the young camp counsellors *sharing their marijuana*, which was not as serious a charge.

I never really knew if they ever arrested, or convicted the actual "head guy" of the drug ring. I do not believe that the Mounties realized the stringency of the Rules of Evidence that they had to go through in order to prove their case. They were sure that they had gathered enough to prove the conviction of the accused. Unfortunately, much of that evidence did not pass the scrutiny of the Rules of Evidence established for our courts. We have precise rules of evidence and sometimes, even when you are sure you have identified the guilty party, you have to have every *jot-and-tiddle* and trace on the evidence. On one case, a Mountie had been tired after his shift; he had seized some evidence and locked it in the trunk of his car overnight, instead of taking it down to the police safe for lock up and identification. At the trial that evidence was denied because it had been kept in the trunk of his car overnight—he could not prove he had control over it for the entire time!

Once again, I became faced with prejudicial treatment—the Federal Government denied me a "junior counsel fee" for the hours I had spent keeping track of the evidence for my husband at that trial. They figured I had been helping David all along, and that I knew the case, so I was not entitled to any additional compensation. This rankled me! It also reminded me of another case I had worked on. A will had been unclear as to the distribution amongst the deceased sons of the testator (person whose will it is) and so the judge wondered if the widows of those sons should have their share—if so that should be argued, and the widows should be represented. I had been helping David with the case. Will interpretations were my idea of real fun—I enjoyed the interpretation of the language, and the intention of the testator, so I volunteered to represent the widows. The trial was adjourned until I did some paperwork on the widows' interests and the case law that would support the widows having a share and an interest. At the end of that trial, I was denied a counsel fee. I engaged a Toronto lawyer to go to the Taxing Officer at Osgoode Hall, to have the fee re-examined, and to get a ruling on the award of said fee, and the amount. The Taxing Officer reviewed my application, but I was still denied. Another example of the impediments a woman trying to make her way in my time had to face!

LEAVING THE FARM—1975

The second time David was approached to take a position on the Bench we decided to take the offer. The lure of a pension was the coin that won the decision. We had made absolutely no preparation for our retirement income, operating as though we would always be practicing law. We never thought we would slow down, or have health problems that would make it impossible to keep up the tempo that we had been living at. It was becoming apparent that our pace of life was getting too much for David. We knew our local judge had an easy life. He would hear one motion to the Court in the morning and then go home for lunch and have a nice snooze!

Well, were we in for a shock—it was not like that in Windsor, where David was sent. It was the policy of the government of the day, not to appoint a judge where he had practiced. There were only three judges in Windsor. One of them, Judge Bruce J. S. Macdonald, had been in a motor accident and was not recovering as quickly as expected. He had been a former military officer, and a Prosecutor at the Nuremburg Trials. He was also getting on in years, and with the accident and his failing health, he was not able to take his share of the load of backlogged cases that the Windsor court had acquired.

However, David's first posting was actually in Sarnia. I stayed on at the farm so that Cam could finish his Grade 13. Cam was president of the student council and he was striving for good marks so he could get into U of T. It was a heavy year for him. Quite frankly, I did not want to move in that year—I guess I had not realized how tough it was going to be to sell the farm and all the animals that we had collected.

We had tried to start a Golden Retriever kennel when we had the opportunity to buy a handsome, British-import male Golden. Laird was striking, a stunning specimen, so we bought him a bitch for his third birthday. He became an *unplanned father*, knowing sooner than we did when the little bitch came into her first heat! We had left her in a stall in the stable and he had dug a trench that you could break a leg in, to get into that stall! She was pregnant too young, but the pair was very fruitful, producing 20 pups in two litters! I was trying to see that the puppies went to good homes—scrutinizing the prospective purchasers, asking if they were prepared to take long walks with the puppies, or if they had a large property, because those little golden puppies, which looked like teddy bears as babies, were not going to be that size for very long. Their father weighed around 80 pounds!

Laird ran about five miles on his own every day; besides running with us when we rode out on the horses. I think he bred every bitch within five miles of our property. Some of our neighbours were quite appreciative, though; we got a phone call from one of them one night saying: "Don't worry, your male retriever is down here, but we got a bitch in heat; will you leave him to visit with her for a couple more days?" Apparently his pups were very well known and well accepted in the neighbourhood.

Then there were all the horses to consider. Cam had boarded some friends' horses and we still had our Austrian riding master's horses as well. We advised Cam that he should give up boarding horses because his school year was so heavy, but he said, "Heck, I've only got 12 horses to look after before school; I go to school with kids that have 30 or 40 cows to milk before they catch the school bus—they think I have a soft job."

We tried to reduce the stable, but it was difficult. We had some foals that we had raised and two of the fillies were doing well at the local horse shows. I had a terrible time making sure those fillies went to good homes. We decided to keep the dapple-gray mare we had bought for Cam. She had been well trained as a hunter/jumper and she was qualified as a foundation brood mare with the Hunter Improvement Society. Cam had even ridden her *to the hounds* one day, with the Toronto and North York Hunt Club. Cam received a verbal commendation from Clifford Sifton, the Master of the Hunt, for the fine ride he had that day.

There is a background to that story of Cam being invited to join the hunt—when I was a junior member of the Eglinton Hunt Club, I had a crush on Clifford Sifton. The Sifton family were the founders of the Winnipeg Free Press. I thought Clifford was more careful and mindful of his horses than most of the other young *swains* that competed in the Saturday afternoon jumping classes. He was not a show-off like those who were just using the horses as vehicles to demonstrate how daring they could be when taking the jumps. So I am not sure if the crush I had was actually on Clifford, or on the way he handled his horses. Of course he would not have known me from a hole in the wall—I did not have the right pedigree, and my father probably did not deal with the right stock brokers in order to have any social engagements with Clifford's family.

However, much to my surprise, years later when the Eglinton Hunt Club started looking for a property outside of Toronto; the Spensley's, from that area, (I had ridden with Ted Spensley at the Hunt Club) put me in touch with Clifford Sifton who was in charge of the search for properties. I corresponded with Clifford, suggesting some available land in our region. They had already relocated once to Bayview, when the property on Avenue Road north had been expropriated by the Department of National Defence for an Air Force training and medical research site.

E.P Taylor had his breeding stable in Bayview, too. I have a picture of my dad and me riding by his place. Bayview started to be built up with country estates of wealthy people from Toronto, so the Club started looking for a location farther away from the suburban traffic.

Cam, on our Dapple Gray

We knew we definitely had a splendid horse for the hunt in the Gray, and we got ambitious about Cam's excellence in riding too—he had won all the local trophies, both junior and senior. We took Cam to the stable of one of the Elder boys who had been prominent in show jumping. As a member of the Hunt Club, I remember them learning to jump. The Elder's stable was just west of Toronto and they trained Olympic and competitive riders, so we thought Cam and the gray mare would do well at that level of training and competition.

When we arrived, we saw the rigorous training Cam would have to go through and we were told he would also have to have a second-string horse, in case the gray mare was injured before a competition. David and I decided the whole thing was too rich for our blood; and, that it could also impede Cam's educational opportunities.

However, with that brief exposure to these competitive riders, and with my correspondence with Clifford Sifton, Clifford, who was the joint "Master of the Hunt" of the Toronto and North York Hunt, invited Cam to ride to the hounds with him when the clubs had a joint meet. Cam rode his mare behind Clifford at the hunt.

Clifford Sifton wanted to buy the mare, not just because she was a good hunter, but also because a dapple-gray would look first-class on a hunt scene with a rider in hunting "pink," the traditional red jacket of the Hunt. We continued to keep in touch as to prospective locations, and his interest in Cam's gray mare. Clifford also commended Cam on his ride, saying that he did a splendid job of "keeping in his pocket!"

~

Some of the happiest years of my life were spent on the farm. If truth be told here, I must tell you that I was devastated to have to leave my home and live in an *empty nest* that needed work. I had waited so long to have a horse of my own and our move to the farm had provided me with that life-long dream. A farm like David and I had would have been my father's dream as well—he had always contemplated retiring on a small acreage. Father had made an offer on a ten acre property on Steeles Avenue, just east of Yonge Street, but Mother thought it was too far from all her favourite shopping spots. Unfortunately, his offer was not accepted and because of the way my mother felt about living in the country, he did not *up the ante*. I wished he had—I think I was as devastated for him as he seemed to be for himself—he and I had always dreamed of having horses one day. My mother often reminded me, though, that I would not be able to pal around with my father forever, and he could not count on having me by his side indefinitely either.

I was feeling terrible about having to move away from my friends, too. I had enjoyed the Lindsay scene: Art Guild, theatres, my neighbours, and the many good clients we had friendships with during our time there. I was happy. On the other hand, I felt that David needed the recognition of advancement, and an appointment to the Bench is the height of a lawyer's career. It is the highest position that a successful and dedicated lawyer can have in deference to his contribution to the Bar. I felt David had earned and deserved that recognition. Even so, I will never forget how terrible I felt when I loaded the gray mare into a horse van with some racehorses, and then had to load my little Quarter Horse mare that I had bought as a *green-broke* three year old. Under Joe's tutelage, she had come along beautifully in elementary dressage and green jumper classes. I stood at the top of the ramp and I do not think I ever felt worse as I gazed over the farm we were leaving.

Eventually, we found a buyer for the farm, Mr. Nesbitt. He was an interesting oddball of a person. He had made his fortune as a mining prospector. Nesbitt had some fascinating ideas, gleaned from his experiences of living in the north. He thought he could extend the growing period for edible crops by starting the crops early, under pyramids. He carried on these experiments in our dressage ring.

On the other hand, his wife's ideas of interior decorating appalled me. The house *had* beautiful hardwood floors, but she covered them with red broadloom! I had to swallow my disappointment. I had put beautiful wallpaper in the big country kitchen—scenes from the hunt! She painted over it!

Emmy, our goat saved me the trouble of finding her a home because she walked back to the farm where we had bought her. She had been in the habit of doing that anyway, every spring, to be with her favourite *billy* when she got *in the mood*! When she was finished her *business*, her former owner would phone us to fetch her. She presented us with twins almost every Easter—she and that old, stinky billy goat were very productive! At the time of the farm sale we had a set of twin goats, but they were not difficult to find homes for because a lot of *horsy* people wanted goats as companions for their horses.

Emmy had reminded me of an old high school memory of a goat I had met at the livery stable where I had volunteered to clean stables and look after sick horses on my Saturdays. One day, when I was bending over, pumping water into the horse trough with the old fashioned pump handle, that goat nailed me in the rear-end. I fell, head first, into the water trough!

~

Another matter that I had to deal with in Lindsay was the winding up of our lifetime's work at the law firm. Now that David was a judge, he had to give up all commercial interests in the firm. As his wife, I could not have any financial interests in the firm either. We sold the business to our junior partners, taking back some long-term mortgages—we gave them very favourable terms to purchase the firm and the building. Those boys got rapid advancement when David and I left town! I closed out our files, passed them on to the juniors and then introduced the clients to the new owners of the firm. This was another difficult time for me—I had helped to build that firm, working side by side with David. A lot of my labour had been pro bono—because of the times—because I was a woman! I knew David deserved this posting; but, I had also helped him to get where he was. As pleased as I was for him, it was not easy for me to leave everything behind!

SARNIA AND WINDSOR

David

Cameron, David, Thelma, Bruce

A Windsor Star Press photo outside of Kingsville's Anglican Church of Rector Jim Stephenson confessing to Judge David Thomson his problem of giving up smoking; upon which Judge Thomson put a fatherly hand on Jim's shoulder and said: "Pray my son, Pray!" This was witnessed by a visiting American Archbishop, who remarked on Jim's unusual congregation!

DAVID'S ACCEPTANCE SPEECH

My brother judges, my wife, our boys, hounored guests, members of the Bar of Lambton County, members of the Bar of Victoria-Haliburton County, my friends from Lindsay, ladies and gentlemen...

I do sincerely thank Judge Mackenzie and Judge MacDonald for their kind words and advice, Mrs. Randolph for her kind words of welcome, Mr. Hill for his words of wisdom, and Mr. Lang for his promise to assist and his words of welcome.

At a time such as this, there is a tendency to reminisce. I well remember the day of my admission to the Bar, as I am sure all lawyers remember entering the profession of law and donning our first gowns. The immediate reaction was that at least there were no more exams, the party that night, the knowledge that we could now go out and earn our living and pay back all those debts which had accumulated while attending college and law school. But at the same time, there was a deep realization in myself that I had entered the profession of law, the pro-

fession of the last liberal art. My province was now to aid in the administration of justice, to assist the oppressed, to uphold the weak, to control against the strong, to defend the right to expose the wrong and particularly to find out deceit and to expose it in all its forms. I, like you, have found in my practice of law that law is a profession of the highest standards of public service, a profession one can practice with honour and with reward, a profession one can lead with honour and dignity and with respect of others.

I found as time went by that I have developed a high opinion of other lawyers, with all their faults, they stack up well with every other profession. They are better to work with, better to play with, better to fight with, and not necessarily the least—the better to party with.

Today is the time of steady legalization of human activities, the law now penetrates every nook and cranny of life. Because of this, the law must grow and change with every new development of society and the community.

Long ago the restrictiveness of the common law had to give way to that great mistress of the law, the law of equality, the law of change and conscience. Equality still to this day gives us an opportunity to interpret with changing times. I feel it is our duty to use it, not to let it become a restrictive law, but within the framework of it to interpret it in its broadest form to fit the changing concepts of today's lifestyle.

There is a phrase that is being used a lot today, a phrase that I don't like and it is "law and order." Its connotation is that there are two things, 1) law and 2) order. I feel if we interpret the law as to changing needs and develop law so that it will fill the community needs, then an orderly society must of necessity follow.

I realize that there are commissions appointed to advise on these changes but I submit that within the framework of the Bar and Bench, these changes can be made—let us all strive to make these interpretative changes.

Today I leave behind my silks, the rough and tumble of practice I so dearly love, but I accept this new mantle that has been placed upon me with a deep sense of responsibility, humility, and excitement. I can only say to you that I will do my best to fulfill this office, I can do no more.

I can recall once as a young lawyer sitting in the Court of Appeal and hearing an extremely forceful lawyer continue a line of argument that the Court had admonished him to discontinue. After three admonishments on the particular point, he continued—he was

Dave Thomson County Judge

Judge D. M. Thomson

Justice Minister Otto Lang today announced the appointment of David M. Thomson Q.C. of the town of Lindsay as judge of the County Court for the County of Lambton. Judge Thomson will succeed Judge R. A. Carscallen, who retired Dec. 31, 1973.

D. M. Thomson, 52, was admitted to the bar in 1948 and was created a Queen's Counsel in 1961. He was a member of the law firm of Thomson, Logan, Thomson and Glass of Lindsay.

then advised by one member of the Court that he was losing patience. The reply by counsel was, "My Lord, patience is what you are paid for." As I start my duties, I ask for the reverse. I ask the Bar for their patience, but if you feel that I am wrong, don't be too patient, don't hesitate to appeal, then all of us may learn something.

I want to thank my partners, my staff, and my friends of the Bar in Lindsay; and my friends from Lindsay for coming this distance. I know I shall miss their many years of friendship and loyalty. It has been said, and you may have heard this before, that behind every successful man there is a disbelieving mother-in-law. However, what success I have attained has been because of the understanding and assistance especially from my wife who during our married years has been the mother of our boys and my partner in the practice of law— also assistance from my partners and my staff – no words that I can use can express the deepness of this feeling of gratitude, accept my thanks.

I am looking forward now to a new life, new friends, a new community, a new challenge. I hope to reach your expectations. Your Honours, members of the Bar, ladies and gentlemen, I thank you.

~

The boys did not move to Sarnia with us. Bruce was still at Lakefield College and Cameron was in his first year at U of T. I, on the other hand had no choice—I will admit that I had a good life—David did his best to make me happy, but it was still a very difficult time for me—one I would like to forget.

Actually, I did not spend much time in Sarnia, due to the fact that I was trying to settle matters in Lindsay. I found a neat little efficiency apartment for us. It was the ideal location on Point Edward Peninsula, with a golf course on one side and the courthouse on the other. David could walk to work. Sarnia's courthouse was quite beautiful. It had been Prime Minister Diefenbaker's dream of the ideal courthouse. The security for judges was much better there than in any of the other courthouses we had been in. There was a private elevator to the judge's chambers, because when dealing with desperate criminals, there was usually a group of their friends and family members close by—there was always the concern that they may not be there with the best of intentions.

When I visited David, I spent most of my time house hunting. I worked with all of the real estate agents in the area, so as not to show any preferential treatment. When you are married to a judge you have to be very careful not to give the impression you are favouring anyone in particular. David was extremely conscientious about that. We had had good interaction with all of the lawyers in Lindsay. I knew some of the lawyers in Sarnia and Windsor, too—some of whom were former classmates of mine; but David discouraged me from socializing with them. His point was that he could not be seen to have special friendships with any one member of the Bar. Because of my husband's circumspection, it ended up being a very lonely time of life for me.

I did find an ideal little Cape-Cod cottage, just outside of town, at Forest. It had about ten acres and a small barn in which we could keep a pair of horses. I tried to persuade the owners to sell; the woman was on the verge of retirement and I think she could have been tempted with enough money. However, we began to notice that David's health was being jeopardized by the fumes from the petrochemical industry in Sarnia, so we were hesitant to purchase anything in that area.

David went to London to confer with allergists about the problems he was having. The allergist said, "Don't ever go back to Sarnia; you are allergic to the petrochemical fumes." When I returned to collect his clothes from the apartment, his camelhair jacket reeked of petrochemicals. That made it even clearer to me that he could not live there.

> **Judges exchange benches**
>
> SARNIA — Judge David Thomson's nose and Sarnia's chemical valley are not compatible.
>
> The 55-year-old judge has a doctor's certificate saying he is allergic to the distinctive odor of the city's petrochemical industries.
>
> So after two months of trying to make a go of it, Judge Thomson is looking for greener and cleaner pastures.
>
> For the next couple of weeks he will be working in Windsor courts while Windsor Judge Michael Meehan presides in Sarnia court.
>
> Chief Judge W. E. C. Colter will try to arrange other temporary exchanges until a permanent move can be made. Since such moves are approved by the federal justice minister, it is not likely it will be made until after the July 8 federal election.
>
> Judge Colter has been sending replacements to Sarnia from London and Goderich.
>
> Judge Thomson, appointed to the Bench in February, had a law practice in Lindsay.

Fortunately for us, a judge in Windsor was unhappy and in 1975, he offered to switch benches with David. The atmosphere in Windsor did not seem to bother him on the days when the wind was blowing the right way. On other days, when the wind blew the pollution from the Edison plant in Detroit up our way, David had some problems breathing, but not as drastic as had been in Sarnia.

I was attracted to the change of scene, especially Windsor's university. I was looking forward to either taking up a part-time appointment at the university law school, or taking some courses myself. I actually applied for an appointment as a part-time lecturer. Most of the professors there had never practiced law and they were taking courses over at Ann Arbour, Michigan. One of our causes was to try to keep Canadian law this side of the border because the area was strongly influenced by its proximity to the United States.

I received a letter from the university, with an offer of a lecturing position in "Contracts 101." After all the different aspects of law I had been through, "Contracts 101" sounded pretty dull. The man who was teaching "Wills and Estates," and "Estate Planning," a field in which I had acquired extensive expertise, had divorced his wife—he did not want to earn enough to have to pay her support, so he had taken the part-time lectureship. I turned the "Contracts 101" offer down.

However, while in Windsor I did take some interesting and useful courses, Media and Local History. Windsor was home to the first university to have its own television station. I learned the background of running a Station, and the discernment of different forms of advertising—making intelligent choices, and not being swayed by advertising hype.

~

We had managed to keep two of our riding horses, the gray mare and my little Quarter Horse; but the Quarter Horse had not done well. She had contracted *shipping fever* during her trip in the transport with the racehorses. I was having a difficult time finding a nice pasture in the Windsor area, like the one I had found in Forest. The land around Windsor was intensively cultivated in soybeans and corn, and the water was sulphurous.

I finally found a place, 15 miles from the house we bought on the shore of Lake Erie. It had the pasture land the horses needed. The greatest downfall was that I had to drive on a narrow, two-lane road with six foot ditches on either side, in order to exercise the horses. David did not have time to ride anymore, so I went mostly on my own. He was busy learning the new job, gaining friendships, bonding with the other two judges, and working late over the cases he was hearing. To compensate, I would ride one horse after the other. One day I received a tongue-lashing from the farmer who boarded them. My mare had shied at a bird that had flown out of a bush and she had stepped on two or three of his precious soybeans. He advised me of the market price of soybeans, and of the extent of the damage I had done—a most embarrassing moment for me. But it really was not my mare's fault either—farmers in the area used to have shotguns firing at automatic intervals in order to scare the crows away from the crops—those shotguns scared my little mare too!

The house we bought was the one owned by the judge David replaced—it was a disaster! The judge and his wife had split up, so he was batching it in the house. We had no idea that the house had been flooded and that the carpet was mouldy underneath, until I developed a terrible allergy to mould and mildew. We began to find traces of it on the walls behind the furniture and in the bathrooms. There was nice tiling in the bathrooms, but the grouting was full of mould. I fought valiantly to clean it up, but the allergy got me down and I found the only place I could get real relief, aside from the riding stable, was at the curling rink. I also took up golfing because there was one of the prettiest golf courses in Ontario, in Kingsville. Golf never really appealed to me; it just ruined a nice walk. It was not relaxing playing with competitive people whose only motivation was to reduce their handicap. I just wanted to get out of the house, in the fresh air.

CAM'S CANOE TRIP

Cam had done his thesis, at the U of T, on Sir Alexander Mackenzie's route to the West, when he was looking for a West Coast port to open up for the fur trade. Cam wanted to replicate Mackenzie's canoe trip, rather then jogging around Europe like so many of his friends did after graduation. During the summer of 1978, Cam and his elementary school friend, Rick Wood, who had just graduated with a degree in Kinesiology, prepared themselves for the trip. Rick was the perfect companion choice. He put Cam through rigorous fitness training, which I heard included 100 sit-ups every morning before breakfast! They took the train to Rocky Mountain House in British Columbia, and picked up a specially reinforced Kevlar canoe that had been made for them by Woodstream.

The boys struck out from Rocky Mountain House in June. Unfortunately, the canoe dumped just below a falls in the Saskatchewan River, when water surged over a dam at a power plant. They lost a lot of their equipment, including Cam's tape recorder that he had used to record interviews along the way. He also lost the one woollen jacket he had, and goodness knows what else; but it was a good lesson for them to learn—they would now definitely remember to lash everything down in their canoe!

They had signed a contract with CBC radio to call in a report of their experiences to the Don Herron's CBC morning show at every town where there was a CBC station. When I was out trying to learn how to play golf, I would carry a little transistor radio with me so I could follow Cam's progress. I remember the day I heard about the canoe tipping—I tried to reassure myself that my son was still alive—no doubt my golfing did not improve one bit that day!

~

I thought about setting up a branch office in Kingsville, as I had previously done in Fenelon Falls. A former classmate was practicing law in Windsor, so I spoke to them about the idea. My intention was to have a specialty practice restricted to my area of expertise in wills, trusts, and estates. The Windsor office would send one of their juniors to the branch office in Kingsville, to assist and learn from me—they would handle all the other areas of practice.

This was a fine line for me to cross, though, because there was the feared impression from some Bar members, whose practices included a lot of estate work, that I was going to move in on their territory and take business away from them—that would be unethical. I had taken the Ethic's course at U of T Law School—I was very knowledgeable and conscientious about ethics and I had no intention of ever appearing before my husband's court for such a violation! I was only going to give advice on wills and estates; it was my intention that any appearances before a Windsor court would be in the hands of the junior. This project never materialized because of all the controversy.

I actually realized how difficult it was going to be when I went to the first Bar dinner that David attended in Windsor. The current president of the local law association informed my husband they did not bring wives to such events! My husband proceeded to inform him that I was fully qualified to be there! I quickly sought out the treasurer and paid my dues as an accredited member of the local law association. That encounter made me realize how difficult some senior members of the Bar were going to make it for me—I felt that I had had enough of these battles. On the whole, lawyers in Windsor were fairly good comrades—the prejudices seemed to lie with a small number of the older members of the Bar who were still not too accepting of women who practiced law. Maybe they gave me such resistance because they were afraid I would use my position as the judge's wife to swing more business from their office to the one that I was going to be associated with—foolish thinking on their part—David and I would never warrant such distrust.

~

David had a heart attack on Valentine's Day, February 14, 1977, two years after we moved to Windsor. He was sent to London, Ontario for bypass surgery. I always felt that he returned to work much too soon. He was advised to work half days, but David was so conscientious about the expense of having a jury earning their daily fee that he would not dismiss them early on his account.

The trial he had taken on was an incredibly heavy one—the theft of auto parts from Detroit factories, and the smuggling of those parts across the bridge and into Windsor for re-sale on the black market. There was quite a ring doing this, and there were Customs agents who were paid off to *wink* when they went by. The evidence was gathered by RCMP officers because it involved a cross-border offence. The RCMP gathered the evidence with video recordings of these frequent passages of trucks that were thought to contain the smuggled goods, and of the boarder guards who winked and nodded when they went by.

This trial also presented the first *video evidence* ever accepted in a Canadian court, and it fell to David to make that onerous decision of admissibility, whether to accept or reject this kind of evidence. Finally he made a ruling, with restrictions, as to the conditions of gathering such evidence—"first and best hand" was to mean first-hand observations of an event. David ordered that the Mountie who had held the video camera to record the evidence of the pay-off of a boarder security guard, also swear that he was there at the time and saw with his own eyes what he had recorded, before it could be entered into evidence. David was certainly put through the ringer about his decision—there were several judges who did not agree with him. At the ensuing judges' annual meeting he was called upon to present a paper defending his decision. As a result of taking on this

Judge continues recovery

County Court Judge David Thomson is in satisfactory condition at Hotel Dieu where he is recovering from a heart attack he suffered Feb. 14.

His wife, Thelma, said today that the judge is doing well but no date has been set for him to be released or return to the bench.

Senior Judge Carl Zalev said today that Judge Thomson was complaining of chest pains that day and he convinced the 56-year-old judge to go to the hospital.

It was at the hospital while getting a checkup, that Judge Thomson suffered the attack.

His illness, plus the fact that Judge Bruce J.S. Macdonald is now classified as a supernumerary judge (semi-retired) as well as working on the Malden inquiry, have left the county court level work to be divided between three judges, said Judge Zalev.

He said the backlog of criminal jury trials is getting longer, with the number of cases being committed to trial from provincial court, usually being greater than the number of jury trials resolved in a week's time.

The idea of a supernumerary judge, he explained, is to lighten the workload for Judge Macdonald, and allow a new judge to get experience and help cleanup any backlogs.

Judge Macdonald has been a supernumerary judge since Sept. 1, and the federal government has known of his intentions since last July, said Judge Zalev, as he awaits a new judge to be appointed to fill out his staff.

To help ease the workload, said Judge Zalev, two county court judges, one from Sarnia and another from Toronto, will hear cases here this month. One will be here for a two-week period and the other for one week.

onerous trial, David's health continued to fail and he had another heart attack.

David was advised by the cardiologist to take early retirement. He was earning a yearly salary of $80,000 and the other judges suggested: "Don't submit your resignation yet; wait 'til we get it up to $100,000." This was something that was in the works. David's retirement income would be based on the number of days he had worked on the bench, calculated at the rate of pay he had been receiving at the time of retirement. This calculation is in the *Judges Act*. David waited until the pay raise and then his cardiologist submitted a letter regarding the state of David's health, directly to the chief judge. Chief Judge Coulter wrote him back: "I'd rather have a friend in a retired judge, than a memory of one." This was in the fall of 1979.

In reality, David was only a judge for five years, but those five years took a heavy toll on him because of his work load. He oversaw most of the jury trials until another judge was appointed in the place of the one who had retired. Once again, I found myself uprooted from my home—not that I had ever really felt at home in Windsor. We had a difficult time selling that house and ended up completely renovating it to make it more attractive. The renovations took an entire year— we were lucky to get our money out of the sale. Chrysler had just filed for bankruptcy, so the area was financially depressed.

~

We decided to move back to the Kawartha Lakes region. Bruce Glass had become the international president of the Kinsmen Club and he was on an extended tour of their clubs. He let us stay in his home while we searched for our own. Our decision not to settle right in the town of Lindsay was brought about because so many of our old clients found their way to our door to ask when we were coming back to work. Many of them were even asking me if I would review the wills I had made for them. We realized we could not do that to the juniors to whom we had sold our practice. We had sold on the understanding that we would never reappear in competition with them. We decided to search out some of the retirement properties in the surrounding Lake District. There were numerous attractive areas where people had renovated their summer cottages, winterizing them for retirement. We bought a home in Victoria Place, just outside of Bobcaygeon, where there were good boat docks and a nice sandy beach.

MOTHER'S PASSING

Before the car accident, which had taken the life of my mother's sister, Mother had had a tumour in her bowel removed. The doctor and I conferred and decided not to tell her that it was malignant—she was a fussy *worry-wart* type and we thought she would recover better if she did not know. I arranged for her to stay at the farm during her recovery. Fortunately, there was a ground floor bathroom; Mother could not do stairs. I put a hospital bed in our living room to make it easier to tend to her needs.

The living room of the farm house had big windows overlooking the wooded area. Mother could hear the coyotes and wolves howling in the woods at night and she thought we were in the middle of the wilderness! I suggested that if she looked out the windows, she could see the bright lights of the hamlet of Cameron. She was just not comfortable in a country setting—she was a city girl.

When her health improved enough, we would take her out to dinner to the "Beehive," a nice golf and country club just outside of Bobcaygeon. It had just the right style of service for her, but every time we drove there a black bear would amble across the road ahead of us, heading for the town dump across the road. This confirmed to Mother that we were indeed living in some terrible, godforsaken hinterland!

Mother had given my boys the game *Twister* which involved contortions of the body. Since she was occupying our living room we could not entertain privately. A young lady that had a crush on Cam, and her family, came by for a visit one day and the boys got this game out. Obviously, my mother had no idea what *Twister* entailed! After listening to the kids giggling and carrying on over this game, and seeing this girl who was giddy over Cam—when this family left mother said: "Oh I can't stand your drunken parties around here!" Mother could be so naïve that way!

I guess, in some ways, my mother and I just totally misunderstood each other. I had been trying to create a quiet and circumspect atmosphere for her convalescence, and then, one day when I was not home she phoned a cab/limousine company to pick her up and return her to Toronto.

By this time Mother had given up the house at 17 Elderwood; it had become quite rundown. It needed rewiring, a new furnace, and there was plaster breaking off the walls and ceilings. She found an apartment on Avenue Road, next to the music library. I was hoping my mother would renew her interest in music, but she did not like the noise of the Avenue Road traffic. Plus, a member of Diefenbaker's cabinet was living in the neighbourhood with Gerta Munsinger, with whom he was having a scandalous affair. Mother said she could see him walking his dogs in Peter Pan Park across the road from her—she was also not happy about dogs being in the park where she liked to walk! She felt the neighbourhood had really deteriorated.

Mother passed away in 1979. David was recovering from his bypass surgery and we were in Arizona at the time. I took a red-eye flight back to Canada, to make the funeral arrangements. Upon her passing we had access to some capital to reinvest for our retirement income. This was another factor that helped David to accept the early retirement his doctor had ordered.

Letter from Cam to Thelma after passing of her mother—

Dear Mother:

I have no idea when this letter will reach you. My position is such that I am afraid I have been no help to you over the period of your mother's death. However I want you to know that my heart is with you through this ordeal you must be facing with her death and Dad's illness.

Perhaps my relationship with Nana was not as close as most grandparent-grandchild ones. Yet I still feel her death very keenly.

I know you are a strong person and will be able to bear up to the situation, I only hope this note will be of some small help in knowing you have all my sympathy and love. Love, Cam

ARIZONA—1980

David's sister, Grace; David and Thelma

During this period David was extremely anxious about his sister Grace who was wintering in Arizona. Grace had been a high school teacher, teaching English and History, and her other interests in life were more directed to the arts. Financial matters were something she was not well equipped to handle. Grace had learned to enjoy the outdoor life with Rex, her second husband. When they decided to winter in Arizona, they had purchased five lots around a golf course, and she learned to golf. They put a pre-fabricated mobile home on one of them. David was worried because Grace had inherited a substantial amount of money when her first husband had passed on; he felt we should have a winter home near her in Arizona so that he could keep an eye on her interests.

While we searched the area, we rented a place near her home, but she took such control of our lives in her *schoolmarm* manner that we decided we would be better off not living too close. Finally, we found an area that appealed to us for its natural environment. We were not looking for a golf course; we just wanted a place to ride and walk, and to look after David's health. The fact that a golf course was close by was a bonus. The need of forming the habit of taking a daily walk had been impressed on David by his cardiologist.

House in Arizona

We built our little place in the desert, out in the foothills. It was in a river valley with more vegetation than the area to the south, and it was only about a one hour drive to David's sister. We built a very modest, simply constructed bungalow, base price of $69,000. It consisted of a cement pad poured on the desert floor, stuccoed over cement block walls, and a partly flat roof with red tile. It was a very attractive and comfortable three-bedroom home. We spent several winters there. I am sure David's life was extended because of it, for his health improved a great deal.

A bonus for me was that there was a livery stable close by. I had a good time there, and when they recognized that I was familiar with horses they let me take a horse out—of course not for free—the going rate was $25.00 per hour. It was a beautiful place to ride along the river valley and I was able to witness the sights of the flora and fauna (wildlife) in a way that I would not have been able to if I had been on foot. The horse scent did not bother the desert creatures, as mine would have, so I was able to get up close to some very interesting ones.

David and I took an interest in learning about that environment. We purchased a Sierra Club book to advise us of the dangers and the strange critters we might run into in the desert, and how to deal with them.

This turned out to be an exceedingly pleasant part of our lives. When early retirement had been thrust upon him, David had taken a course in photography at Haliburton School of Fine Arts. Photography gave him some motivation to take his daily walks. He became an exceptionally wonderful nature photographer.

TRIPS WITH DAVID

MEXICO...

After buying the farm, and when David undertook to learn to ride, we took a trip to Mexico to the famous international riding school at San Miguel "d'Allende," where people from all over the world went to hone their riding skills. David wanted to learn to ride properly, he did not want to ride like a cowboy. We actually attended this riding school two winters—1972 and 1973, in the month of March, which was a good time to get off the farm. March was usually windy and sleety, and so wet that we could not let the horses out for fear they would ruin the pasture.

This wonderful riding school was run by an American and was very efficiently administered. He had hired Mexican cavalry officers to teach us.

In order to rate our riding skills we had to sit on a barrel, which was hung on ropes that were attached to four posts. There was a saddle on the barrel. The instructors took great delight in putting every candidate for the riding school through the process of mounting this barrel, and then, they would pull on the ropes to see how well we could stick in a saddle—and that is how they decided which class we went into.

We stayed in a nice little hotel in the town of Saint Miguiel d'Allende, the weekend we arrived, in order to get used to the sun and the altitude. They advised that people from lower altitudes should not undertake strenuous physical activity when they first arrived in that thin air. With David's history of cardiac problems we were particularly conscious of this.

The riding school had a nice, family-style hostel. We associated and exchanged experiences with everybody at mealtime at one big long table. It was very interesting to learn why some of the couples were there, and some of the other different things they were doing. For example, there was an excellent art and language school in San Miguel—some of the couples would split up, one would be doing the riding, and the other would be studying art or sculpture, or the Spanish language at the school in town.

The Mexican cavalry officers pretended they did not understand English, so the Spanish I had taken at Laval came in handy when we were in Mexico. I understood the commands—like when they would asked us to canter—*"el gallopeala el a de"*—"to the left lead foot," or *"el a deroacha"*—"for the right lead foot."

It was good training! Before we rode in the ring we had a one hour lecture on horse and stable management, and horse ailments. Every horse owner should be aware of such things. Then we had two hours of riding and training in the ring, followed by a one hour ride into the countryside to loosen the horses up because they could get muscle-bound from riding in the ring. There was an old airstrip where we were allowed to gallop the horses, full out, if we wanted to—–like the Mounties did on their charge!

One day we were practicing the trot and David started to run out of breath. He rode into the middle of the ring to pause and catch his breath, and the instructor said: "You can't do that! You gotta do the other side too, or your horse will be muscle-bound!" Poor David was gasping for breath and he had to go around again the other way, so the horse would have a balanced exercise!

The horses were well trained, but if a horse did misbehave, one of those cavalry officers would take him in hand and teach him a lesson. I got to ride the sweetest little gelding; his name was "Canejo," Spanish for "rabbit," and he loved to jump! The instructors told me that in the previous session Canejo had had a heavier rider and he was just delighted to have a light rider this time. He did such a wonderful job of jumping, under me, that the instructor wanted me to compete with the advanced riders in the final competition. I knew that if I did, David would want to, too. He had not acquired the same horse sensibility that I had; I was a more experienced rider—I knew when the horse was tensing his shoulder muscles and about to do something different than he was being asked to do—David had not ridden enough to know those things! David and I were taking lessons together, so I stayed in the same class with him, even though I was a more experienced rider and could have moved up to another level. I did not mind, actually, because since I had become a mother I had begun to take more caution when riding—not taking the same risks as I had when I was younger. And, when I had ridden at the Hunt Club, it had been a different style of riding from what these international riders were teaching us. They said, "Hunt riders ride on the kidneys of the horse." That was true—the riding seat for the hunt is much farther back, whereas for jumping you need the forward seat. Actually, the riding school had a hard time finding a saddle to fit my small stature, so when I returned for the second year, I took my own little pony club saddle. That worked much better for me and the dear little horse I was riding!

BARBADOS...

David and I both loved sailing and we found out that our Scottish doctor, Duncan Colterjohn and his wife, Liz, loved sailing too. We all decided to take a winter vacation in the Caribbean Islands. We rented a sailboat, along with a captain and a young woman who crewed for him, and cooked the meals.

The contract for the sailing trip was for two weeks and we were to sail out from Antigua. We thought we had better go a few days earlier to get used to the sun before setting out on our sailing venture. We rented a little jeep and drove to the west side of Barbados, which was less touristy, and less expensive than the windward east side of the island. We had some out-door fun in the sun and swam in the ocean. We stayed at a little inn and just across the road was a goat pasture. The goats reminded me of our Emmy. We could see those goats from the veranda of our inn—I went over to try to make friends with them!

From there we took a ferry boat over to Antigua, where we set out on our sailing adventure. The young woman who made the meals did a wonderful job. One meal I remember, in particular, was a cucumber soup, very refreshing for the tropical temperatures.

We stopped at numerous little islands, which were all independent of each other, so we had to have a local official come aboard and give us a pass to sail in their waters. Some of these officials were very amusing. The captain said all they were really looking for was a drink before they signed their names to our pass!

The captain was very reluctant to let us *handle* his ship; he did not trust our sailing skills. However, when we were heading back to Antigua we got what is called "the kicking jennies." You could not go wrong sailing in a nice steady wind like that, so the Captain broke down and let us take over on the trip back. That was a wonderful adventure!

Dear Cam:
This is our means of locomotion here — and it works very well — no trouble with cold starts

Love:
Mom & Dad

VIA: AIR MAIL

To:
Mr Cam Thomson
Maple Brae Farm
RR #2,
Cameron
ONTARIO
CANADA.

Dear Cam:
I have made some personal friends here too. This family lives across the road at a beautiful abandoned Great House. I hope we don't have one of their kids for dinner. Love, Mom.

(Mr. Cam Thomson, Maple Brae Farm, R.R. #2, Cameron, ONTARIO CANADA.)

CAMPING DAYS...

After Cam got the job at Woodstream, he built a Kevlar canoe for his father and me. It was custom made, with nice comfortable seats and a live-box for fish. He put a lot of nice extras on our canoe.

Our engineer neighbour, Bill Dahl, taught us how to get it on top of the van that we had bought for our *golden days*. He worked out pulleys and ropes attached to the front and back bumpers, so that David and I could pull our Kevlar canoe up on top of our van. We had great fun taking this canoe places, and we also had some great adventures fishing with Cam and his friends.

THE MEDITERRANEAN...

David and I took Greek and Roman History as a half credit course when we were in Law School and we had been so enthralled with what we learned that we had promised ourselves that someday we would take a trip to see the sites of the cradle of civilization. It was not until the last year of David's life that we managed to arrange such a trip.

He had spent most of the winter of 1986-87 in the hospital in Scottsdale, Arizona, for extensive abdominal surgery. We had spent the summer of 1987 trying to build up his strength so that we could take a Mediterranean cruise that fall. In October we set out. David was unable to take the immunity shots that he needed for the North Africa part of the cruise, so we joined the ship afterward, in Naples, Italy. We had a fascinating time, cruising through the Mediterranean islands, stopping at different ones for day trips ashore.

Ephesus, an old sea port, which is mentioned in the Bible, was just fascinating—I wished we had been able to stay there longer. The ship dropped anchor just outside of Istanbul. We had a couple of days touring there, which was absolutely captivating—an entirely different experience. I wished I had known the language because the people seemed so engaging.

Unfortunately, David had a number of sick days that kept him in the cabin, but there was a wonderful British ship's doctor who attended him when he was unwell. This trip was certainly one of biggest highlights during our life together.

David and Thelma with the ship Captain

FAMILY GROWING UP

Neither one of my boys made the decision to follow in their parents' footsteps—maybe they were tired of lawyers. We had often invited out-of-town counsel, at the last minute, to share our meals; hence we had less food for the boys. We had a saying on those evenings—family hold back—which meant "no second helpings!" The boys did not always like having to share their supper! Another possible reason might have been that as county lawyers, David and I were constantly getting phone calls, just as we would sit down to supper. Plus, we were away from home quite a bit, mingling within the community.

CAM

Cam had mentioned that when he started at U of T he had been toying with the thought of entering law. In the back of my mind I began to picture scenarios I had seen happen in other family firms, when the eldest son finished his education and then joined the practice. The younger partners who had been *holding the fort* were often overlooked. The son was usually given a position equal to the younger lawyers that had worked hard to build the practice. I was mindful of the affect on those who worked for us, and who had been so personally loyal to David and me. They had worked hard in the office, and in the community, to help build up the practice. I knew I would definitely want to make it fair to them if Cam did decide to enter the firm.

Thankfully that situation never transpired. Cam told me that when he went to U of T he did not like the Law students—maybe they were too serious for him—like his mother. He began to take a more intensive look at History, which was an interest of both his father and my father. My father had taken evening history courses at the U of T as long as his health would allow. David and I were always talking history. Wherever we travelled we would look into the historical background of places beforehand; it made our trips more interesting. Cam graduated from U of T with an Honour Degree in History.

~

Cam's first job was in Niagara Falls, with Woodstream, the company that had built the canoe he had used on his cross-country canoe trip. He worked on the factory floor slapping *Kevlar* onto the canoe frames. It was a dirty job, but those were tough times for his age group. There was a big after-war "baby boom" and numerous young people were having a difficult time finding work. Rick, Cam's friend that had been with him on the canoe trip, and who had a teaching degree, was even having a hard time finding a teaching position. He and his wife ended up teaching in a northern Native community.

Cam had stayed up all night preparing a resume when he had heard that the company president of Woodstream was going to be interviewing prospective job seekers. When he laid his resume on the desk, the president noticed Cam's name and asked: "Are you the boy who paddled one of our canoes 1,300 miles?"

Cam said, "Yes."

"Well I don't need to look at your resume, you're hired! You're in the canoe business."

As Cam worked his way up in the company he discovered that they were so labour intensive that they proved unprofitable. He had to submit a report to that effect. At the time, Woodstream was making the Fenwick fly-fishing rod, as well, so they transferred Cam to that division of the company. He had an interesting career finding the graphite for the rods and setting up three factories to make these exclusive Fenwick rods. I was dazzled when Cam told me that he could not keep up with the demand for the $1,200 rods! I remember my first fishing rod was a bamboo pole from a hardware store!

When Woodstream was bought out by Berkley's, an American company, the year of the Free-trade deal, Cam was told to close the three rod factories. That was incredibly painful for him because Woodstream had been like a family environment—they even had a daycare centre in the factory. Cam was asked to work in Berkley's Mississauga plant where they made plastic handles for frying pans.

He was not interested in that job. Some of the previous staff of Woodstream suggested to the Berkley management that Cam would be the ideal candidate for them to send to Taipei, Taiwan to set up a rod factory there.

Donna, the young woman whom Cam eventually married on June 6, 1981, had started coming out to our farm when she was in Grade 11. Her father had been sent to Lindsay to open a new branch for the Bank of Nova Scotia. She helped with our riding program for the developmentally disadvantaged kids. She also took private riding lessons from the Austrian cavalryman, Joe. It was quite apparent to me, by the way she looked at my son, that she was smitten with Cam from the onset. Donna obtained her Masters in Library Science. After graduating, she took a job in the library at McMaster University in Hamilton, Ontario. Her first two years there were quite difficult because many of the older librarians resented the fact that she was their senior, due to her education in the new computer methods of cataloguing books.

Cam and Donna's Wedding (Bruce, Donna, Cam, Thelma, David)

Eventually, Cam and Donna bought a home in Grimsby. Their first son, Alistair was born while they were living there. David was still alive then and we had a nice family gathering to celebrate our grandson's christening. David's brother, Ross, performed the ceremony. Cam was away in Taiwan a lot and eventually the company offered him a permanent job there. They flew Donna over to visit with him during the Chinese New Year, but after talking it over they decided against such a big move, preferring to raise their family in Canada.

By the time our second grandson, Callum, was born, David's health was failing rapidly. In fact, he passed away not long afterward. Cam and Donna purchased the home they are currently in because they were outgrowing their Grimsby home and Donna wanted to be closer to her job at McMaster. They have done a wonderful job decorating, according to their taste—it is filled with souvenirs from Cam's many travel adventures.

One trip, in particular, comes to mind—a "trapper's rendezvous" they went to in East Quebec. Cam was still doing a great deal of outdoor recreation when they were at the Green Lane house. He had qualified to have a trap line and he would snowshoe around his trap line each morning. Cam was sure he could win a snowshoe race, but in the end a skinny little Quebecois, about half Cam's size, beat him!

They had another trip to Chesapeake Bay when Cam was invited by the Governor of Maryland to participate in a shoot there. I guess Cam had met the Governor at one of his company events and he admired what a good shot Cam was. Cam had been a good shot when we had lived on the farm—he could knock off the groundhogs that were making holes which could break our horses' legs. And he had wonderful vision, like his father. When David had his eyes examined for the Air Force they made him go back for another examination because they could not believe how sharp his vision was! Cam won the water fowl hunt at Chesapeake Bay in Maryland, and he won a beautiful *Berretta*, an imported European gun. However, having won the shoot, it fell upon Cam to be the host for the following year's hunt. I do not think Cam and Donna were too happy about that because the trip put a strain on their resources. It had been a freebie the first time, as a guest of the Governor of Maryland, but the second time they had to pay their own way!

BRUCE

Bruce had decided that he wanted to be a veterinarian. David and I had felt that Cam might have been headed in that direction because of his love for animals, however Cam figured his science was not strong enough for veterinary college. It turned out that Bruce had a mind for science and math; he was admitted to the pre-vet course at Guelph University. I do not know whether the teacher's strike in Toronto had an effect on his admissibility, but at the end of the first term he was put on *rogation* (skipping a year—try again later). Bruce had elected to stay in a men's residence at the University and I believe that he might have been dazzled by the fact that there were so many girls on the campus—quite a distraction for a young man who had attended a private boys' boarding school!

Bruce had played English *rugger*, cricket, and football at Lakefield; apparently, he had been a good sprinter. He tended to be overweight and the boys at Lakefield used to call him, "The Jelly Bomb." Despite his size, though, he could move quickly and effectively. His father and I asked him not to play football; we wanted him to concentrate on his studies because we knew it was going to be difficult for him. He said that with all the girls on campus that he had to work his frustrations off somewhere—the football field was the best place he knew of to do that!

At the end of the first term, the school did not actually fail Bruce, but they did tell him he needed longer to mature and that he should reapply again in a year or two. By then we had bought the Bobcaygeon property and Bruce elected to take Biology at Trent University in Peterborough. He lived in the house while we were in Arizona. In theory it was a good idea, but in the end it turned out to be impractical because of the distance between Bobcaygeon and Peterborough.

Bruce had bought himself a second-hand *Gremlin* car. At our Windsor home, he had been associating with boys who rebuilt classic cars and he had gotten involved in car maintenance. He was sure that he could maintain the little car. Unfortunately, it was not reliable for the winter trips to school, and his attendance suffered. He did well in Biology, but dropped two other courses. Bruce did not complete his degree.

Then the computer came on the scene and Bruce proved very adept at it. He took a computer technician course at Sir Sanford and was on the Dean's Honour List. David and I had high hopes that Bruce had found his niche. Bruce also showed an interest in designing prosthetics. He was hoping he could find work in that field with Johnson and Johnson, who had a plant outside of Peterborough. We were happy when we heard that he had an interview with them, but then they moved their plant to Mexico.

Bruce always kept up with computer technology. He had his own computer business at one time, but went through several partners who bilked him—he was too trusting. Eventually, Bruce opened a computer repair business, but he started getting severe chest pains and was told he needed bypass surgery. At the age of 47 he had a four-vessel bypass. The doctors thought he had done well in surgery; however, when he was recovering in his room some of the grafts gave way. He had to be rushed back into surgery. Bruce was comatose for a month and we were fearful that he might be brain damaged by such a long period in a coma. When he awoke, he was suffering from amnesia. I sent a lot of our family pictures to Bruce, with the hope that they would help him to regain his memory. He is still struggling to recover.

Bruce lived with Nancy for about 20 years before they were married. Nancy has quite a different background, but I am very pleased that she has been supportive of Bruce. After the Johnson and Johnson job did not work out, a good friend of Bruce's, from Lakefield, called and said that he had bought two Palmac Pet stores with his inheritance and he had found out that the manager of the one he had in Cobourg had his finger in the till. "You are the most honest man I know; will you come and take over the Cobourg store?" he asked. Bruce took his friend up on the opportunity. His knowledge of animals came in very handy there and he had a few successful years running that store. Eventually, his friend sold the business. Bruce and Nancy live in Niagara Falls, Ontario, now.

GRANDSONS—ALISTAIR AND CALLUM

Callum and Alistair

As I mentioned earlier, David passed away not long after the birth of our second grandson, Callum. David and I had spent many of our winters in Arizona, so had not actually been a large part of our grandsons' lives. After David's passing I was still much more of a casual acquaintance to the boys. Donna's parents, though, were around quite a bit. Cam and Donna would leave the boys with her parents when they took trips. I was grateful to them because their help allowed Donna to go on some interesting excursions that Cam went on, in connection with his work. They were very devoted to Cam, Donna, and the boys, whereas I was a drop-in, occasional guest on my way to and from Arizona.

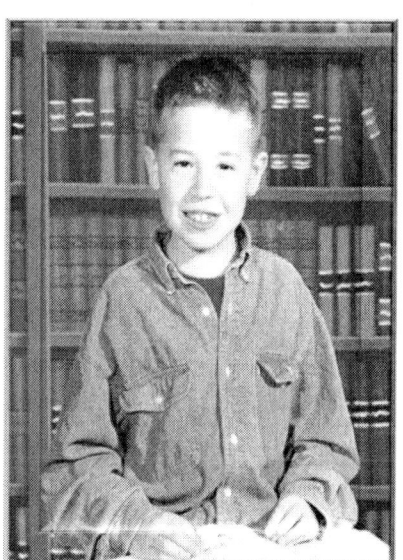

As the boys grew up, Cam often took them fishing and hunting, teaching them the finer points of fly-fishing. Both Alistair and Callum love the outdoors.

Alistair and I at Devil Lake, at Thanksgiving

Cam and his boys—Alistair and Callum

AN EYE-OPENER FOR ME

It was on December 17, 1984 that I had my heart attack. I was out walking my Cairn terrier, Craigy, in the desert. I liked to walk at sunrise; David liked to walk after his afternoon nap. The morning walks gave Craigy the chance to run on the golf course's soft grass, instead of the hard desert sand, which was rough on her tiny paws. That particular morning things were quite damp because it had been a rainy night. There were big, deep puddles on the cart path around the course, so I hiked up into the higher ground. Somehow I just keeled over backward, hit my head on a rock, and was knocked out.

Craigy was on a leash and of course I had let it go when I blacked out. She ran down to the golf course, to some Mexican workers, and started barking. She looked so agitated that the Mexicans realized she was trying to tell them that something was wrong. Fortunately for me, two members of that crew were related to the Mexican woman, Maria, who was helping me with my household maintenance, and with nursing David, so they knew the dog belonged to me. They followed her to where I was lying.

I was just coming around and the first thing I saw was two Mexican men looking down at me. They assisted me to my feet and helped me home. I decided to lie down for awhile. There was a branch of the Mayo Clinic in the area, which sent a young doctor up to that community once a week. I knew that the next morning was his day there, so I thought to stay in bed for the rest of the day and go to the clinic in the morning.

When the doctor examined me he said he thought it would be a good idea for me to check into the hospital and have some tests done. Well, I felt that one heart patient in the family was enough! I had no idea I was a candidate, too. David was being followed by a good Canadian cardiologist, Carmen Brooks, who was practicing in Arizona. Brooks took over my case. In fact, Brooks had done his internship under Doctor McKelvey, who had been my father's cardiologist at the Toronto General Hospital.

Brooks and his colleagues were great fans of David's because David had spoken at a medical legal conference about the high cost of the doctors' specialist insurance and the unconscionable awards against insurance companies in the United States. These awards made their premiums high. Norman Bell spoke for the insurance companies. He was quite a flamboyant California lawyer and he boasted about the big jury awards he had obtained. David took him to task.

I was put through a battery of tests—a whole week! I think they liked the colour of my *Blue Cross*! By Christmas Eve they told me I definitely needed bypass surgery. Doctor Brook's surgeon friend, Doctor Fisk (the surgeon who did the actual surgery) was trying to gather up, and convince, his team of 20 people who assisted him with his bypass surgeries that they were needed for surgery on Christmas Eve, 1984. Thankfully, the entire team responded. They had all met me when I was undergoing the testing—I guess they thought I was worth saving because every one of them showed up on Christmas Eve to give me a five-vessel bypass!

I was released from the hospital ten days after the surgery. It was a difficult recovery period. I wanted to go back to our house, but David thought I should stay in the motel that was close to the hospital. It was in downtown Phoenix, and it was dirty and noisy. I told David that I just needed to come home to sleep—home was the best place to recuperate, and it was not as though I did not have help. The nice little Mexican girl I had coming to help me when David was not well was still with us. She was very knowledgeable and perceptive. She helped me with everything, including the plumbing and wiring. She was a smart girl and I think if her English had been better she could have done anything. I taught her enough English that she got a job as a busboy in the golf course clubhouse. In return she taught me some Spanish.

I went home with a big incision on my chest. I made a good recovery, doing what I was told, but I will never forget how difficult it was to walk my first half block. The cardiologist saw me every week and wanted me to report how long it was taking to walk a mile—I told him that half a block was a hard struggle. I do not want anymore surgery; I would not have the drive and the motivation, now, that I had then. Of course, then I had a sick husband I had to look after—David was my motivation—I needed to get well enough to look after him.

RETURN TO BOBCAYGEON—DAVID'S PASSING

David was not well when we bought the Bobcaygeon place and moved there, but he loved the outdoors and boating. When David was in high school he had worked for the Peterborough Canoe Company during the summer months, when his father was a pastor at the little church on Stoney Lake. David had become very knowledgeable about boating and repairing outdoor motors. Part of his job had been to deliver rental boats and canoes to the cottages. He thought that the location on Pigeon Lake, in a retirement community that had about two acres around each home, was the ideal location for us.

I think the home we bought had one of the best shore views in our community. The homes on the lake had outside decks; we added to ours, by wrapping it all around the house. We spent most of our time there. I was not keen on the decorating tastes of the previous owner. The woman, Rusty, was a redhead—I think she decorated the place around her coloring—even the carpeting was rust-coloured! Anyway, despite the interior, I enjoyed sitting on the deck, reading with my husband.

Unfortunately, David's health was failing fast and this meant frequent trips into the emergency room at Rose Memorial Hospital in Lindsay. I knew some of the doctors there, having previously served on the hospital Board, but there were a lot of new doctors in town by then, too. I think that some of the older doctors who knew us were reluctant to tell us what they perceived was wrong with David. It took a new, young doctor who was working in Emergency to blurt out that he thought it was leukemia.

David was referred to the Oncology Department at Sunnybrook Hospital for the final diagnosis, which we obtained on July 1, 1988. To treat the leukemia, he was put on a program that involved frequent trips to the emergency room for transfusions. The type of leukemia David had was destroying the white cells in his blood and when he got weak he needed a blood transfusion. Quite often these trips into the emergency department would be late at night because that is when David would suffer the most. This was very strenuous on me because the hospital was about 28 miles from our house.

There was another complication—David had a rare blood type—Type-O. Quite frequently the Lindsay hospital did not have his blood type, so they would keep him on intravenous solutions until the Type-O blood arrived from Toronto. We spent many long, tedious hours in the emergency room. These trips increased as his illness progressed and his general health declined.

Thus the boating that David so loved did not amount to much; but, I must say that he did buy himself the best boat he had ever had in his life. When he felt well enough he would putter around on it. In fact, it was such a well equipped boat, and such a size that when I tried to sell it after his death, when the gas prices skyrocketed, nobody wanted a gas burner like that anymore.

Cam and Bruce were not around to help out much during this time. Bruce was working in Cobourg, and Cam was in Niagara Falls, with the Berkley Company. They were absorbed in their careers and I believe they were unaware of how quickly their father's health was failing. That left me to take care of David on my own. I did inform them that their father had leukemia—Cam visited when his dad was first hospitalized. In truth, though, I kept the extent of their father's illness fairly quiet because I did not want to worry the boys unnecessarily. But the trips to emergency increased, and so did the trips to Sunnybrook as the reports on the quality of David's blood became more discouraging. It was tough on me. I did have a lovely Portuguese girl and her helper come to the house once a week to help me out with general household maintenance, though.

For my own release during this difficult time, I had joined the Anglican Church choir at the church of the Epiphany in Bobcaygeon. I had many friends there and the Rector was an amazing man, an ideal visitor to the sick. Even though my husband was Presbyterian, the Rector's visits to David were the highlights in his week. The Rector had a new joke to tell every time he dropped by. The man had a broad background of life experiences, having been a microbiologist before he decided to become a clergyman. He and the members of the church choir helped me tremendously throughout this time.

David had such a zest for life that he refused to accept the fact that his days were slipping away. He did not go into the hospital until he started on chemotherapy for the leukemia; he was at home up until his last four days of life. He was feeling so poorly that he elected to try the chemotherapy. The first day he started on the chemotherapy, David's cardiologist ran out to the parking lot as I was leaving. "You know you better get your affairs in order, your husband will be gone by Christmas. Don't discuss anything with him, he has such a positive attitude and will to live—that's the best thing he's got going for him," he informed me.

David did not want to think of not getting successful results from the chemotherapy; he was optimistic it would cure his leukemia and that he was going to live on. When I finally did tell his family, they certainly did rally around, especially his elder brother, Reverend J.K. Ross Thomson. I have to pay tribute to him because as soon as he heard the diagnosis he said: "If a bone marrow transplant would help, count on me first, before you even think about your boys as an option."

That was one of the most difficult periods of my life because David and I had been so open and honest with each other about everything in our lives. Concealing from him the fact that he was not expected to survive the chemotherapy was difficult. His cardiologist believed that the chemo would be too much for his heart—after four days that proved to be true. David expired on the fourth day of his treatment, on the morning of Saturday, November 8, 1988.

There was a federal election on at the time and Bruce Glass was running for the Federal House. He was speaking at meetings in Bobcaygeon. I was anxious to attend, so I squeezed in an afternoon debate. While I was at the meeting, David passed away. He died, sitting in an armchair, while the nurses were making his bed. After Bruce's speech, I had returned home. Fortunately, the Portuguese girl was at the house when I received the phone call that David had died, so I was not alone.

Cam and Bruce came home immediately when I notified them of their father's death. I was relieved that they accepted my decision to not tell them what I had been privy to. David's family was a great source of comfort, too. His sister, Grace, phoned the rest of the family for me.

I was overwhelmed when Ross and all of his family arrived for the funeral. Ross had four children and they each came with their spouses and children. One of the little two-year-olds tackled the floor lamp in the middle of the living room when I had all the guests back to the house after the funeral. I thought I would be expected to serve afternoon tea to everyone. That was such a stressful occasion—I think I was absolutely overwhelmed, and in a state of shock.

Judge David Thomson, first Chamber of Commerce president

A longtime lawyer and judge who began his career in Lindsay has passed away. Judge David M. Thomson, 67, died Tuesday at the Ross Memorial Hospital.

A private family funeral service was held today (Thursday) at the Mackey Funeral Home.

The Honorable David Moffatt Thomson was a man who took an active interest in the community. Since 1979, he and his wife Thelma had lived in Victoria Place, while wintering in Arizona. He was "a man with the natural grace to make all he met feel better about themselves," his family said.

David Thomson came to Lindsay in 1948 to practise law in the firm of Cunningham and Thomson. His wife joined his firm in 1949. The couple lived in Lindsay and Fenelon Township.

In 1974, he was appointed judge of county court for Lambton County in southwest Ontario and subsequently to the County of Essex and Counties and Districts of Ontario. He retired to come back to the area in 1979.

Thomson was the charter president of the Lindsay Chamber of Commerce in 1951-52. He acted as president again in 1964. He was a past chairman of the Victoria County Board of Education and a member of the Lindsay Law Association.

Thomson was a member of St. Andrew's Presbyterian Church in Lindsay, the Kiwanis Club, the Lindsay and Fenelon Falls curling clubs and was an active Liberal.

As a lover of the outdoors and wildlife, he was a keen hunter, fisherman and horseman.

Thomson is survived by his wife, sons Cameron and Bruce, one granddaughter, two sisters and one brother.

Judge David Thomson

PAGE TWO "THE POST", LINDSAY, ONTARIO, THURSDAY, NOVEMBER 10, 1988

A POEM FROM A FRIEND, STAN PITTS—TO DAVE

(Stan Pitt was the newspaper owner/editor in Lindsay)

It seems like only yesterday since Dave and Thelma came
To the little town of Lindsay to seek fortune, fun and fame
With their shiny new diplomas and their beckoning to the Bar
They set up their orange crate office on William North, by gar!

While Dave held forth in the front room to greet the client rare,
Thelma tried hard in the back room to make dinners out of air.
And so this dauntless couple with a measure of "true grit"
Kept their noses to the grindstone till they conquered bit by bit.

Quickly business gained momentum and the profits likewise grew,
Until Dave with his old cronies could take off a day or two.
I was glad to share the friendship of this gay and motley crew
And to be a willing partner in the crazy things we'd do.

There'd be times when we'd go fishing on Lake Temagami
The greatest little fishing group that ever you did see.
Once David shot a black bear, that with a rumbling roar,
Turned and chased our mighty Dave, through the cookhouse door!

Or perhaps a-hunting we would go, to shoot a deer or two
And fill our bellies to the full on Pollock's rare goose stew,
Or spend a frosty evening around a great log fire,
Swapping yarns and telling tales of which we'd never tire.

Remember Dave, old Les's hound, with long and droopy ear,
With a proper setting of his tail, he'd hunt rabbit, quail or deer.
He could track a chipmunk 'long a fence, his old heart all a-flutter,
And once back in the hunt camp, he consumed two pounds of butter.

On many a summer afternoon when things were sort of still,
We'd all with one accord; appear to "overlook a hill."
With ceremonious flourish we'd throw the cork away
And pass the jug from hand to hand to complete a perfect day.

It seemed there could be no ending to the many pleasant things,
That come now floating backward on memory's fragile wings,
But the old gang's sort of fading now with even Dave a-goner,
As he moves to Sarnia's greener fields with the title, "Your Honour."

But no matter what his title to others in the land,
He'll be just "Dave" to those left in our fading little band,
It won't be because we're lacking in respect, good heavens no,
It will be because of what he is, that he would have it so.

So David, while on complex laws you're busy cogitating,
If you should find the process sometimes most aggravating,
Don't let the heavy burden make of your life a wreck,
Just lean right back and laugh out loud—and think of us, by Heck!

~

After David passed away, I was undecided what I was going to do with the rest of my life. After all, I was only 66 and I still had some life left in me! I did not want to just sit around! I felt so privileged to have had the education I had and thought that I owed something back to society for the privileges that I had enjoyed. I decided to look into taking some courses. When I mentioned this to Bruce Glass, he prepared an office for me at the firm, thinking it might be a good idea if I returned in a consulting capacity for wills and estates.

Courts usually take a break over the Christmas holidays, so Osgoode Hall would offer Continuing Education courses to help practising lawyers keep updated on their specialties in law. That year, they were offering a course on wills, and estate planning—right down my alley. However, after taking the course, I found that the attitudes of practising lawyers and their clients had changed. This new approach was difficult for me to accept. Many of the lectures were about what measures one ought to take to protect themselves from their clients, especially those who lacked testamentary capacity. For example, when I was practising, if I had a person with a *fragile* mind wanting to make a will, I would just phone the family doctor and get his opinion on the situation. Family doctors and family lawyers worked together in close knit circles, then. It was mentioned at the course that Mount Sinai Hospital in Toronto had the best questionnaires for examining a person of questionable capacity. The Law Society recommended that such an individual be tested before a lawyer take on the responsibility of making their will. This sounded terribly time consuming and expensive to me, especially for the clientele of modest means in Lindsay.

This experience also made me very concerned about the casual way I had practiced law—times were definitely changing. Gone was the mutual trust. People were suing their lawyers at the drop of a pin if they were not satisfied with their services. Complaints were pouring in to the Discipline Committee of the Law Society and this worried me if I were to return to practicing law. I was at a point in my life where I did not need to open myself up to those kinds of stresses––I turned down Bruce's offer and pursued other interests.

Another problem I faced was getting rid of the Bobcaygeon house; I could not stand living there any longer—too many memories. As occurs in most retirement communities, after a cycle of ten years, there is movement of sales, due to couples experiencing either severe illnesses or the death of their partner. A condominium development was being constructed on the river just outside of Bobcaygeon. It was near shopping facilities, so numerous people in our retirement community began moving out in order to be closer to the conveniences.

When I put my place up for sale there were seven other houses in that community on the market. I engaged a splendid woman decorator to help me with redecorating. I put in a rosy-beige carpet and painted all the garish walls a coordinating shade of beige. Those two changes made the inside of the house look twice as large. By Christmas, the place still had not sold and I really did not want to stay there any longer. David Logan's son, Hugh, and his wife, Patty, both had big education loans to pay off and they were looking for a place where they could be housed economically. I decided that if they would agree to allow the house to be shown for sale that they would be the ideal tenants. I would charge them a nominal fee and they would pay their own utilities. Patty did a beautiful job of maintaining the house. I owe them a great deal of credit that my house sold first amongst the seven that were on the market.

~

After my move back to Lindsay, I sang in the choir in St. Paul's Anglican Church. They were planning to go to Oberammergau in Germany in the spring of 1990 to see the *Passion* play, which is performed every ten years. I had not wanted to put down the necessary deposit and commit myself to going until I had my Bobcaygeon home sold. When it finally sold in March 1990, I was able to plunk down my money, but I had joined the group so late that all of their reservations were made. I was sort of the *fifth wheel* on the trip, being the ninth person to go. Despite that, it was a very interesting experience.

The travel agent who was arranging church trips that season went broke and we had to solicit another one. They shortened the tour by about ten days. Everywhere we stopped for an overnight we had to find a place for me to stay. It was exciting because I got to stay in separate accommodations from the group. In Lucern they put me in the same Bed and Breakfast as the bus driver. Two members of the group walked over that night to make sure my accommodation was satisfactory—and that I was not sleeping with the bus driver! Besides the fact that I had my own room, he did not appeal to me. One of the men offered to take my room and let me bunk in with his wife. I thanked him but said I was already settled in.

When we arrived in Oberammergau, I was housed in the stable of the family of the man who was playing Joseph of Aramathea in the *Passion* play. They had converted their stable into single guest rooms for people that were attending the performance. They were a fascinating family. The man was a captivating and dedicated individual. He would take time to visit with everyone at suppertime. He even wore his costume when he peddled his bicycle to the performances. He was a carpenter, but had given up working for a year in order to practice and perform in this play. Everybody performing in it had done the same. Occasionally, I managed to have lunch with my group and compare notes on how everyone was enjoying their time. Being a last minute add-on, I found that my seat at the performance was not in the best location; I had to peek around a post to see what was going on—but it was still a wonderful experience. The music and voices were superb!

The bus trip back through Bavaria was fascinating, too. We went through the Black Forest and visited some historic sites. I am truly thankful that I managed to sell the Bobcaygeon property in time to make that wonderful trip. It had been an adventure that had not appealed to David. I felt elated that I had finally made it.

ELDERHOSTELS AND TRIP TO SCOTLAND

There was another thing I had always longed to do that had never appealed to David––the idea of staying in "elderhostels." The Canadian head office was in Kingston, Ontario. Elderhostelling was a wonderful program that was held at different universities. One could stay in a university residence and take lectures in numerous subjects. When I saw the fascinating courses that I could take, over the ten years (1988 - 1998) after David's passing, I took ten of them.

David had never desired to live in a university residence; I had longed to when I was going to university. My father was paying my tuition and felt that since I lived in a nice home I should be there for the family supper at six o'clock. Several of the clubs that I wanted to join met at seven p.m. and this made it difficult for me. There were so many other evening activities on campus that I would have loved to be able to stay for, too. In a university residence I could have taken advantage of them. But, Father said it was out of the question. He had numerous other financial obligations to members of his family. Bottom line was—I had a good home—I was expected to commute.

The first elderhostel that I went to was at Dalhousie University in Nova Scotia, where I took a course on searching the family roots. Next on my list was Acadia University in Wolfville, Nova Scotia, where my father's uncle had practiced law. I fell in love with Wolfville. While there, I met some of my dad's cousins. They were most interesting. I think if I had been younger, I might have made my retirement home there. One of the cousins was a professor at Acadia. He was the mushroom expert in the Botany department. The course I took at Acadia was on the Fundy tides; thankfully I was still fit enough to walk the beaches along the Bay of Fundy. The professor who conducted those outdoor experiences was absolutely wonderful. He taught us a great deal about the local environment.

The big excitement in the evenings was for everybody to gather on the steps of the university Administration building and make bets as to when the Chimney Swifts would come down the chimney, where they nested every night. It was the most peaceful holiday I ever had. I did not watch television, or turn on a radio that entire week! Anyone I have ever talked to, who has visited Acadia, declares it is a breathtaking place with all of its natural habitat, and the picturesque Bay of Fundy. And not to be left out, there are some good restaurants there, too. One of the side trips offered was to the dykes that were built by the Acadians. The Acadian history just fascinated me.

The next summer I went to the University of Western Ontario in London, to take a course on medical legal ethics. I think that if I had been younger I would like to have gotten into that field, it was intriguing. A recently divorced friend accompanied me to this one. We stayed in the old London Hunt Club, which was located by the river, a nice place for morning walks. I stayed there for two elderhostels.

~

"DeNure's Tours" of Lindsay was going to do a tour of the Highlands of Scotland and my heart skipped a few beats as I thought of how wonderful it would be if I could take that trip. When I had the daycare in the basement of our first house, Fred DeNure used to drive a town bus. After his regular nine o'clock *get to work business* was finished, he would pick up the toddlers who came to my daycare. He was so nice, chatting up those little kids. I thought Fred was wonderful, so did Bruce. After we moved the daycare to downtown Lindsay, Fred would still bring Bruce home. Sometimes I would notice the bus idling out in my driveway. I would rush out, thinking that something was wrong—Bruce would laugh and say: "Oh, I'm just chatting with Mr. MANURE!"

I have digressed, though—back to my planned tour of the Highlands of Scotland. In order to prepare for this trip, I went to an elderhostel at Crieff, just south of Guelph. A professor at Guelph University was giving a course on the Reformation in Scotland. I wanted to be well informed about Scottish history before my trip, because I knew that such knowledge would enrich my experience.

I just loved the elderhostels at Crieff; they were located at the Maclean family's country estate. It had been a family farm, but had been developed into a retreat centre for church groups and elder hostels. It was beautiful, reminding me of the farm. I walked through the woods in the morning before the lectures.

So, off I set on the DeNure's tour to the Highlands of Scotland—and I went alone! This is another thing that is so wonderful about elderhostelling—you do not have to go as a couple. I loved to table hop—that was an excellent way to meet the greatest variety of new friends with common interests.

While in Scotland, I put an advertisement in the *Flying Scotsman*, the weekly newspaper that most wandering Scots read. I thought that, just maybe, I would try to find Iain, to discover what had become of him. My desire was simply to connect with an old friend, not complicate my life, or his, with any emotional entanglements. I had seen enough problems that people could create for themselves when I had practiced law. When I saw where Iain came from, I noticed how beautiful it was—like Haliburton, Ontario!

We stayed at a wonderful little country hotel in Pit, in the Lake District, in the middle of Scotland. We were able to take day tours from there; distances are not great in Scotland. There was probably about 70 miles to the sea on either side of where we were. The day we went to Dunoon, where Iain was born, I was really tempted to leave the group to search for the MacAulay family. But I did not. I have no idea what stopped me. Maybe it was the thought that Iain was probably happily married to a nice Catholic wife and that they might have had a dozen children. I was no home wrecker!

Actually, the fact that Iain had been a Roman Catholic was another reason that had helped me make my decision not to go to Scotland in 1946. Iain had downplayed his Catholicism by saying that he went sailing on Sunday mornings instead of going to mass, but I figured if we had ever had a family that would be a sticking point for me. He would be under pressure from his priest to bring his children up as Catholics—something I did not think I could do.

So I left the Highlands of Scotland with naught but the memories of a wonderful trip and the musings of what might have happened to an *old love*!

~

After Scotland I went to an elderhostel at Trent. It was not quite the same comfortable environment as other hostels, but the course I was going to take outweighed that situation. Trent University was also trying to get a program started whereby they would have a village for educated seniors who were willing to tutor and mentor students. They were putting up some nice manufactured homes along the Otonabee River, a beautiful setting. Since I had always admired Lester B. Pearson's work of reconciling nations to solve mutual problems, I thought that living on campus and mentoring a student would be an ideal retirement project. If I did that I would get my courses for free, and there were numerous courses I wanted to take.

At Trent, I took a course on international relations. The professor was fascinating! His father had been a *batman* to an officer in the British army in South Africa. A batman is the individual who looks after an officer's uniforms and belongings. The officer thought highly of his batman and he undertook to educate the batman's son, who turned out to be my professor at Trent University. I thoroughly enjoyed that course.

~

I returned to Crieff to take a course on Stonehenge. I was starting to slow down physically, and Crieff's location was somewhere I could drive to quite easily. Norma Gill, my former doctor in

Lindsay, had an interest in Stonehenge, as well. She had visited the site in England and she was full of its theories and lore. Since her husband Peter had been killed in a terrible car accident, Norma was having a difficult time. I called her up—sure enough, she joined me.

~

In 1996 I had to have angioplasty surgery, in Arizona. That really started to slow me down, physically. I decided it was time to give up elder hostelling, and Arizona.

DEALING WITH THE PROPERTIES

As I have already mentioned, the Bobcaygeon property David and I had owned, did not sell until March 1990. It was a pretty scary time for me, owning the three homes, two in Ontario and one in Arizona. In the past I had seen clients suffer severe financial setbacks under the same circumstances. After the Logan's moved into the Victoria Place, I had put down a deposit on a condo in Lindsay. I picked an end unit, which had more privacy. Since the unit was still in the early stages of construction, I made arrangements with the developer not to close the purchase on the condo until I sold the Victoria Place house. Meanwhile, I paid him the going rate of interest on what I owed. I continued to winter in Arizona.

~

Finally, at the end of 1998, I decided to sell the condo I had bought when I sold the house in Rio Verde, Arizona. Unfortunately that was a very rainy winter! Arizona brags that they only have five rainy days a year—well, there was an entire winter of them that year, owing to the "jet stream!" At last, in March 1998, I received two offers. One was from a couple who were counting on an inheritance for funds and who wanted me to hold a mortgage until their money came through. I had done enough work on estates to know that those kinds of financial arrangements could be a bit dicey, at the best of times. I accepted the second offer, a cash deal from a man who wanted my house as an investment until his own retirement. However, he informed me that he was not ready to retire yet because he had to wind up his business in Detroit. He figured it would take him at least a year, so I rented the place from him during the winter. I took advantage of the extra time I had there to sell off what I could of my collectables and prepared the rest to ship to Canada. I also looked around for a cheaper location in the nearest town, Fountain Hills, where I would be closer to medical care, my dentist, and grocery shopping. It was a nice little town and I figured that I could carry on alone if I had a smaller place.

~

I enjoyed my time in Arizona. I belonged to the Art Guild, and a music circle that had beautiful chamber music concerts in gorgeous homes, on Sunday afternoons. It was a nice life, but I began to find it increasingly difficult to live on a 65 cent dollar. Everyone knew that it was going to be my last year at the Rio Verde house and they were *wining and dining* me—throwing me numerous farewell parties. I was also in a production that the choir was putting on about the history of the community. In addition to all of that, I attended exercise classes three mornings a week. Because of the exchange rate, my lifestyle was beginning to get a bit cramped. I found it difficult to keep up with my friends. I could not dress in the customary style expected to go to the  Country Club. And then to top it all off, just because I had sold my house and was only renting, the Country Club confiscated my Country Club charge card! There was a noticeable class distinction between owners and renters and it appeared I had become a second-class resident!

I decided I needed a job to help me out financially. I applied for, and got, a part-time job as a receptionist at a real estate office—the permanent receptionist wanted her weekends off. I thought it would be an interesting job—after all, I did have some real estate experience. Before I could start, though, I had to go down to the Department of Justice in Scottsdale to obtain a *green card*, a necessary document to hold a job in the United States. I was refused a card. I was told I could practice law if I qualified for the Arizona Bar, which meant I would have to write exams. I guess it boiled down to the fact that I could not take a job that any American could do.

Things began to fall apart for me. As I mentioned earlier, in 1996 I had to have angioplasty surgery (insertion of a balloon to clear the clogged arteries)—that really set me back. I was also fairly alone in Fountain Hills, since I was new to town. I joined a choir at the Presbyterian Church and befriended a recently widowed lady, Luella Parsons. She was a tremendous help to me during my recovery. The doctors insisted I have somebody stay with me for the first 24 hours after my surgery. Being as independent as I was, I had not thought that would be necessary, but I was quite confused during those first 24 hours—I could not even remember where I had put my breakfast cereal! I was very thankful to Luella for staying with me.

After the surgery, I felt so weak that I began to rethink my plan to continue going back and forth between Lindsay and Arizona, especially now that I was alone. Travelling was becoming difficult, and no longer enjoyable. After careful consideration, I decided that the time had come to give up that lifestyle. Another reason was that I had to pay for quite a bit of my medical care in Arizona. I had

paid for my cataract surgery in 1998 and my *out of country insurance* would not pay for the angioplasty because I had a pre-existing cardiac condition. That cost me $5,000. The cataract surgery also cost me $1,880 more than the original estimate because I was charged an additional "facility charge"—I was a foreigner! I had been paying taxes in Arizona for 20 years; I did not think I was a foreigner!

Painting in the desert

Thelma's paintings, including a self-portrait (bottom – centre)

One thing that I did not want to miss, though, was a memorial service at Rio Verde's Memorial Garden. David and I had been active in starting this custom and there was a memorial to my David there. I enjoyed the open-air services we had for those we loved, who had passed on. We held these on All Saint's Day, known as *La Noche des Meurts* to the Mexicans. The last year I was there, I convinced them to have a piper play a lament for my David. When I went up to the piper to thank him, he was crying!

Farewell party at Rio Verde

LINDSAY

I still lived in Lindsay when I was not elderhostelling, or wintering in Arizona. I had numerous friends there—Joan, our former office receptionist; my doctors, Norma and Peter Gill; and our law firm members. They were comforting associations. I joined the church choir as a summertime replacement soprano. Most of my Lindsay friends invited me to spend the weekends with them at their summer cottages. After moving into my condo, I realized it was the first time since 1953 that I had actually lived in Lindsay during the summer. After David and I had built our cottage on the lake, we had spent most of our summers there.

But, not being one to sit idle, I looked around for things to do. Lindsay had a fine summer theatre that I enjoyed being able to go to again. I could not attend when David and I lived in Victoria Place because it was too far to come in for an evening at the theatre. Norma and Peter Gill were very kind to me, as well. Whenever there was a senior citizen special at the local movie theatre that they thought I would enjoy, they would call me up. We would also go out for a light supper at my favourite restaurant, "Joel's." The Gills and I had promoted and helped "Joel's" get started. I enjoyed their friendship and companionship again.

Members of the law firm were very kind to me, as well. They would take me out for lunch on such occasions as the anniversary of my husband's death, or his birthday, and they included me in their firm and law association dinners.

In earlier years I had been involved in the formation of the Lindsay Art Guild, which had grown out of an evening drawing class. We promoted struggling young local artists. I purchased some of their works at various sidewalk and garden sales. I still have many of these pieces. I volunteered at the art gallery on Sundays, figuring if I got dressed up for morning church service I might as well help at the gallery in the afternoon. I served tea and welcomed visitors.

75ᵀᴴ BIRTHDAY—SEPTEMBER 1997

JOEL'S on Cambridge
1-705-324-1752

OCALA ORCHARDS

SEYVAL WHITE WINE
made entirely from
PORT PERRY GRAPES

JOEL'S 7 TOMATO SALAD WITH
MARIPOSA DAIRY'S GOAT CHEESE
ON BUCKWHEAT GREENS
* * *
LEMON & ELDERBERRY SORBET
* * *
LINDSAY FALL FAIR
RESERVE CHAMPION LAMB
OR
KARL'S KINMOUNT RAINBOW TROUT
STUFFED WITH LEMON & DILL
* * *
FARMER'S MARKET VEGETABLES
* * *
RIDGE ROAD APPLE CRISP
WITH WOODVILLE MAPLE SYRUP
AND HUCKLEBERRIES
* * *
COFFEE OR TEA

It was my idea to throw myself a 75ᵗʰ birthday party. I thought it was a tremendous accomplishment that I had actually made it to that age, after having the bypass surgery in 1984. I had only expected to live about ten years after that, because that was all the medical profession offered me. But I was a good patient—I did what I was told and thought that since I had made it to such a remarkable age, I ought to celebrate it with the friends who had helped David and me along the way. Our lives had been greatly enriched by those good friends. Their support in our early struggling days had meant so much to me—what better time to show my appreciation than my 75th birthday! I had no idea at the time that it would be my last hurrah in Lindsay.

I wrote the invitations on the day of Princess Diana of Wales funeral—it was the only news on the radio! I usually listen to the opera Saturday afternoons, a lifetime habit of my parents that I continued with, even when David had called it *caterwauling*.

I arranged the party at Joel's. I had enjoyed seeing his success in starting a restaurant business in what used to be the lunchroom of the old bus terminal. Joel had studied culinary arts in Europe and it showed. Joel and I had a great time designing the menu. It took several lunches to plan because I wanted to celebrate all the local things to be enjoyed—the fish from the nearby trout farm, and the produce from all of the good friends I had at the Farmer's Market. Joel planned everything on the menu to be bought locally, if possible. I believe that the only import on my birthday dinner menu was the wine from Port Perry.

There were about 30 guests, including the farm families that had helped David and me to settle into country life, and our junior partners at the firm. My sister-in-law and her son, and a couple of friends came from Haliburton. My guest list had grown as people heard about my party! The restaurant had to close their main section, but they did leave a few tables in a small room for outside patrons.

I arranged this event myself, not wanting to lay the responsibility of celebrating that epic moment in my life on my children. It was a great occasion—we had the grandest time sharing old memories.

MOVING TO BRANTFORD, ONTARIO—MAY 15, 1998

I had been in Lindsay for ten years, but I had come to the realization that it was time to move on. I also wanted to be closer to family. I was comfortable in the condo, but things were changing. Peter Gill had been killed in an unfortunate vehicle accident when he and Norma were on their way to Florida—one of my sources of support and comfort gone. Many of my other friends were having health and family problems, as well. To top it all off, the law firm was changing too. David Logan had already been appointed to the Bench, and then Bruce Glass was appointed. What a record—our five-lawyer firm produced three High Court judges! I wonder if that is something of a record.

During the last week of October, 1997, I was staying with Cam and his family for a few days before my departure to Arizona for the winter. I was still keeping up my habit of a morning walk, and on one of my walks I noticed that the house next door to Cam had a "For Sale" sign on its front lawn. I stopped to take a good look at the house and its surrounding buildings. There was a big shed on the property, which would be ideal for the storage Cam needed for his boats and sporting equipment; or, maybe even a place to keep a horse! Of course I knew I would never be able to get another horse, so technically, I bought the shed for Cam. This place looked like it was made to order for me! I knocked on the door. No answer. I walked around the property, taking in the beauty of the setting. I was getting more and more excited, thinking that this was serendipity. I gave Cam the "Power of Attorney" to put in an offer-of-purchase for me.

Living in the house next door to my son Cam also had another bonus for me—I would be close to my grandsons. They were so interesting—of course their grandmother thinks they are the most brilliant and fascinating boys to walk this earth. Since moving there, my grandsons have provided me with a great deal of inspiration, and have given me a renewed interest in my life. At the time, I felt I could contribute to their lives, as well. I thought that with my love of history, it would make for interesting dinner conversations. I looked forward to rehashing family historical events and their relationship to current events, feeling that would be an important part of the boys' educations. Of course, while we were at it, I would be sure to ramble on about some of the notable and enterprising people amongst their ancestors.

Just before Christmas, 1997, the Logan's visited me in Arizona. When they returned to Ontario to celebrate Christmas with their family, I accompanied them and asked if they would drop me off at Cam's place. I spent the holiday season with my family and had an opportunity to see the inside of the house, on which I had made an offer. I found it very acceptable. The interior woodwork was honey oak, much like the woodwork that had been in the farm home I had loved. I dickered with the seller. Someone had given her the idea that she had listed her place at too low a price. She was holding out for more money because she thought the shed added extra value to the property. I spent many sleepless nights waiting for one of the succession of offers to be acceptable. Cam drove me to Lindsay to list my condo there for sale, as well.

~

Coming back to Brantford held another attraction for me—Iain MacAulay—although I did not even think of this when I looked at the house beside Cam. If you remember, it was just outside the Brantford Armouries on Brant Avenue where I had pledged myself to wait for Iain. The old feelings that surfaced the first time I drove past that bench overlooking the river came as a shock to me; I thought I had put that experience in my life behind me. I had been true to my promise to David to try to forget the man who first made me *feel like a woman*. I had had a number of platonic male friends during the war years and when the veterans returned home I learned that many had gotten married overseas. After that summer of 1946, I had been en route to being a career woman, building a life on my own. Of course David had also convinced me of my path when he asked me to share my life with him—personally and professionally. I thought I had been true to my promise to David, but being in Brantford stirred up some old, haunting memories.

When I drove around town I tried to pick the less busy roads, finding Brantford very difficult to navigate. The street names were not consistent, changing from one block to the next. I discovered that from where I live my favourite way into town is via Mohawk Road, which is more of a country drive. It has fewer busy intersections, where those with compromised vision and slowed reaction time have a less difficult time driving. Each time I come into town that way I pass the Armouries, and every time I pass that bench overlooking the Grand River I think of the day I promised Iain that I would wait for him—a most fascinating man who added a lot to my life and learning during a war-ravaged time.

~

Cam and Donna made a big effort to have me over for supper every Sunday, however it did not take me long to see that my son and daughter-in-law had no time to make a social life for me in Brantford. I started looking at what there was around to interest me.

I began attending events at Glenhyrst Gardens and thought I might do some volunteer work there, like I had at the Lindsay Art Guild. But that scene did not turn out to be comparable at all. Then I noticed there was a University Women's Club that held an afternoon book club—that was just my cup of tea.

I met some of the women in the afternoon book club when I attended the 100th anniversary celebration for the IODE (Imperial Order Daughters of the Empire) at the John Peel Restaurant on Dalhousie Street. The IODE was one of the groups I had joined in Lindsay, while trying to build my clientele. At one of their annual meetings I had proposed a notice of motion to change the name to the *Daughters of the Commonwealth*—the older members shot me down in flames! It was inconceivable that they would change their name! That group had started during the Boer War, to bring comfort to the families of soldiers who were fighting. The organization was celebrating its 100th anniversary soon after I moved to Brantford. I thought—"There's a place where I could meet some women of my own generation."

The ladies that belonged to the University Women's Book Club encouraged me to attend and that has been a real godsend to me. They met in each others homes, so I got some ideas of how to decorate the house I had bought, with all the dribs and drabs of furniture and paintings I had collected over the years. I enjoyed the friendship of those women tremendously. You really get to know a person when you spend several hours with them, discussing the books they have enjoyed, and what they gleaned from them. It is interesting to discover what different people get out of the same book. I had found some kindred spirits.

~

At the time of this writing I am in my 89th year. That is a good ripe age—actually, I am over-ripe, long past my *best before* date! I have had a few health concerns in the last few years. I think the main, immediate problem for me is that I have had to give up my morning walks, which I felt were an important part of my well-being. I have peripheral artery disease, poor circulation to the hands and feet. I think that the various lipids and cholesterol lowering medications I have been on have had the side effect of wasting away my calf muscles. Those muscles that once impelled a horse over a jump are gone! I really miss my morning walks, especially with a dog. So this physical deterioration in my life is a great disappointment. I used to love to swim—Cam's pool was a great attraction for me, but he never kept it warm enough to suit me. I found that the shock of temperature change is hard on a cardiac patient, causing, in my case, palpitations, or fibrillation. I am also finding that I have the cardiac fibrillation more frequently now—more because of emotional stress rather then physical, and I am finding I need a lot more rest.

My one grandson, Alistair, and his significant other, Sarah, will be getting married this spring, 2011. When the family had a hard time dealing with their cohabitation without benefit of clergy, even though it was hard for me to accept too, I accepted that more than I would accept them getting into debt to rent accommodation elsewhere. They lived in my basement for two summers. Alistair has been a great help to me and he has trained his young brother, Callum, to be my *Refuse Management Engineer.* Callum comes over before garbage day and helps me organize and get the garbage out to the road for pickup.

Alistair and Sarah now have an apartment in Hamilton. She is working and taking extension courses; she wants to be a social worker. Alistair is in his fourth year of English and Humanities—sounds like English and History to me, but they name things differently now. For the past two summers they have both worked at a private summer camp for autistic children. They say that they are better paid than most summer camp jobs because it is a 24/7 job; some of these children can never be left alone. I felt sorry for Sarah when we had a birthday party for her and she said that was the first time in eight weeks that she had been able to sit down to a meal without having to feed somebody else—so that gives you some idea of the dedication that working with autistic children takes. Alistair worked with six autistic boys. Last summer one of them attacked him and he had to go to Emergency to deal with his injuries. Apparently some of these children can be very unpredictable. There are varying degrees of autism—hopefully research will develop the special knowledge needed to help some of these individuals live fulfilling lives.

BEING RECOGNIZED ON TELEVISION

In the spring of 2010, whilst in the midst of working on my memoir with Mary, I received a phone call from Holly Doan. She informed me that she was doing a documentary on professional women in the 1950's, and that it had been recommended to her that she get in touch with me. Since I am usually up for a challenge, even at this age, I said that I would be delighted to be interviewed.

When Holly arrived we did the make-up application, while her cameraman set things up in my basement. Once I was ready for the camera, we headed downstairs. It looked like a professional studio. Holly fired questions at me about what it was like to practice law in the 1950's, narrowing in on family law and the changing times after the war years. The documentary is set to air in March 2011. I look forward to seeing what I look like—*under the lights*!

Prepping for the interview, and the interview

50th class reunion of the Bar Admissions Class—1999
(Thelma—3rd row, 4th in on right)

EPILOGUE

The bonus of living a long life is to be in a position to tell tales on contemporaries, and then to enjoy the perks of those who cater to you, so that you will say something nice about them...

When I started to write my memoirs, I was triggered by an article in "Nexus," which was written by Mayo Moran, the dean of the U of T Law School, whom I admire very much. She is a tremendous woman, and much to be admired and respected. The article is about the struggle to handle your affairs like a reasonable person and not be carried away by emotion and the events that hit you in your life. One of the things that persuaded me about my father's thinking about a legal education was that he asserted that having a trained legal mind, learning logic and the application of pure reason to problems, without being carried away by emotion, was very valuable training for life. It equips you to deal with your own personal problems in a way that is superior to most areas of education—like Trudeau's *Reason Above Passion*. I wanted to respond to that article and that was part of my focal point when I first began to put together my memoir.

If I were to advise young women who are considering law today I would encourage them to look on it as acquiring a trained mind that is not subject to the emotion of the moment, but is capable of taking a longer, broader view of the problems that life presents.

I would also say to them to plan it around a life—if they work for a big law firm, for the big dollars, then they will have to forget about trying to have a life because they will have no control over their time. They will be working for billable hours every waking hour—and a lot of the ones when they should be sleeping, as well. In some of my darkest moments I wondered if I was wasting the talents with which I was entrusted, as my father's partners had alluded to, by having a family. But then I would look at what I had—a loving husband, two wonderful boys—and a life. And I knew that I had made the right choice for me.

The nice thing about the life that David and I had created for ourselves, when we left behind the big city dollars and developed our practice in a small town, is that even though we did not make the big money, we had a life. We had family time together—time to enjoy our respective hobbies, and to include our boys in those outdoor experiences. I joke sometimes that my oldest son has made a career out of fishing! There are rewards to sacrificing the big dollars—indescribable rewards in feeling that you can use your education to help people who have not had the opportunity to acquire one. I felt tremendously satisfied when clients expressed appreciation for the help I gave them. I would walk down the streets in Lindsay, years after my retirement, and people would come up to me and say they could not forget what I had done for their family. Many of the incidents I could not even remember, but it was gratifying to hear such praise and respect.

Those clients were the ones who were willing to take a chance on a female lawyer in those times—they trusted me. And when I did a good job for them, I was rewarded with tremendous personal loyalty. David and I were lucky to have had the same type of loyalty from the junior partners that joined our practice—we were fair with them, and they stayed with us instead of striking out on their own.

It is very difficult to come to the crossroads in life where you are faced with the decision of whether to accept the *big bucks*, or not, and have to make the decision of whether the sacrifice they demand will be worth it. Many women give up having a family in order to have that prestige. I did not do that and I am content with that decision. In fact, I believe that I ended up with the best of both worlds!

I will leave you with what I tried, through my lifetime, to live by—the Prayer of St. Francis of Assisi. This was one of the songs we sang when I was in the church choir. I hope that I have lived up to it, at least in some small part...

Prayer of St. Francis of Assisi

Lord,
Make me an instrument
Of your peace;
Where there is hatred, let me sow love;
Where there is injury, pardon;
Where there is doubt, faith;
Where there is despair, hope;
Where there is darkness, light;
Where there is sadness, joy.

Oh Divine Master,
Grant that I may not so much
Seek to be consoled as to console;
To be understood as to understand;
To be loved as to love.
For it is in giving that we receive.
It is in pardoning that
We are pardoned.
It is in dying that we
Are born to eternal life.

THELMA'S SPECIAL MEMORIES

Whenever I hear this poem, I think of David and the times we wandered the woods together, partridge and duck hunting, and falling down into the long grass beside a field of stubble ... and, the possible conception of our first son, Cam...

<u>Autumn Leaves</u>—by Frank Sinatra

The falling leaves drift by my window
The autumn leaves of red and gold
I see your lips, the summer kisses
The sun-burned hands I use to hold
Since you went away the days grow long
And soon I'll bear old winter's song
But I miss you most of all my darling
When autumn leaves start to fall...

And for Iain—my Scot...

<u>Ae Fond Kiss</u>—by Robert Burns

Ae fond kiss, and then we sever
Ae farewell, and then forever
Deep in heart-wrung tears I'll pledge thee,
Warring sighs and groans I'll wage thee.

Who shall say that fortune grieves him,
While the star of hope she leaves him
Me nae cheerful twinkle lights me,
Dark despair around benights me.

I'll ne'er blame my partial fancy:
Nothing could resist my Nancy
But to see her was to love her
Love but her, and love forever.

Had we never loe'd sae kindly,
Had we never loe'd sae blindly,
Never met—nor never parted—
We had ne're been broken-hearted.

Fare thee weel, thou first and fairest
Fare thee weel, thou best and dearest
Thine be ilka joy and treasure,
Peace, Enjoyment, Love and Pleasure.

Ae fond kiss, and then we sever
Ae farewell, alas, forever
Deep in heart-wrung tears I'll pledge thee,
Warring sighs and groans I'll wage thee.

MEMORIES OF THELMA

Dear Mary:

     I have often been asked what it was like growing up in the late 1950's and early 1960's with a professional woman for a mother. I think the assumption is that it was so unusual at the time that I must have suffered some way, due to it. However, when I look back at my early childhood I can honestly say I did not realise there was anything unusual about it at the time. It is perhaps a common human infant experience to feel your mother is just like all other forces of nature. Just like the sun and the moon, my mother was always there and exactly as she should be.

     While I was a pre-schooler my mother took time out of her legal career to stay home with me and my younger brother, so in many ways there was nothing unusual about my early childhood. When I look back on it now, it was a very happy boyhood. Through my hazy memory of Lindsay, Ontario, 50 years ago, I see a Norman Rockwell type of stereotypical small town. I remember Mom giving me a carrot in the mornings to take out to the milkman's horse, which delivered milk and eggs to our home every day. We only had one car that Dad had to take to work, so we walked almost everywhere. To save her back, I can remember my mother taught our family dog to pull in a harness. She used a wagon in the summer and a sleigh in the winter to pull my brother and I, and the parcels or groceries, when we walked downtown.

During this time Mom and a couple of other ladies started the very first co-operative daycare in the community. Initially, it was in our basement and backyard. This was a pretty ideal situation for me as I got to stay home with my mother, but every day a bunch of kids came over to play. Later, as the daycare grew it was moved to above a store on the main street. The store was owned by Mom's friend, and the daycare continued to operate for many years.

I don't think I ever realised that there was anything unusual about my mother, until I was well into school and started to go home with my friends, and met their mothers. Even then, it was not Mother's career that made her stand out. It was her sense of humour and playfulness, compared to the rather tired, worn and dull mothers that most of my friends had. Mom always had some sort of little game or tease going on that made every day fun. For example, I remember several times a week, when she was doing laundry, my brother and I would sit on the dirty sheets while she dragged them down the long hall to the washing machine. She called this game "the last train to Baghdad" in reference to flying carpets.

As I grew older and gained more independence, she went back to work full-time. However, she always had an arrangement with a nice local lady who would be at home when we walked home from school, or for lunch. We had several of these ladies over the years. I remember them all as being kindly—they made wonderful lunches, including fresh baked cakes and pies. This was the first indication I had that perhaps my mother was not perfect. These ladies were much better cooks!

Mom was always a great lover of the outdoors and she passed this on to us boys. She was very supportive of us doing anything outside. In those days, before anyone considered child abductions, we used to run wild all over the countryside, exploring, building tree forts, fishing, and tobogganing. On Saturdays I can remember Mom packing us lunches and putting them in a backpack, and then we would head out with our friends for a full day in the woods and fields around our home, not returning home until dark.

Mom was quite an outdoors person herself, and an accomplished angler and hunter. Certainly it impressed a lot of my little friends when I told them my mother had her own shotgun. Her real passion, though, was horses and she often took us to riding stables when we were young. When we moved out to a farm, she was able to fully indulge this passion by having her own horse. She rode several times a week, winter and summer. Mother continued to work on improving her riding skills, taking lessons, and traveling to Mexico for advanced courses in horsemanship. I seemed to have inherited her talent and interest in anything equestrian. We spent many weekends traveling to compete in horseshows and fall fairs, throughout my teen years.

It was really in my high school years that I started to appreciate how unique my mother was. In the early 1970's the "Women's Movement" was forefront in the news. My female classmates were all excited by the revolution in gender politics that was going to allow them to have careers and professions the equal of men's. They all seemed to feel that they were on the cutting edge and were the vanguard of this societal change. I would go home and look at my mother who was 30-40 years ahead of them in doing the same thing—without the support of a whole movement and women's groups with political influence. She did it all on her own, with her usual intelligence and happy determination. I know she encountered barriers, but she just found her way around them, and through them. Somehow, she did this without ever seeming angry or bitter about the male dominated world that she not just survived, but also thrived in.

My mother, Thelma Thomson, had a remarkable career in law, but she was a wonderful mother, as well. Our home was a happy and exciting place to live. There was always a lot going on. It was full of animals, activity, and the noise of lots of coming and goings of friends, clients, and neighbours. There were great stories, laughter, and songs—and Mom was always at the centre of it all!

Cameron Thomson

Dear Mary:

What can one say about a woman they have known all their life? As my mother she is the world to me. She went through many tribulations during her life, yet always seemed to overcome them with a smile. A couple of the stories I'd like to relate to you will show my mother's concern and love for her family.

One instance that comes to mind is the almonds on the green beans. This happened on the farm, I believe, after a busy day of riding and dealing with the army riding master, Joseph Bauer. She was preparing dinner for the family, trying to accomplish several things all at the same time. And, as usual, she wanted to have everything perfect. However, when she was roasting almonds for the green beans that she was making for dinner, she burned the almonds! She was so mad at herself and she burst into tears because everything wasn't perfect—even after a day's hard riding. She was always such a perfectionist, probably the quality that helped her to succeed so much throughout her life.

~

Another instance happened as I was learning to jump a horse. I was riding Jack, a beautiful strawberry roan with a full blaze down his nose, and a long, flowing mane. It was my first time jumping and I couldn't quite get it right. I kept leaning forward when I approached the jump, and that was the wrong position to take. Colonel Bauer had his lunging whip and he had that habit of cracking it right between my shoulder blades—almost. This one time I was leaning too far forward and right after the jump there was a hard right turn—the horse made it, but I didn't! I left a dent in the aluminum barn wall, about two feet off the ground, when I landed against the wall! I had the wind knocked out of me. My mother was rushing to my aid. Colonel Bauer yelled to her—"woman get that horse under control, immediately."—which she dutifully did. I think Colonel Bauer recognize that he had pushed me a little too hard that day. So that Christmas he gave me a four-inch strip of ribbon off his *iron cross* medal that he had earned in World War II. I still have it, with the card he wrote—"to Bruce for valour on his first day jumping."

Bruce Thomson

Dear Mary:

I remember David speaking to my high school class about the practice of law, when I was in grade 12. He was very open and informative—a pleasant person to hear describe his career. He made law appear to be very interesting and enjoyable.

I was visiting family in Lindsay during my articling year and met a member of the firm. I had known this person at Queen's Law. He was planning to move to Ottawa, which was home town for him. He suggested that I would find the Thomsons, and Dave Logan, an excellent group with whom to work. I followed up with the group, and my wife and I met them. We seemed to take to each other as old friends.

There was no difficulty working with a husband and wife team. Each practiced very effectively. David conducted a significant barrister's practice, and did so very well. Thelma was an estates expert. All of us went to Thelma for advice on estates work that we were doing. Thelma not only knew her field well, but also she had an excellent manner of conveying information to others, i.e. a good teacher. Although Thelma grew up in Toronto, she fit in perfectly in rural Ontario. Clients associated with her with confidence and admiration. She was very much a person who contributed to her community when doing volunteer work. Thelma, David, and Dave Logan all recommended participating in volunteer work in the community, both as a means of being a good citizen, and also as a means of getting our names in front of the public for the development of our practices.

I started with the firm in 1971. By that time, women were more visible in the legal profession so that women did not run into some of the biases that Thelma had in the 40s and 50s. I remember Thelma telling me about appearing before the Ontario Court of Appeal in the 1950's, when she was about 8 months pregnant. One of the justices made the error of referring to her as Miss Thomson. In the 50's that could carry quite a stigma for a woman. Without missing a beat, Thelma stepped to the side of the podium, turned sideways, pulled back her barrister's gown and said: "You will notice, My Lord, that it is Mrs. Thomson." A very embarrassed male Court of Appeal Judge almost crawled from the bench. That was an example of how Thelma was prepared to make a point directly, firmly, but without disrespect.

I think that in rural Ontario, Thelma found acceptance as a lawyer. Probably, she found more difficulty with some male members of the profession, than with the public. Some men just could not get with the program that women are people who are intelligent and capable of practicing law and serving as judges. I know of one male lawyer in the area who was from the same generation as Thelma and David—this person was of the old school—he thought that a woman's place was in the home. Perhaps jealousy played a role in the attitude of this person. My first trip to the Court of Appeal was the result of this lawyer handling a legal matter in a way that blindsided Thelma so that a future transaction was jeopardized. The Court of Appeal justices were aggressive to the appellate counsel representing the client that this male lawyer had represented—to the point of stating that the conduct was in the category of "sharp practice." One Justice referred to the conduct of the other lawyer as practicing "the pounce theory" when blindsiding the lawyer in Thelma's position. We won.

When Thelma was an articling student, the attitudes of many male members of the bar were sexist. Probably those men today would be embarrassed at how they conducted themselves with female students and female lawyers.

My wife was an x-ray technician, and she told me that when she graduated in 1967, the male sexist behaviour was prevalent. In addition, male x-ray techs were paid more than women, simply because they were men. It stuck in every woman's throat because very often the male was not the best technician.

I think that the male shortcomings toward women in the law made the women even better lawyers because they rose to the challenge.

I have always considered working with a woman as my first boss the best experience I could have had. I saw a lawyer who was very good at her profession. I did not see a woman when looking at Thelma. And Thelma was a very attractive woman, too. In effect, my experience with Thelma made me gender blind. I recall at one of our local law association meetings, one of the male lawyers made some sexist comments to a female lawyer (and this was in the 90s)—the male was trying to be witty; however, his comments embarrassed the female colleague and many male lawyers present. I spoke to the errant male lawyer, later, explaining that I thought he had embarrassed our fellow member of the law association. To his credit, the lawyer said: "I guess I should apologize." And further to his credit, he did. He felt very ashamed of himself that he had embarrassed a colleague whom he liked and respected. He had crossed the line.

Thelma had done some deputy-judge service in family and youth court before David was appointed. As she described that experience, she brought a broader dynamic to my view of practicing law. David was appointed to the County Court Bench on January 24, 1974. I always maintained contact with Thelma and David after they moved from Lindsay, and when they returned to the Lindsay area. As David described the career as a judge, I thought a judicial career could be most interesting. Then, in July 1981, Dave Logan was appointed to the County Court Bench and I continued to have an inside understanding of the career. When I was appointed in November 1997, the shift to the bench was like changing gears while driving a car with a stick shift. When I walked into court for the first trial, I wondered if I had made the right decision, but within two minutes I was thinking to myself: "Oh, I'm going to love this job." And I have. It is very enjoyable, challenging, and interesting.

Thelma has continued to be a vibrant and intelligent friend. I have been very fortunate to have known her since 1971 when we began working together. As a human being, a friend, a lawyer, "she's a keeper."

All the best—Judge Bruce Glass

SOME OF THE PEOPLE I KNEW
AND
WHAT BECAME OF THEM

Mary Eugenia Charles—First female lawyer in Dominica—also the first female prime minister of Dominica

Louis Fox—Chief Justice of Jamaica, then returned to Canada and worked for the Legal Aide system

Royce Frith—Became a leader in the Federal Senate. Later became Canada's high commissioner in London, England

Fred Kelsick—Attorney General of the Winward Islands

Betty Robson—Ontario Court Judge

Bob Spratt—Ontario Attorney General Department

Sydney Dymond—Ontario Court Judge

Judy LaMarsh—Secretary of State during the Trudeau years. Also wrote "I Was Only a Bird in a Gilded Cage"

Walter Gordon—Minister of Finance

Larry Parnell—Solicitor General

NOTE FROM THE AUTHOR

Working with Thelma has been quite the experience, and adventure. It gave me a deeper insight into the conflicts many women had to endure as they stepped out into what was considered *a man's world*. No one—male or female, should ever take for granted the struggles that these women endured along their paths.

I found, throughout the interviewing process, that as independent a woman as Thelma was, she still deferred much to, first her father, then her husband. Even so, she was a bona fide pioneer in law—the first female lawyer in small town Lindsay, and a constant advocate for women's rights, especially in the areas of wills and estates.

One of the most difficult areas I faced while interviewing Thelma was getting her to talk about *her feelings*. After months of interviewing and discussions, she called me one day and suggested that I watch the movie "Pleasantville" so that I would know what it was like to live in the 1950's, and I would also know why it was so difficult for her to answer many of the questions I asked her, especially those relating to emotional feelings. I informed Thelma that I had seen the movie, and then I asked if she had ever seen the movie "Mona Lisa Smile," which is about a young teacher with radical ideas, teaching in a private girls' school in the 1950's. Thelma said no; I suggested she watch it, so I leant her my copy. I felt that she would relate to that movie because she had attended Branksome, a private girls' school in Toronto.

After watching the movie, Thelma called me and the emotion began to flow—she had so related to that time ... she told me how she had given up her own personal ambition of working in the Foreign Affairs Department, in order to appease her father's wish for her to become a lawyer, and also to help David pursue his career ambitions. There was such vibrancy in her voice when she talked about the *red carpet* being rolled out for returning veterans in 1945, and that no one even wanted to interview a woman for government jobs—especially in the Foreign Affairs Department. Thelma related to me that during an interview for an Articling position, the interviewer told her that she was foolish for even trying to get such a job—why would anyone want to consider hiring a *flip* of a girl like her! Just another example of the prejudices women had to face then.

There was another area in Thelma's life that she finally admitted to me that she *settled*—she chose a man she thought would be more constant and reliable to build a home and family with—not that she had not enjoyed a wonderful life with the man she married—Thelma had nothing but praise for her husband David, and the good life they had together. In fact, much of her memoir sings praises to David and his accomplishments.

But, there was always a longing in her voice and her eyes when she spoke of Iain MacAulay, her Scot—her first real love. He made her heart flutter and she has often wondered how her life would have turned out had she taken him up on his offer to join him in Scotland that summer, when he had sent her the 300 pounds. I think I will write the alternate story one day—just for Thelma—just for the love that never came to fruition.

Thelma mentioned that her father actually liked Iain—he enjoyed bantering with him at the table, finding Iain to be very intellectual and mature. Thelma even divulged that had she had her father's blessing to go to Scotland, she just might have done so. She did confide, though, that her mother was partial toward David.

Thelma was on a roll that day. I questioned her about her relationship with her mother, suggesting that I had the feeling that it was a very strained one. She disclosed to me that she felt her untimely entrance into the world had put a crimp in her mother's desire to become a concert pianist, because her mother had gotten pregnant on her honeymoon.

In reality, though, hearing that bit of information, in many ways, Thelma's mother had also settled for other than what she really wanted in life—like so many young women have had to do throughout time—even now. Some of the "old attitudes" of educating a girl only enough to be of support to an educated man, had rubbed off on Thelma's mother, from her mother's era. Thelma's mother had never been totally onboard with having Thelma go to law school to become a lawyer—some of the reason being that it used up the money that she felt could be better spent entertaining in the manner that she would have liked to.

Thelma loved to go fishing with her father, an activity that irked her mother to no end—fishing was not something a proper young woman should be doing! I asked Thelma how her mother had accepted her learning to ride horses, then. I could see the smile over the phone—that was okay because Thelma was meeting the right people—those with pedigrees and old money! I laughed. She laughed.

In conclusion, I think there were more than one road not taken in Thelma's life—the road to Scotland, and the road to her desire to work with the Foreign Affairs Department—she settled—first, by becoming a lawyer—but she just wasn't any lawyer. Thelma actually earned two degrees—her second one being a Doctorate of Juris Prudence.

Secondly, she married David, but that wasn't really *settling*, was it—it was still to an amazing man who loved her, and together they accomplished a great deal— two wonderful sons, a law practice which produced three judges, and a lifetime of memories.

So, having said all that, maybe the roads not taken were the ones that were not supposed to be. Thelma—thank you for allowing me onto one of your roads!

Mary M. Cushnie-Mansour

Note: *I have related Thelma's story to you in the "first person," in order to capture "her" voice. Also, excerpts from Thelma's letters have been recorded exactly as she wrote them, for the sake of authenticity. I have also done my best to be accurate with names and places, according to Thelma's memory of the events that unfolded in her life.*

I extend my thanks to Brenda Ann Wright and Bethany Mansour for helping me with transcribing, scanning, organizing and editing Thelma's biography.

Mary M. Cushnie-Mansour

ABOUT THE AUTHOR

Mary was born on November 15, 1953, in Stoney Creek, Ontario, Canada. She is a freelance creative writer who now resides in Brantford, Ontario with her husband, Adel (Ed).

In March 2006, Mary completed a freelance journalism course at the University of Waterloo, after which she began writing freelance articles and a fictional short-story column for the Brantford Expositor.

Mary has published, under her publishing company, *Cavern of Dreams*, four poetry anthologies: *Life's Roller Coaster, Devastations of Mankind, Shattered,* and *Memories*; and a collection of short stories, *From the Heart*. She also writes children's stories, novels, plays and songs. Her first published novel, "Night's Gift" was released in March 2011. It was awarded an "Editor's Choice" designation from the publisher, IUniverse.

Mary is active in the writing community. For several years she ran a creative writing program, *Just Imagine*, for the Grand Erie District School Board. Mary is always encouraging those who have a love for writing to follow their dreams, even to the point of helping some see their own work come to fruition.

Check out Mary's web-site for more information on her and her other writings … www.cavernofdreams.ca

~ *Mary M. Cushnie-Mansour* ~

The many faces of Thelma—A 20th Century Portia!